Jane Austen

The Woman

Also by George Holbert Tucker

- Abstracts from Norfolk City Marriage Bonds (1797–1850)
- Bedlam Without Bars
- Cavalier Saints and Sinners
- A Goodly Heritage: A History of Jane Austen's Family
- More Tidewater Landfalls
- Norfolk Highlights, 1584–1881
- Tidewater Landfalls
- Virginia Supernatural Tales

Jane Austen

THE WOMAN

Some Biographical Insights

GEORGE HOLBERT TUCKER

Foreword by John McAleer
Professor of English, Boston College

ST. MARTIN'S PRESS
NEW YORK

Scholarly and Reference Division,
St. Martin's Press, Inc., 175 Fifth Avenue,
New York, N.Y. 10010

First published in the United States of America in 1994

Printed in the United States of America

ISBN 0-312-12049-4

Library of Congress Cataloging-in-Publication Data

Tucker, George Holbert.
Jane Austen the woman : some biographical insights / George Holbert Tucker.
p. cm.
Includes bibliographical references and index.
ISBN 0-312-12049-4
1. Austen, Jane, 1775-1817—Biography. 2. Women novelists, English—19th century—Biography. 3. Women and literature—England—History—19th century. I. Title
PR4036.T83 1994
823'.7—dc20 93-35954
CIP

Interior Design by Digital Type & Design

In Memory of My Beloved Wife,

Elizabeth Braxton Williams Tucker

(1904–1993)

Contents

Acknowledgments

Although a lack of space prevents my acknowledgment of all of the individuals and institutions in the United States and Great Britain who have assisted me in the research for this book, the following should be specifically named: Oxford University Press for permission to quote from *Jane Austen's Letters to Her Sister Cassandra and Others* and the *Memoir of Jane Austen,* by the Rev. James Edward Austen-Leigh, both edited by the late R. W. Chapman, and from other publications relating to Jane Austen; the Bodley Head for permission to quote from *Jane Austen's Sailor Brothers,* by J. H. and Edith C. Hubback, and *Jane Austen, Her Homes & Her Friends,* by Constance Hill; the Fellows Librarian of Winchester College for permission to quote James Austen's poem on the death of Jane Austen; Mrs. Lawrence Impey, for permission to quote from the invaluable *Austen Papers 1704-1856,* and other important family manuscripts and publications; the Jane Austen Society for permission to quote from its annual reports and other publications; the trustees of the Jane Austen Memorial Trust for permission to quote from its manuscript holdings; Mrs. Joyce Bown for copying entries in the Steventon parish registers; the great-grandsons of Admiral Sir Francis Austen for permission to quote from a manuscript of Anna Austen Lefroy; Helen Lefroy for her unfailing interest and help; Deirdre Le Faye, the acknowledged authority on biographical matters relating to Jane Austen, for her valuable assistance and criticism; Jean Bowden, curator of Jane Austen's House, Chawton, for her help; Robert S. Harrison of the record office of the House of Lords for special help with the chapter dealing with Jane Austen and scandal; Park Honan for his help and enthusiastic encouragement; the late Eliza George Parke, Mary Eugenia Parke, Caroline Heath Tunstall, and Elizabeth Calvert Page Dabney for their support and interest; John A. Parker, Jr., head of the general reference department of Kirn Memorial Library, Norfolk, for obtaining copies of Austen-related books and articles from magazines and other publications through interlibrary loans; Ruth Walker for her abiding interest and encouragement; James R. Henderson III for reading and correcting the manuscript and for suggestions for its improvement; David J. Gilson for his keen interest in my work and for help with research problems; Mildred ("Millie") Johnson for making the final typescript; my esteemed friend Professor John McAleer of the English Department of Boston College for his perceptive and beautifully written foreword; and last, but not least, my late wife, Elizabeth Braxton Williams Tucker for her unfailing encouragement and support.

FOREWORD

The biographer of Jane Austen must seem to many beleaguered modern readers to be someone who has taken on the Rumplestilskinian task of converting a legacy of small change into large bills. In considerable measure blame for this situation falls on successive generations of Jane Austen's collateral heirs who, for more than a century, held hostage such oddments of her personal history as had fallen to their lot, while, from time to time, trickling out random facts that seemed to confirm the validity of the biographical image on which they had agreed. As Deborah Kaplan had perceived, one consequence of this process is that Jane Austen's life "tailored to reveal only maidenly affections within a network of family loyalties . . . is duller than it need be." Recent biographers, striving to remedy this deficiency, have hit upon the stratagem of stirring her life into the brew of the turbulent times in which she lived. Regrettably, the result has been a seething cauldron to the surface of which Jane Austen only intermittently rises. Now, however, George Holbert Tucker, after fifty years of patient, yet relentless, research, has found the way to convert the mountain of Austen small change into substantial notes. As the heap dwindles, so does the dullness. Seen from the perspective Tucker gives us, in *Jane Austen the Woman,* she will never be the same again. From the opening page onward, chapter through chapter, without a moment of uncertainty, she is brought to life. At long last the crumpled, censored family image is ready for permanent dismissal to the dustbin.

Gone now, thanks to Tucker's integrity, is the demure old maid—the spinster recluse. No longer need biographers feel constrained by her brother Henry's evangelical affirmation: "Short and easy will be the task of the mere biographer. A life of usefulness, literature, and religion was not by any means a life of events." No longer need we see these words reiterated as Douglas Bush does, apologizing for a life with "few dramatic events." Or worse still, as M. A. Bold recasts them: "Of her unsensational life there is little to chronicle. She took her world as she found it, wishing for nothing better."

Twenty-five years ago, Howard Babb protested, "Most of Jane Austen's critics are obsessed by a sense of her limitations." That was the plain truth. Let the myth of uneventful domesticity illustrate this fact for us. In 1918 A. Edward Newton wrote: "Jane Austen was actually as shy and retiring as Fanny Burney affected to be. She could hardly have presided gracefully in a drawing-room in a cathedral city—much less have been at home among the wits in a salon in London." Sixty years later Vladimir Nabokov was still insisting: "Can we rely on Jane Austen's picture of landowning England with baronets and landscaped grounds when all she knew was a clergyman's parlor?" It is this false image that George Tucker topples from its pudding-stone pedestal.

And what of claims advanced by others that Jane Austen's vision of society was ahistorical? All too typical is Harry Levin's endorsement of it: "It never occurred to Jane Austen that the young officers who figure as dancing partners for her heroines were on furlough from Trafalgar and Waterloo." Was Francophile Levin unaware that two of Jane Austen's brothers, those among her siblings closest to her in age—both of them, Francis and Charles, future admirals—were out on the high seas helping to sink the French fleet while their sister Jane, ever in active correspondence with them, gloried in their exploits? Had he never remarked that the action of her novels does not carry up to the battle of Waterloo? Can we complain that Jane Austen centered none of her action on the French Revolution when, as Tucker reminds us, Sir Walter Scott, her contemporary, "wrote of the France of Louis XI, not of that of Louis XVI," and Shakespeare never wrote a syllable about the Spanish Armada. Tucker confirms Christopher Kent's estimate of this brand of Austen bashing: "The concern of literary critics with historical dimensions of Jane Austen's canvas betray limitations in their conceptions of history more than limitations in her art."

To take up another absurdity of Austen criticism: What of the common supposition that she was a stay-at-home, had never ventured north of the Trent? This claim Tucker refutes with hard facts. It is a matter of record that Jane Austen traveled often and on treacherous roads that took the lives of her cousin Jane Cooper; her beloved confidante, Madame Lefroy; and of James Wyatt, architect of Fonthill, which he built for the novelist William

Beckford (allied by marriage to the Austens); and crippled the great Humphry Repton who had landscaped the estates of her mother's kinsmen.

The myths have burdened us with a myriad of books that have tried to confer variety on a life that daily confronted more reality than most modern scholars experience during a month of Sundays. George Tucker compels us to ask, Is it really necessary to assess Jane Austen in a context of what Nietzsche, Freud, Foucault, Lukacs, and Heidegger thought, or Shaftesbury, Richard Price, and Theophrastes held? Why, Tucker inquires, take the reader on a wearisome tour through the groves of academe when what is truly needed is an encounter with Jane Austen as she actually was? As a writer who has steeped himself in the period in which Jane Austen lived—as someone who has, for more than half a century, annually reread each of the novels—George Tucker has not only confronted Jane Austen with the competence of a professional researcher and historian, but he has consistently exceeded those standards ordinary investigators have certified as adequate and has studiously collected pertinent, original source material. Not only has he discerned the existence of unsuspected, untapped sources, he has run them down and authenticated them, with full documentation. Often he has put in correct focus aspects of Jane Austen's life and achievement, which doctrinaire scholars have dealt with haphazardly, brushed aside as inconsequential, or ignored altogether. Tucker not only has a true feeling for Jane Austen's world as it was, he shows us that the great revolutions of her time were dealt with inherently in her novels. He has not only had his own concentrated research to draw upon, but he has made himself thoroughly familiar with the findings of all contemporary Austen biographical explorations, cross-examined the authors of such works, and, more often than not, recruited them as members of his own research team. This has been possible because the reputation he has earned, as author of *A Goodly Heritage,* his seminal study of Jane Austen's ancestral heritage, has not only singled him out as someone whose knowledge and judgment are a resource of indisputable merit—it, in fact, has identified him as the Schliemann of Austen scholarship.

In *Jane Austen the Woman,* Tucker confirms the justice of David Monaghan's contention, put forward when the bicentennial of Jane

Austen's birth was being celebrated in 1975, that "the great events of her day were at the center of her consciousness . . . To write of 'three or four families in a country village' was then the very way to write about the condition of England . . . her contemporaries . . . would have recognized that she was directly encountering the kind of moral questions that had to be answered if a society based on a code of duty and obligation to others was to flourish." Monaghan thus speaks out more boldly than Warren Roberts, Parke Honan, Oliver MacDonough, and others who have surmised that, to show her responsiveness to the events of her time, nothing more is needed than to acknowledge the involvement of those whose lives touched her personal world, and to remark occasional asides, in her letters, to distant battles, slavery, rising prices, and powdered wigs. Half a century ago the redoubtable Ralph Chapman marked out a more fruitful line of inquiry. He had found, he said, "some striking parallels between Jane Austen's names, of person and places, to real names, or names in other books, and suggested that she felt the need of a framework of reality, in names and houses and scenery, on which to build her fictions." This framework of reality Tucker now has brought into view. With an intimacy that is his by entitlement, because of his industry, Tucker has evaluated various aspects of Austen's personal history—her milieu, friendships, romantic attachments and her extensive reading, her response to current events, her religious orientation. His objective has been not to tell us more about Jane Austen as a novelist but to produce on Jane Austen, as a woman, a theme and variations. *A Goodly Heritage,* which gave Austen scholarship the solid footing it hitherto had lacked, makes this new book not only a necessity but a gangplank to reality.

Replete with radiant insights and facts that hitherto went undetected by a legion of Austen sleuths, Tucker's *Jane Austen the Woman* brings us cozily into her private world. Here we find that the exuberance of the girl who wrote the juvenilia was not quenched by the responsibility that fell upon her to shape her early ventures into fiction into major novels and then crown that achievement with three new masterpieces written with an almost breakneck speed that brings to mind the genius that impelled Shakespeare, Dostoyevsky, and Faulkner when they hit their stride.

Little disclosures first whet our appetite—the likelihood that the Austen's neighbor, William John Chute (kin of Horace Walpole's friend, John Chute), a robust, outdoor man, was possibly Sir John Middleton's prototype; that Sand Barton, Devon, could be the original of Barton Park; and that Jane Austen's cousin Edward Cooper, prone to writing "letters of cruel comfort," might have been Mr. Collins's prototype. How instructive, too, to realize that an allusion to "Regency bonnets," in *Catharine or The Bower,* makes it probable that this first approach to her mature style dates back to 1788-89, three years earlier than anyone hitherto surmised. And what, by the way, was the Regent doing when, at his behest, Jane Austen was shown through Carlton House? Consulting the court calendar, which, hitherto, no one else had thought to do, Tucker found "Prinny" shooting partridges on the manors of the Marquis of Anglesey.

Jane Austen's life even touched the lives of other writers. Consider her predilection for Crabbe and Cowper. We learn that her Aunt Jane Leigh-Perrot's cousin, William Welby, was Crabbe's intimate friend, a conduit, therefore, providing the Austens with knowledge of Crabbe. To clinch the contact, Welby's son, William, married Aunt Jane's admired niece, Wilhelmina Spry. Cowper's cherished confidant was Joseph Hill, the very London barrister who served the interests of Jane Austen's uncle, James Leigh-Perrot, and her cousin, Thomas Leigh. In 1806, Austen was much in Hill's company when they both were guests at Stoneleigh Abbey. Yet another Hill, Herbert Hill, uncle of the future poet laureate Robert Southey, married Jane Austen's long-standing friend, Catherine Bigg. Had Jane Austen not broken her engagement to Catherine's brother, Harris, Hill would have been her brother-in-law. Cassandra Cooke, Jane Austen's cousin and spouse of her solicitous godfather, Samuel Cooke, was not only a friend and neighbor of Fanny Burney's, she was, herself, a published novelist. Sir Egerton Brydges, her putative cousin, also wrote novels. Jane Austen, furthermore, was not vainly boasting when she spoke of kinship to Beckford, author of *Vathek.* Lady Albinia Bertie, aunt by marriage of Jane Austen's brother James, was married to Francis, Beckford's uncle. Joanna Leigh, blood cousin to Jane Austen, was married to yet another Beckford.

For a further literary association Tucker reminds us that, just seven years after Jane Austen's death, Lord Byron's body lay in state for two days at the London town house of Jane Austen's favorite niece, Fanny Knight Knatchbull. That Jane Austen could have held her own at any literary salon is also evident when we learn of her quip concerning a possible delay during a visit she made to London—"I should inevitably fall a sacrifice to the arts of some fat woman who would make me drunk with Small Beer." It is, in fact, a robust reference to the fate of Moll Hackabout—a country girl snared by a procuress, as shown in the first plate of Hogarth's "The Harlot's Progress." Can this be the utterance of Jane Austen, the parson's daughter, whom posterity stations in a vicarage parlor demurely tending the tea table? And how we would like to have been present when, on another London visit, this sharp-witted woman was an evening guest of one of the great master spies of the era, who, a year hence, together with his wife, was struck down by an assassin in a bloody moment today's tabloids would put in screaming headlines.

"Invention," observed Sir Joshua Reynolds, whose vigorous creative life ended just as Jane Austen's began, "strictly speaking, is little more than a new combination of those images which have been previously gathered and deposited in the memory; nothing can come of nothing." George Tucker, knowing this well, has not been intimidated by Henry Austen's declaration that his sister "drew from nature; but never from individuals." Torrid scandals, with almost punctual regularity, gave notoriety to the lives of many people whose lives touched Jane Austen's. While it is tempting to seize on George Tucker's remarkable chapter on Jane Austen's anything but squeamish awareness of these events as designed to refute those who insist no suspicion of sexual passion ever entered her head, the purpose of this chapter, revealing her interest in the scandals of her time, far exceeds so narrow a goal. The squeamishness of her critics themselves has left unharvested till now this fertile cropland of insights. For our benefit the forthright Tucker has been left to gather in an abundant yield that the faint of heart have refused to confront. In a book that rattles, in every chapter, the bones of yesterday's Austen scholarship, page after page of this chapter astounds and titillates us.

At last the truth is in the open. The family biographers were not trying to keep Jane's personal history low-keyed because she would have found any other approach intrusive. They were catering to their own prudery. Jane Austen was not afraid of the truth—

quite the contrary, as G. K. Chesterton put it: "Jane Austen may have been protected from the truth but precious little of the truth was protected from her." In the nineteenth century, at Stoneleigh Abbey, one of the citadels of the ancient Leigh family from which Jane Austen's mother sprang, an eye was perceived peering out from behind a floral painting. When this overpainting was removed from the canvas it was found that it had hidden an admirable likeness of Charles I. To save their king, the "loyal Leighs" had resorted to this stratagem. In a sense George Tucker has now removed the pretty posies superimposed on Jane Austen's true likeness by well-meaning but ill-advised guardians of her reputation. His book, for the time being, must occasion embarrassment among those Austen scholars who never looked farther for Jane Austen's true image. But it can only occasion rejoicing among those who want the real Jane Austen restored to the light.

Jane Austen the Woman will stand with Deirdre Le Faye's *A Family Record,* which goes as far as perceived facts could go as a main source for future Austen biographies. Tucker's book points out the direction that, henceforth, conscientious biographers must take. Never again will Austen biographers be free to assume that everything worth knowing about Jane Austen already is known and that future biographies must find their substance in the further sifting of revealed facts or in such subtleties as faddist criticism stumbles upon or imagines it has discovered.

JOHN MCALEER
Webster Island, Duxbury, Massachusetts
September 27, 1993

Austen

John Austen of Horsmonden (d. 1620)
m. Joan Berry (d. 1604)

Francis Austen (fifth son, d. 1688)

John Austen (d. 1705)
m. Jane Atkins

John Austen (d. 1704)
m. Elizabeth Weller, by whom he had, among other children:

Francis Austen (1698-1791)

William Austen (1701-1737)
m. (1) Rebecca Hampson (widow of William Walter, M.D. by whom she had one son, William Hampson Walter, who was the father of Philadelphia, James, and Henry Walter). → (2) Susannah Kelk (no issue)

By his first wife, William Austen was the father of:

Philadelphia Austen (1730-1792)
m. Tysoe Saul Hancock

Elizabeth (Eliza) Hancock (1761-1813)
m. Jean Capot de Feuillide

Hastings de Feuillide

Rev. George Austen (1731-1805)
Rector of Steventon and Deane,
m. Cassandra Leigh (1737-1827)

and two other daughters

(1) Rev. James Austen (1765-1819) m. (1) Anne Mathew (by whom he had Jane Anna Elizabeth Austen, who married Rev. Benjamin Lefroy and had issue)
(2) Mary Lloyd (by whom he had James Edward Austen [Austen-Leigh after 1837], who had issue, and Caroline Mary Craven Austen)

(2) George Austen (1766-1838) He was mentally defective.

(3) Edward Austen (1767-1852; Knight after 1812) m. Elizabeth Bridges (by whom he had Fanny Catherine Austen [Knight after 1812], who m. Sir Edward Knatchbull, and ten other children).

(4) Henry Thomas Austen (1771-1850) m.
(1) Eliza de Feuillide, his first cousin (no issue)
(2) Eleanor Jackson (no issue)

(5) Cassandra Elizabeth Austen (1773-1845) never married

(6) Francis William Austen (1774-1865) He m. (1) Mary Gibson (by whom he had six sons and five daughters)
(2) Martha Lloyd (no issue).

(7) JANE AUSTEN (1775-1817) never married

(8) Charles John Austen (1779-1852) He m.
(1) Frances Palmer (by whom he had four daughters)
(2) Harriet Palmer (by whom he had three sons and one daughter).

Leigh

Sir Thomas Leigh (1498-1571;
Lord Mayor of London, 1558-1559)
m. Alice Barker, alias Coverdale. Leigh was descended
from Hamon de Legh, Lord of the Moiety of High Legh,
Cheshire, temp. Henry II. He was
the father of, among others:

Rowland Leigh of Longborough and Adlestrop
m. Catherine Berkeley

Sir William Leigh of Longborough and Adlestrop (d. 1632)
m. Elizabeth Whorwood

William Leigh of Adlestrop (d. 1690)
m. Joanna Purry

Theophilus Leigh of Adlestrop (d. 1725)
His second wife was Mary Brydges,
a sister of the first Duke of Chandos,
by whom he had, among others:

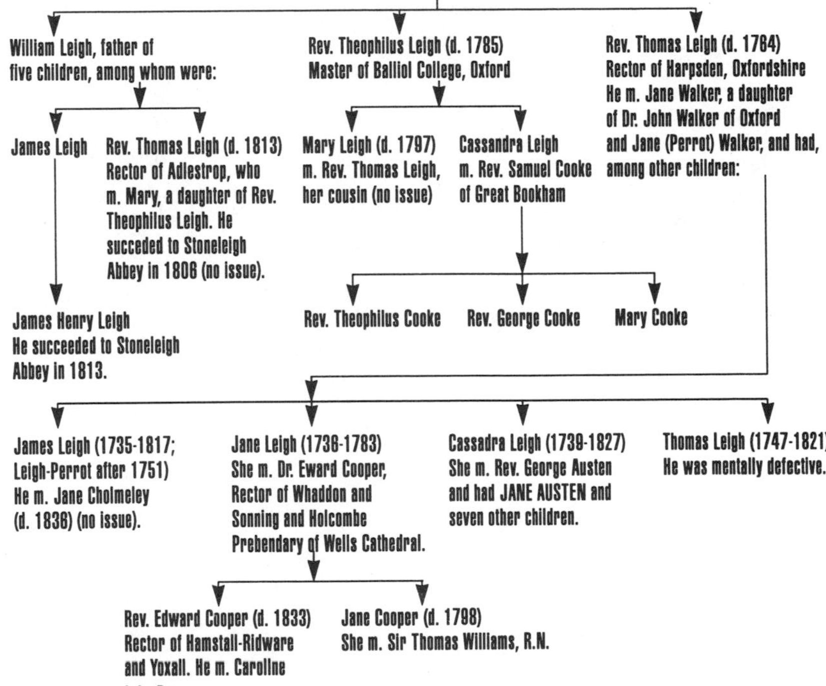

Jane Austen

The Woman

JANE AUSTEN

The only known contemporary likeness of Jane Austen, this pencil and watercolor sketch was drawn by Cassandra Austen around 1810. It is now in the National Portrait Gallery, London.

CHAPTER

1

Presenting Miss Jane Austen

In December 1815, when Jane Austen declared, "I think I may boast myself to be, with all possible vanity, the most unlearned and uninformed female who ever dared to be an authoress,"[1] she was indulging in playful self-deprecation. Nothing could have been further from the truth. Not only was she well read, knowledgeable concerning the theater, music, politics, religion, and the fine arts, she was also keenly attuned to the exciting period in which she lived. These assertions can easily be verified by a careful reading of her surviving letters, which also reveal that she was a flirtatious and occasionally sharp-tongued girl who matured into a compassionate but critically objective woman of genius.

This reassessment is a radical departure from the Jane Austen described by her earliest biographers. Until 1870, when the *Memoir of Jane Austen,* by her nephew James Edward Austen-Leigh, was published, the only previous account of her personal life available was the "Biographical Notice of the Author," written in 1817 by her brother Henry as an introduction to the posthumous publication of *Northanger Abbey* and *Persuasion.* In it, despite Jane's emphatic assertion that ". . . pictures of perfection . . . make me sick & wicked,"[2] Henry Austen began the post-mortem canonization of his sister by declaring:

> Though the frailties, foibles, and follies of others could not escape her immediate detection, yet even on their vices did she never trust herself to comment with unkindness. The affectation of candour is not uncommon; but she had no affectation. Faultless herself, as nearly as human nature can be, she always sought, in the faults of others, something to excuse, to forgive or forget. Where extenuation was impossible, she had a sure refuge in silence. She never uttered either a hasty, a silly, or a severe expression.[3]

As anyone familiar with Jane Austen's letters will immediately realize, these pietistic assertions cannot be supported by facts.

Later, Henry Austen expanded his earlier biographical account in a preface to the edition of *Sense and Sensibility* published by Richard Bentley in 1833. By then, he had exchanged his former role of a sophisticated London banker for that of "an earnest preacher of the evangelical school," causing him to tincture his updated appraisal of his sister with the following even more ponderous religiosity:

> Perhaps these volumes may be perused by some readers who will feel a solicitude respecting the authoress, extending beyond the perishable qualities of temper, manners, taste, and talents.—We can assure all such (and the being able so to do gratifies us more than the loudest voice of human praise) that Jane Austen's hopes of immortality were built upon the Rock of ages. That she deeply felt, and devoutly acknowledged, the insignificance of all worldly attainments, and the worthlessness of all human services, in the eyes of her heavenly Father. That she had no other hope of mercy, pardon, and peace, but through the merits and sufferings of her Redeemer.[4]

This sanctimonious cant was the verbal equivalent of the approved icon of Jane Austen that her family had apparently agreed by 1833 to present to the world. Once the impression was fixed in the minds of an increasingly moralistic and sentimental public, a further step was taken by Cassandra Austen, Jane's beloved but cautious older sister, to insure that no contrary evidence would survive to cast doubt on Henry Austen's evangelically slanted twaddle. Before her death in 1845, Cassandra looked over her younger sister's "open and confidential" correspondence "and burnt the greater part."[5] Some of the relatively few less revealing letters from Jane to herself, which she saved, were further censored with scissors, after which she either gave or bequeathed them to some of her nieces.

These and other Jane Austen letters, which were already in the possession of her nieces Anna Lefroy and Caroline Austen, were used by James Edward Austen-Leigh in preparing the *Memoir*. Even so, the greater number of Jane's letters to her niece Lady Knatchbull (the former Fanny Knight) were not discovered until after the latter's death in 1882. These were published in part by Lady Knatchbull's son, the first Lord Brabourne, in 1884, with a dedication to Queen Victoria.[6] Since then, a few other letters written by Jane Austen to her naval brothers or friends have surfaced, but they still bring the total to fewer than 150, a pitifully small number to have survived from the hundreds she is known to have written.

Fortunately, those that remain were edited in 1932, with a revised and corrected edition published in 1959, by R. W. Chapman, a labor of love that finally made every known Jane Austen letter completely available for the first time. Chapman's edition has been updated by Jo Modert's *Jane Austen's Manuscript Letters in Facsimile* (1990), which reproduces every known letter and fragment of Jane Austen's correspondence.

Chapman's and Modert's editions of the letters are therefore the only reliable primary sources for a reappraisal of Jane Austen as a credible human being since enough first-hand biographical material remains in them to indicate what she was like. Before the letters were available in Chapman's and Modert's editions, however, an entirely different Jane Austen had been foisted on the public by sentimental biographers. Using the *Memoir* as their primary source, these romancers succeeded in transforming their subject into a cozy spinster who wrote entertaining love stories as a pastime in the intervals between amusing her nieces and nephews with parlor games or accompanying their impromptu dances on the piano. Most of the biographies that have been written of her from the time of the *Memoir* until the present have therefore exaggerated the "dear Aunt Jane" legend so markedly that the vividly human and coolly objective Jane Austen as revealed in her novels and surviving correspondence has been largely ignored.

Although the *Memoir* preserved much valuable biographical information, it nevertheless succeeded, because of its overcautious familial piety, in fixing Jane Austen in the minds of several generations of readers as merely a gentrified author of witty and skillfully plotted romances. Fortunately, ample contrary evidence has surfaced since the publication of the *Memoir* to reveal that the real Jane Austen was not only a credible blending of genius and human fallibility, but was also richly endowed with an infinite variety of cultural interests.

Jane Austen was born on December 16, 1775, in Steventon rectory in Hampshire, England, where her father, the Rev. George Austen, was the incumbent as well as the rector of the neighboring parish of Deane. His family had risen to prominence and prosperity in the Weald of Kent during the reign of Elizabeth I by way of sheep farming and the manufacture of woollen cloth.[7] Her mother, born Cassandra Leigh, came from a higher social class, being descended from the Leighs of Cheshire, an aristocratic family that traced its descent from Hamon de Legh, lord of the Moiety of High Legh at the time of Henry II.[8]

Because of the frightful incidence of infant mortality at that time, Jane was privately baptized the day after her birth,[9] at which time she became the goddaughter of the Rev. Samuel Cooke, vicar of Great Bookham in Surrey, who had married a first cousin of Jane's mother. Cooke later became a close friend of Madame d'Arblay (Fanny Burney), whose novels Jane Austen greatly admired. Her godmothers were Jane, wife of Francis Austen of Sevenoaks, Kent, the wealthy solicitor uncle of Jane's father, and Jane, the wife of Dr. James Musgrave, rector of Chinnor, Oxfordshire, a relation of Mrs. Austen.[10] Because of the severity of the winter of 1775-76, Jane's public christening in her father's tiny medieval church did not take place until April 5, 1776.[11]

Jane was the seventh of eight children, whom she playfully referred to in one of her letters as the Hampshire Austens.[12] These were: James, who succeeded his father as the rector of Steventon;[13] George, who was mentally abnormal and did not live with the family;[14] Edward, who was adopted by his distant cousins, the Knights of Godmersham, Kent, and who took the surname of Knight after the death of his adoptive mother in 1812;[15] Henry Thomas, Jane's favorite brother;[16] Cassandra Elizabeth, Jane's beloved only sister;[17] and Francis William and Charles John Austen, both of whom eventually ended distinguished careers as admirals.[18]

After living at Steventon for twenty-five years, Jane moved with her parents and sister Cassandra in 1801 to Bath, where they remained until after the death of her father in 1805. With her mother, Cassandra, and Martha Lloyd, her lifelong friend, she then lived in Southampton from 1806 to 1809. In July 1809 all four women moved to Chawton, in Hampshire, where Jane remained until May 1817, when she went to Winchester because of ill health. She died there, unmarried, on July 18, 1817, and was buried in Winchester Cathedral.[19] Four of her novels, *Sense and Sensibility* (1811); *Pride and Prejudice* (1813); *Mansfield Park* (1814); and *Emma* (1815), were published while she was living at Chawton. Her two other novels, *Northanger Abbey* and *Persuasion,* were brought out in December 1817, a few months after her death.

Since there is only one authentic contemporary likeness of Jane Austen, the well-known pencil and watercolor sketch on the front cover of this volume made by her sister, Cassandra, now in the National Portrait Gallery, London, it is necessary to consult the recollections of those who knew her to record how she appeared. The first description was written by her father. On December 17, 1775, the day after her birth, he informed his Kentish sister-in-law, Susanna Walter, in a letter that Jane resembled her brother Henry, who was four years her senior and who grew up to be the handsomest of the Austen sons.[20] Later, in July 1788, when twelve-year-old Jane was visiting her Austen relations in Kent in the company of her parents and sister, she was described by Susanna's daughter, Philadelphia, as being "very like her brother Henry, not at all pretty & very prim, unlike a girl of twelve," as well as "whimsical & affected."[21] Evidently Jane was not long outgrowing that stage, for in 1791, when she was sixteen, her cousin, Eliza de Feuillide, reported that she and Cassandra were "perfect Beauties & of course gain 'hearts by dozens.'"[22] That same year, Eliza further described them as "two of the prettiest girls in England."[23] One year later, when Eliza was visiting Steventon, she amplified her earlier descriptions to Philadelphia by writing: "Cassandra & Jane are both very much grown (the latter is now taller than myself) and greatly improved as well in manners as in person, both of which are now much more formed than when you saw them. They are I think equally sensible, and both so to a degree seldom met with, but still my heart gives the preference to Jane, whose kind partiality to me indeed requires a return of the same nature."[24]

Many years later, Jane's niece Anna Lefroy recorded an amusing recollection concerning her Austen aunts dating from her Steventon days. In recalling Jane and Cassandra's visits to Deane rectory, where Anna lived with her father and stepmother, she wrote: "I remember the frequent visits of my two aunts, & how they walked in winter through the sloppy lane between Steventon & Deane in their pattens, commonly worn at that time by Gentlewomen . . . I cannot remember distinctly the face of either Aunt at that earliest period to which I have referred, only their general appearance, & especially the shape, the set that is, of their bonnets, for the bonnets themselves were in all respects—both as to material colour & trimming precisely alike—but it was my amusement to guess, & I could always guess right which bonnet & which Aunt belonged to each other—"[25]

As far as is known, these are the most memorable early descriptions of Jane Austen as recorded by those who knew her during her Steventon days. Nor are any descriptions of her person to be found in her surviving letters from the same period, other than the fact that she had already begun wearing caps similar to the one shown in Cassandra's later drawing of her. In a letter to her sister in 1798, Jane wrote: "I have made myself two or three caps to wear of evenings since I came home, and they save me a world of torment as to hair-dressing, which at present gives me no trouble beyond washing and brushing, for my long hair is always plaited up out of sight, and my short hair curls well enough to want no papering. I have had it cut lately by Mr. Butler."[26]

Jane moved with her mother, sister, and Martha Lloyd to Chawton in July 1809. There are several graphic recollections of her person, characteristics, and accomplishments dating from then until her death in 1817. The first comes from Henry Austen's "Biographical Notice of the Author" prepared by him in 1817 as a preface for the posthumous publication of *Northanger Abbey* and *Persuasion*. It reads:

> Of personal attractions she possessed a considerable share. Her stature was that of true elegance. It could not have been

> increased without exceeding the middle height. Her carriage and deportment were quiet, yet graceful. Her features were separately good. Their assemblage produced an unrivalled expression of that cheerfulness, sensibility, and benevolence, which were her real characteristics. Her complexion was of the finest texture. It might with truth be said, that her eloquent blood spoke through her modest cheek.[27]

Henry Austen was not entirely original in his description of Jane's high coloring, for he borrowed his simile from this description of Sophia Western in Fielding's *Tom Jones:* "Her complexion had rather more of the lily than of the rose; but when exercise or modesty created her natural colour, no vermillion could equal it. Then one might indeed cry out with the celebrated Dr. Donne:

> *—Her pure and eloquent blood*
> *Spoke in her cheeks, and so distinctly wrought:*
> *That one might almost say her body thought.*"[28]

To his description of his sister's physical appearance, Henry Austen added: "Her voice was extremely sweet. She delivered herself with fluency and precision. Indeed she was formed for elegant and rational society, excelling in conversation as much as in composition."[29]

Anna Lefroy was less expansive than her Uncle Henry. In a letter addressed to her half brother, James Edward Austen-Leigh, when he was collecting material for the *Memoir,* she wrote: "In later years Aunt Jane's personal appearance must be as well remembered by you as by me. The figure tall & slender not drooping—but well balanced as was proved by her light & firm step. The complexion of that rather rare sort which seems limited to the light Brunette—a mottled skin, not fair, but perfectly clear & healthy in its hue: the fine naturally curling hair; neither light nor dark—the bright hazel eyes to match—the rather small but well shaped nose—one wonders that with all these advantages she could yet fail of being a very handsome woman!"[30]

The description of Jane given by James Edward Austen-Leigh in the *Memoir* is equally vivid: "In person she was very attractive; her figure was rather tall and slender, her step light and firm, and her whole appearance expressive of health and animation. In complexion she was a clear brunette with a rich colour; she had full round cheeks, with mouth and nose small and well formed, bright hazel eyes, and brown hair forming natural curls close around her face. If not so regularly handsome as her sister, yet her countenance had a peculiar charm of its own to the eyes of most beholders."[31]

Caroline Austen, the younger sister of the author of the *Memoir*, was more explicit:

> As to my Aunt's personal appearance, her's [*sic*] was the first face that I can remember thinking pretty, not that I used that word to myself, but I know I looked at her with admiration—Her face was rather round than long—she had a bright, but not pink colour—a clear brown complexion and very good hazle [*sic*] eyes. . . . Her hair, a darkish brown, curled naturally—it was in short curls around her face (for then ringlets were not.) She always wore a cap—Such was the custom with ladies who were not quite young—at least of a morning but I never saw her without one, to the best of my remembrance, either morning or evening.[32]

In commenting on her aunt's personal traits during her Chawton years, Caroline Austen added:

> She was fond of work [i.e., sewing and embroidery]—and she was a great adept at overcast and satin stitch—the peculiar delight of that day—General handiness were amongst her characteristics—She could throw the spilikens for us, better than anyone else, and she was wonderfully successful at cup and ball—She found a resource sometimes in that simple game, when she suffered from weak eyes and could not work or read for long together—Her handwriting remains to bear testimony to its own excellence; and every note and letter of hers, was finished off handsomely—There was an art *then* in folding and sealing—no adhesive envelopes made all easy—some people's letters looked always loose and untidy—but *her* paper was sure to take the right folds, and *her* sealing wax to drop in the proper place—.[33]

Four contemporary or nearly contemporary accounts of Jane Austen's appearance and personal characteristics by others confirm these family impressions. The first was set down by Sir Egerton Brydges, the poet, antiquarian bibliographer, and brother of Jane's early mentor, Mrs. Anne Lefroy, the wife of the rector of Ashe, the neighboring parish to Steventon and Deane. In his *Autobiography*, published in 1834, Brydges recalled: "I remember

Jane Austen, the novelist, a little child: she was very intimate with Mrs. Lefroy, and much encouraged by her. . . . When I knew Jane Austen I never suspected that she was an authoress; but my eyes told me that she was fair and handsome, slight and elegant, but with cheeks a little too full."[34]

The second recollection of Jane Austen is equally revealing. When Mrs. Thomas Mozley, a sister of Cardinal Newman, was visiting the Rev. Fulwar-William Fowle, the rector of Allington, Wiltshire, in 1838, she learned that he had known Jane intimately in his youth from her visits to his father's vicarage at Kintbury in Berkshire. Mrs. Mozley, a great admirer of Jane Austen's novels, included his recollections in a letter to her sister:

> I asked him many questions about her & he gave me a very nice & satisfactory acct. of her—he said she was pretty—certainly pretty—bright & a good deal of color in her face—like a doll—no that wld not give at all the idea for she had so much expression—she was like a child—quite a child very lively & full of humor—most amiable—most beloved—he says the Austins [*sic*] are all clever—clever in a way—they write verses &c rather elegantly & are agreeable—but not superior—that Jane & James [i.e., Jane's elder brother] rose far above the others & were truly superior—the others had much vanity—there was not a glimpse about those 2.[35]

The third and fourth near-contemporary reminiscences of Jane Austen were included in two letters written by the wife of the Rev. Charles Beckford of Southampton after the publication of the *Memoir* in 1870. Mrs. Beckford, born Charlotte-Maria Middleton, was one of the daughters of John Charles Middleton, who rented Chawton Manor from Jane's brother Edward for a term of five years beginning in 1808. From 1809, when the Austens moved to Chawton from Southampton, until 1813, Mrs. Beckford, as a girl, was frequently in Jane Austen's company and remembered her vividly.

In her first letter to a friend who had lent her a copy of the *Memoir*, Mrs. Beckford commented on the well-known engraving of Jane Austen that served as a frontispiece to the volume:

> Jane's likeness is hardly what I remember there is a look, & that is all—I remember her as a tall thin spare person, with very high cheek bones great colour—sparkling Eyes not large but joyous &

> intelligent. The face by no means so broad & plump as represented; perhaps it was taken when very young, but the Cap looks womanly—her keen sense of humour I quite remember, it oozed out very much in Mr. Bennett's [*sic*] Style—Altogether I remember we liked her greatly as children from her entering into all Games &c.

In a later letter, written after Mrs. Beckford had borrowed the *Memoir* for a second reading, she commented: "We saw her often. She was a most kind & enjoyable person *to Children* but somewhat stiff & cold to strangers She used to sit at Table at Dinner parties without uttering much probably collecting matter for her charming novels which in those days we knew nothing about—her sister Cassandra was very lady-like but *very prim,* but my remembrance of Jane is that of her entering into all Childrens Games & liking her extremely."[36]

As for Jane Austen's personality, she was a classic example of a high-spirited, flirtatious, and occasionally satirical young girl who matured into a sensible and compassionate woman. Her youthful ebullience manifests itself in her juvenile writings, now known as *Volume the First, Volume the Second,* and *Volume the Third,* three small copybooks into which she transcribed her earliest attempts at story-telling between 1787, when she was twelve, and 1793, when she was eighteen. These juvenile writings not only reveal a promising literary apprentice endowed with a genius for satirical comedy; they also disclose the pert young author who described herself a few years later as being able to ". . . die of laughter . . . as they used to say at school."[37]

Jane's early exuberance, a characteristic that prevailed throughout her Steventon years, was undoubtedly the basis for the following adverse criticism leveled at her many years later by her snobbish niece, Lady Fanny Knatchbull, who recalled hypocritically (considering she had been Jane's favorite niece): "Aunt Jane from various circumstances was not so *refined* as she ought to have been from her *talent,* & if she had lived 50 years later she would have been in many respects more suitable to *our* more refined tastes."[38]

By the time Lady Knatchbull penned that diatribe the more robust spirit of the Georgian and Regency eras had been repressed by the blight of Victorian primness. Even so, Lady Knatchbull in the same letter did admit reluctantly that during the latter part of her life

". . . Aunt Jane was too clever not to put aside all possible signs of 'common-ness' (if such an expression is allowable) & teach herself to be more refined, at least in intercourse with people in general."[39]

Jane Austen's earliest letters prove conclusively that she wholeheartedly enjoyed the social amenities of the North Hampshire of her youth. This is also vividly reflected in her juvenilia, written to be read aloud to her family, who encouraged her to compose her rollicking satires. That Jane did not hesitate to write about death, drunkenness, deformity, physical injuries, suicide, adultery, illegitimacy, and theft in these early works is therefore hardly in accord with the claims made later by her Victorian and Edwardian kinfolk regarding the rarefied atmosphere of her early environment. Granted, these subjects were treated by the lively young author in a burlesque manner. But the fact that she, as a clergyman's daughter, was even permitted to write about them, and to spice her stories with occasional healthy doses of vulgarity and contemporary slang, is indicative of the tolerance of human fallibility that prevailed in her father's rectory.

As a daughter and granddaughter of Anglican clergymen, Jane was well instructed in the Christian principles as well as the stately ritual of the Established Church of her time. These serious regimens not only underscored the rules of good conduct that she firmly but quietly stressed in her novels, they also gave her an abiding spiritual comfort throughout her adult life. Meanwhile, as a high-spirited girl, Jane devoted most of her Steventon years to the everyday pleasures readily available to a person of her class—dress, dancing, and flirtation—with the hope of an early and financially advantageous marriage. In the meantime, she varied these pursuits with visiting and reading widely from worthwhile literature as well as what she once referred to as the "mere Trash of the common Circulating Library."[40] When these palled, she resorted to the more private avocations of letter writing, needlework, drawing, playing the piano, and singing, at all of which she was accomplished.

Jane Austen never suffered fools gladly, and if the sharp things that appear with relative frequency in her early letters are any indication, it is possible that she was not always cautious in sparing the feelings of others. This brings us to the Jane Austen of about the age of sixteen, and to a statement concerning her at that stage of her development that was made several years later by Mrs. George

Mitford, the mother of the author Mary Russell Mitford. Mrs. Mitford's remark has elicited howls of protest from many of Jane Austen's more squeamish biographers and admirers that would have been unnecessary had they taken the trouble to examine the criticism in the light of contemporary evidence.

Before doing so, however, it might be wise to quote the argument advanced by James Edward Austen-Leigh to rebut Mrs. Mitford's story, if for no other reason than to reveal later that the premise upon which he built his reasoning was false. Declaring that Mrs. Mitford was unconnected with the Steventon area during Jane Austen's girlhood and was therefore in no position to criticize his aunt's behavior at that time, the author of the *Memoir* commented: ". . . for upon Dr. Russell's death, in January 1783, his widow and daughter removed from the neighbourhood, so that all intercourse between the families ceased when Jane was little more than seven years old."[41]

To tell the story as it relates to Jane Austen, in a letter dated April 3, 1815, to her friend Sir William Elford, Mary Russell Mitford said. "*Apropos* to novels, I have discovered that our great favorite, Miss Austen, is my countrywoman; that mamma knew all her family very intimately; and that she herself is an old maid (I beg her pardon—I mean a young lady) with whom mamma before her marriage was acquainted. Mamma says that she was then the prettiest, silliest, most affected husband-hunting butterfly she ever remembers. . . ."[42]

Mary Russell, the mother of Mary Russell Mitford, was born in June 1750.[43] She was the only surviving child of Dr. Richard Russell, rector of Ashe and vicar of Overton, Hampshire, and his third wife, Mary Dickers, a daughter of a wealthy landowner. Dr. Russell and his family, who lived at Ashe rectory, were intimately acquainted with the Austens of Steventon. In 1783, when Jane was seven, Dr. Russell died in his eighty-eighth year. His widow and her daughter Mary then moved to Alresford, near Winchester, a distance of not more than ten miles from Steventon. Mrs. Russell died two years later, at which time her thirty-four-year-old daughter inherited £28,000 as well as considerable property. She was not a beauty, having been described by a contemporary as possessing a "plain face, prominent eyes and bad teeth, and bad complexion" scarcely relieved by a "kind and cheerful expression which animated her countenance."[44]

Despite these physical defects and because of her wealth, Mary Russell attracted several admirers, her final choice for a husband being George Mitford, a ne'er-do-well from a good family with a mania for greyhound coursing and whist, at both of which he was a constant loser. The couple was married at Alresford in October 1785 by Dr. William Buller, then dean and later bishop of Exeter. He was a good friend of Jane Austen's father, who included one of Buller's sons among his pupils at Steventon.[45] At first the Mitfords lived in style at Alresford, making occasional visits to the Ashe-Steventon neighborhood where Mrs. Mitford had grown to maturity. Thus she had ample opportunity to observe the behavior of her friends and acquaintances—Jane's for instance.

Three children were born to the Mitfords, but only one survived. This was Mary Russell Mitford, who was born in Alresford in 1787, when Jane was twelve. By that time George Mitford, to whom all but a small part of his wife's fortune had been entrusted at the time of their marriage, had not only gambled away his own money, but a good deal of his wife's as well. This finally obliged the Mitfords to move from Alresford to Reading in 1791, when Jane was in her sixteenth year.

The evidence provided by Jane's juvenilia plainly indicates that she was flirtatious and lively, with a girl's normal interests. When Mrs. Mitford's own plain looks are considered, it is not difficult to imagine that her censure of Jane as a spirited and handsome young girl would have been in proportion to her own remembered disappointments over her lack of beauty when she was the same age. That Mrs. Mitford's recollections, communicated years later to her daughter, who was also a plain woman, were therefore biased cannot be disputed. But an honest acknowledgment of Jane Austen's cleverness, flirtatiousness, and self-assurance at the time she was writing her juvenilia lends some credibility to Mrs. Mitford's remark even though it continues to distress many of Jane's more sentimental admirers.

An example of Jane Austen's youthful high jinks are the facetious entries she made in the marriage register at Steventon Church.[46] The leaf on which Jane's notations appear is not a part of the actual register itself, but rather an exemplar to indicate how entries should be made on the blank forms of the register proper. As no dates are recorded on the specimen sheet, it is impossible to determine when

Jane made her entries, but it is likely that it was during her teens. The entries read:

> The Banns of Marriage between *Henry Frederick Howard Fitzwilliam* of *London* and *Jane Austen* of *Steventon.*

And:

> The Form of an Entry of a Marriage. *Arthur William Mortimer* of *Liverpool* and *Jane Austen* of *Steventon.*

And:

> The Marriage was witnessed between us. *Jack Smith, Jane Smith,* late *Austen,* in the presence of *Jack Smith, Jane Smith.*

Note that Jane's sly joke in the last entry made the Smith couple witness their own nuptials, which was irregular. Also, as a part of Jane's humorous touch, it is worth mentioning that Henry Frederick Howard Fitzwilliam, the conjectural bridegroom whose banns were to be published, bore the names later given by Jane to Henry Tilney in *Northanger Abbey* and Henry Crawford in *Mansfield Park,* Frederick Wentworth in *Persuasion,* the Mr. Howard who was to marry Emma Watson in *The Watsons,* and Fitzwilliam Darcy in *Pride and Prejudice.*

Jane Austen's surviving letters dating from her Steventon years, beginning in January 1796 and continuing until the end of February 1801, reveal her for the first time as a coquettish young woman of spirit. Her appearance at that time was later noted by her niece, Caroline Austen thus: "She was not, I beleive [*sic*] an absolute beauty, but before she left Steventon she was established as a very pretty girl, in the opinion of most of her neighbors—as I learned afterwards from some of those who still remained."[47] But Jane's outstanding physical feature, then as well as later, was her merry hazel eyes, which she inherited from her father, and which missed few of the subtleties of the human comedy going on around her.

Unlike the more subdued letters of her maturity, Jane Austen's earlier letters are notable not only for their liveliness but also for any number of caustic observations concerning her neighbors that continue to distress the priggish among her admirers. The ability to "shoot folly as it flies"[48] was an integral part of Jane Austen's genius, however, and her ability to use that gift with well-aimed precision is one of the reasons her novels are as readable and relevant today as they were when they first appeared. It is therefore ridiculous to take exception to the occasional uncharitable comments in her early letters as being incompatible with her great talent. The same woman who created Mrs. Norris, Lady Catherine de Bourgh, Mr. Collins, Mr. and Mrs. Elton, and Sir Walter Elliot, to name but a few of her more odious characters, was also fully capable of discerning their counterparts in real life. Moreover, as her censorious remarks were communicated in her private correspondence with her sister and were never intended for publication, she was justified in sharing them with the one person in her family who, at least during her earlier and more tolerant womanhood, was sufficiently indulgent to be amused by her younger sister's occasional malice.

Jane's letters to Cassandra between 1796 and 1801, supplemented by family remembrances of her during the same period, reveal a good deal about her personality. Of greatest importance was her emerging individuality, for despite her obvious enjoyment of the superficialities of society, Jane Austen was basically a very private person. This is demonstrated by a quotation from a letter to her sister written in December 1798, in which she asserted: "I do not want people to be very agreeable, as it saves me the trouble of liking them a great deal."[49] This drawing the line between her private and public worlds was understood early on and respected by Cassandra, her most intimate confidant from early childhood until her death.

Despite the closeness between the two sisters, however, they were temperamentally different. Cassandra was noted for her prudence, whereas Jane's flirtatiousness as a girl was occasionally so impulsive that her older sister would caution her that her excessive vivacity would make her an object of censure. Jane evidently heeded this advice in time, for as she grew older, she became increasingly reserved with strangers. In a later passage in the 1815 letter quoted earlier, Mary Russell Mitford described a visit to Jane Austen at Chawton in that year by a relation of the man who was then pursuing a lawsuit against Jane's brother Edward Knight. Understandably, Jane gave the visitor a cool reception, but in doing so she also indicted her usual behavior to outsiders by her aloofness.

Miss Mitford wrote:

> . . . a friend of mine, who visits her now, says she has stiffened into the most perpendicular, precise, taciturn piece of "single blessedness" that ever existed, and that, till "Pride and Prejudice" showed what a precious gem was hidden in that unbending case, she was no more regarded in society than a poker or a fire-screen, or any other thin, upright piece of wood or iron that fills its corner in peace and quietness. The case is very different now; she is still a poker, but a poker of whom every one is afraid. It must be confessed that this silent observation from such an observer is rather formidable. Most writers are good-humored chatterers—neither very wise nor very witty; but, nine times out of ten (at least the few that I have known), unaffected and pleasant, and quite removing by their conversation any awe that may have been excited by their works. But a wit, a delineator of character, who does not talk is terrific indeed![50]

Fortunately, one of Jane Austen's brothers later unintentionally provided the explanation for Jane's general aloofness toward strangers, to which he added a pleasant account of his sister's usual conduct toward those within her family circle. In a letter written on January 31, 1852, by Admiral Sir Francis Austen, Jane's older naval brother, to Miss Eliza Susan Quincy of Boston, a daughter of a former president of Harvard College, he recalled his sister thus: "In her temper, she was chearful [*sic*] and not easily irritated, and tho' rather reserved to strangers so as to have been by some accused of haughtiness of manner, yet in the company of those she loved the native benevolence of her heart and kindliness of her disposition were forcibly displayed. On such occasions she was a most agreeable companion and by the lively sallies of her wit and good-humored drollery seldom failed of exciting the mirth and hilarity of the party."[51]

Apart from the fact that as a child Jane Austen came near dying of "putrid fever" (i.e., typhoid), her general health was robust during her Steventon years. There are references in two of her letters written in 1799, however, that indicate that she had begun to suffer a weakness in her eyes.[52] But this did not seem to trouble her greatly, and her felicitous young womanhood at Steventon was an extension of her early childhood until December 1800, when she was suddenly faced with a violent uprooting from the Hampshire in which she had always lived. The wrench occurred when her father, then sixty-nine, decided quite suddenly to appoint his eldest son, James, as his *locum tenens* at Steventon and retire with his wife and two daughters to Bath. Jane Austen was staying with her friend Martha Lloyd at Ibthorpe when the decision was made and had hilariously anticipated her return home by writing to her sister, then on a visit to Kent: "Martha has promised to return with me, & our plan is to have a nice black frost for walking to Whitechurch, & there throw ourselves into a postchaise, one upon the other, our heads hanging out at one door, & our feet at the opposite."[53]

When Jane and Martha arrived at the rectory, however, they were greeted by Mrs. Austen, who announced abruptly: "Well, girls, it is all settled. We have decided to leave Steventon and go to Bath."[54] Jane is reported to have fainted from the shock. The move was made early in 1801, and for the next eight years Jane's life was clouded, first by the death of her mentor, Mrs. Lefroy of Ashe, in December 1804, and later by the death of her father in January 1805. Faced with the prospect of having to live on a considerably reduced scale by the latter event, Jane and her mother and sister suffered temporary mental anguish, but this passed when four of her brothers came to the rescue by assuring them of a small but adequate income.

Added to these difficulties, the constant removal from one rented lodging to another in Bath and later in Southampton, and what Jane's niece Caroline Austen referred to as her aunt's "nameless and dateless" romance, which presumably occurred at some seashore place between 1801 and 1804 and which ended tragically, further contributed to her mental unrest to the extent that her literary creativity became practically nonexistent. As a consequence, by 1809, when Mrs. Austen, her two daughters, and Martha Lloyd settled in Chawton, the lively young Jane Austen of the carefree Steventon years had been conditioned by sorrow and emotional suffering.

At Steventon, backed by the assurance of her family's position, Jane was still, even at twenty-five, an ebullient young woman whose youthful cleverness was indulged by those who had appreciated and encouraged her from the time of her precocious childhood. In Bath and Southampton, however, Jane's formerly assured role as an extroverted commentator on the society she frequented was suddenly reversed. As her family was relatively unknown in those places, she was reduced to the role of a cautious observer rather than an outspoken critic. But this enabled her to quietly augment those observations she had already garnered during her first twenty-five years at Steventon with additional nuances of the human comedy played out on a larger scale.

By the time she had settled at Chawton at the age of thirty-three, Jane Austen was a well-traveled young woman for her time. Between her birth and 1809, when she moved to Chawton, she had journeyed across England from Kent in the east to Devonshire and Wales in the west, as well as from Hampshire in the south to as far north as Staffordshire. She had also lived in Oxford, Reading, London, Bath, and Southampton. Knowledge of these places later provided her with carefully observed background material, not only for *Sense and Sensibility, Pride and Prejudice,* and *Northanger Abbey,* which she revised for publication after moving to Chawton, but for the three other novels, *Mansfield Park, Emma,* and *Persuasion* that she wrote there.

Also, despite her ironic assertion that she was "the most unlearned and uninformed female who ever dared to be an authoress,"[55] Jane Austen was not only a well-educated woman for her time and station, "sensible to the charms of style, and enthusiastic in the cultivation of her own language,"[56] she also possessed a good knowledge of French, a familiarity with Italian, and a nodding acquaintance with Latin. Additionally, she was well read in the English classics, particularly Shakespeare, Milton, Johnson, and Cowper, as well as the poets and prose writers of her time. She also had a wide knowledge of British fiction from the time of Defoe until her own period; played the piano and sang passably well; and enjoyed the professional theater. According to her brother Henry's testimony, she continued throughout her life to be "a warm and judicious admirer of landscape, both in nature and on canvas."[57]

Apart from a list of the dates of composition of three of her novels prepared by herself, supplemented by a later and more comprehensive one drawn up after her death by Cassandra, and occasional references in her own letters as well as the fortunate survival of the canceled chapters of *Persuasion* and the manuscript of her last unfinished novel, now known as *Sanditon,* there is little left to reveal the details of Jane Austen's habits of composition during her maturity. Enough is known of her after she moved to Chawton, however, to realize that the nine years of her unwilling residence in Bath and Southampton had matured her to the point that she was ready to begin the second and most important phase of her literary career. The fortunate survival of eighty-one of Jane's letters written between 1809 and 1817, and the recollections of her niece, Caroline Austen, and her nephew, James Edward Austen-Leigh, also preserve vivid glimpses of her during her Chawton years.

In commenting on Jane's daily routine at Chawton, Caroline Austen said: "My aunt must have spent much time in writing—her desk lived in the drawing room. I often saw her writing letters on it, and I beleive [*sic*] she wrote much of her Novels in the same way—sitting with her family, when they were quite alone; but I never saw any manuscript of *that* sort, in progress . . ."[58]

This was further elaborated in the *Memoir*, in which Caroline's brother, in expressing his amazement at the volume of work Jane accomplished between 1809 and her death in 1817, wrote:

> How she was able to affect all this is surprising, for she had no separate study to retire to, and most of the work must have been done in the general sitting-room, subject to all kinds of casual interruptions. She was careful that her occupation should not be suspected by servants, or visitors, or any persons beyond her own family party. She wrote upon small sheets of paper which could easily be put away, or covered with a piece of blotting paper. There was, between the front door and the offices, a swing door which creaked when it was opened; but she objected to having this little inconvenience remedied, because it gave her notice when anyone was coming. . . . In that well occupied female party there must have been many precious hours of silence during which the pen was busy at the little mahogany writing desk, while Fanny Price, or Emma Woodhouse, or Anne Elliott [*sic*] was growing into beauty and interest.[59]

By the time Jane Austen settled at Chawton, she had developed into an assured and appealing woman of the world. She had then reached that rare state in which a happy mingling of sophistication and childlike gaiety of spirit was achieved. She had also put all ideas of marriage behind her, having made the choice, as one writer has aptly described it, between the overuse of the reproductive organs and genteel celibacy.[60] As a result, she came to regard each of her novels as it was published as a "darling child,"[61] the phrase she applied to *Pride and Prejudice* when it came out in 1813. Meanwhile, as one of the "formidables,"[62] as she playfully referred to her sister and herself in a letter dating from her Chawton period, she relished the security of the first permanent home that she had known since her Steventon days, tempering the quiet at Chawton Cottage by frequent visits to her brother Henry in London, and less frequent ones to her brother Edward at Godmersham in Kent. This pleasant routine continued until shortly after the publication of *Emma* in December 1815. In 1816, Jane Austen became seriously ill; a little over a year later she was dead.

The exact nature of Jane's fatal illness was a matter of speculation until 1964, when Sir Zachary Cope, a Fellow of the Royal College of Surgeons, assessed the symptoms as recorded by Jane in her last remaining letters, after which he declared that her death was caused by Addison's disease. This insidious complaint is a progressive atrophy of the adrenal cortex and is attended by weakness, abnormal brown pigmentation of the skin and mucous membranes, weight loss, low blood pressure, and gastrointestinal upsets, from all of which Jane Austen suffered during the last year of her life. The disease was named for Dr. Thomas Addison, of Guy's Hospital, London, who first identified it thirty-eight years after Jane's death.

In commenting on his diagnosis Cope wrote:

> Jane Austen died at 4:30 a.m. on 18 July 1817 at the age of 41 from an ailment the nature of which has never been ascertained, or, so far as I am aware, seriously discussed. No information was furnished by the doctors who attended her, and her relatives were reticent about her illness, so that we are compelled to rely chiefly on the few comments made by the patient herself in her letters that have survived. Fortunately Jane Austen was an accurate observer, and though she made light of her troubles until near the end one can rely on her definite statements.[63]

Cope commented further: "Addison's disease is usually due to tuberculosis of the suprarenal capsules, and it is likely that it was so in Jane's case. The disease runs its course rapidly, indicating an active pathological process that might well account for any fever. Pain in the back has also been noted in Addison's disease by several observers"—a complaint Jane mentioned in the early stages of her illness. In summarizing his findings, Cope concluded: "If our surmise is correct, Jane Austen did something more than write excellent novels—she also described the first recorded case of Addison's disease in her letters of the adrenal bodies."

Cassandra was with Jane in the bow-windowed room in the still-existing house on College Street, Winchester, when she died. In describing Jane's last hour, Cassandra recorded: "I was able to close her eyes myself & it was a great gratification to me to render her these last services. There was nothing convulsed or which gave the idea of pain in her look, on the contrary, but for the continual motion of the head, she gave me the idea of a beautiful statue, & even now in her coffin, there is such a sweet serene air over her countenance as is quite pleasant to contemplate."[64]

Eleven obituary notices announcing Jane Austen's death have been discovered: the first was published in *The Hampshire Chronicle and Courier* on July 21, 1817. The fullest of them, presumably written by Jane's brother Henry, printed in *The Salisbury and Winchester Journal* on July 28, 1817, reads: "On Friday the 18th inst. died in this city, Miss Jane Austen, youngest daughter of the late Rev. George Austen, Rector of Steventon, in this county, and the Authoress of Emma, Mansfield Park, Pride and Prejudice and Sense and Sensibility. Her manners were most gentle, her affections ardent, her candour was not to be surpassed, and she lived and died as became a humble Christian."[65]

Six days after her death, during the early morning hours of July 24, 1817,[66] Jane Austen was buried in Winchester Cathedral. Shortly afterwards her brother James, who was ill and could not attend the funeral, wrote the following somewhat stilted but heartfelt poem lamenting Jane's untimely death.

Venta, within thy sacred Fane
Rests many a chief in battle slain,
And many a Statesman great & wise
Beneath thy hallowed pavement lies:
Tracing thy venerable Pile
Thy Gothic Choir & Pillar'd Aisle
Frequent we tread the vaulted grave
Where sleep the Learned & the Brave;
High on the Screen on either hand

Old Saxon Monarch's coffins stand,
Below, beneath his sable stone
Lies the Conqueror's haughty son:
Immured within the Chapel wall
Sleep mitered Priest & Cardinal;
And honor'd Wickham lies reclined
In Gothic tracery enshrined.

But sure since Williams's purer taste
Old Walkelyn's heavier style effaced
O'er the plain roof the fret work spread
And formed the Arch with lancet head;
Ne'er did this venerable Fane
More beauty, sense & worth contain
Than when upon a Sister's bier
Her brothers dropt the bitter tear.

In her (rare union) were combined
A fair form & a fairer mind;
Hers, Fancy quick & clear good sense
And wit which never gave offense;
A Heart as warm as ever beat,
A Temper, even, calm & sweet:
Though quick & keen her mental eye
Poor Nature's foibles to descry
And seemed for ever on the watch,
Some traits of ridicule to catch,
Yet not a word she ever pen'd
Which hurt the feelings of a friend,
And not one line she ever wrote
Which dying she would wish to blot;
But to her family alone
Her real, genuine worth was known.
Yes, they whose lot it was to prove
Her Sisterly, her filial love,
They saw her ready still to share
The labours of domestic care,
As if their prejudice to shame
Who, jealous of fair female fame,

Maintain that literary taste
In womans mind is much misplaced,
Inflames their vanity & pride,
And draws from useful work aside.

Such wert thou Sister while below
In this mixt Scene of joy & woe
To have thee with us it was given,
A special kind behest of Heaven.

What now thou art we cannot tell:
Nor where the just made perfect dwell
Know we as yet. To us denied
To draw that parting veil aside
Which 'twixt two different worlds outspread
Divides the Living from the Dead.
But yet with all humility,
The change we trust was gain for thee.
For oh! If so much genuine worth
In its imperfect state on Earth
So fair & so attractive proved,
By all around admired & loved,
Who then the change dare calculate
Attendant on that happy state,
When by the Body unconfined
All sense, Intelligence & Mind
By Seraphs borne through realms of light
(While Angels gladden at the sight)
The Aetherial Spirit wings its way
To regions of Eternal day.[67]

Shortly after her death Jane's charm as a woman and accomplishments as an author were acknowledged by John Britton in *The History and Antiquities of the See and Cathedral Church of Winchester.* Britton wrote:

> Among the interments in this pile, is one of a lady whose virtues, talents, and accomplishments entitle her not only to distinguished notice, but to the admiration of every person who has a heart to feel and a mind to appreciate female worth and merit.

> The lady alluded to, Miss Jane Austen, who was buried here, July 1817, was author of four novels of considerable interest and value. In the last, a posthumous publication, entitled "Northanger Abbey," is a sketch of a memoir of the amiable author.[68]

Many years later Jane's nephew James Edward Austen-Leigh, the youngest member of her family present at her funeral, wrote: "Her brothers went back sorrowing to their several homes. They were very fond and very proud of her. They were attached to her by her talents, her virtues, and her engaging manners; and each loved afterwards to fancy a resemblance in some niece or daughter of his own to the dear sister Jane, whose perfect equal they yet never expected to see."[69]

CHAPTER

2

Homes, Environments, and Friends

Jane Austen, either as a woman or as an author, cannot be properly appreciated without a working knowledge of her immediate family and friends, as well as of the environments in which she lived during her brief lifetime. As an author whose chosen field was "pictures of domestic life in country villages,"[1] Jane was fortunate in having been born in rural Hampshire. It was there, during her formative years, that she absorbed the nuances of the type of English society she later depicted in her novels.

Steventon, where Jane lived for her first twenty-five years, was then a microcosm of thousands of similar communities throughout England. Referred to as "Stivetune" in the Domesday Survey of 1068, its history extended back to Roman and Saxon times.[2] Located around seven miles from Basingstoke, the principal town of the area, Steventon is still an out-of-the-way place tucked in between two major modern highways that follow the routes used in Jane's day by stagecoaches. The one to the north links London with Salisbury, Bath, Exeter, and Taunton, while the one to the south connects London with Winchester and Southampton. Access to Steventon in Jane's time was by way of a deeply rutted cart road that was usually in deplorable condition.

Apart from its medieval church, a small stone building dedicated to St. Nicholas, where Jane's father was rector from 1761 to 1801, no other structure now remains at Steventon with which she would have been familiar. Steventon Manor, an imposing sixteenth-century flint and stone house with diamond-paned casements, was razed in 1970 after it had been vandalized.[3] The thatched cottages that housed the farm laborers and their families during Jane's Steventon years were torn down during the early part of the nineteenth century. Even the rectory in which she was born was demolished during the 1820s after it had been damaged by a great thaw that flooded the cellars and rendered the ground floor rooms uncomfortably damp. At that time a new rectory (now a private residence) was built on a nearby hill for the Rev. William Knight, one of Jane's nephews, who was rector of Steventon from 1823 until his death in 1873.[4]

According to contemporary accounts Jane's birthplace was an attractive but unpretentious brick structure of two stories and an attic, with leaded casement windows and sharp, pointed dormers punctuating its steep red-tiled roof. The north or main entrance was approached by a half-circle carriage drive, while the grounds in that area were shaded by elms and horse-chestnut trees. To the south of the rectory were "one of those old-fashioned gardens in which vegetables and flowers are combined" and "a terrace of the finest turf," which Jane's nephew and first biographer suggested in the *Memoir* "must have been in the writer's thoughts when she described Catherine Morland's childish delight in 'rolling down the green slope at the back of the house.'"[5]

Catherine Hubback, a daughter of Jane's brother Sir Francis Austen, in an account of his childhood, described the interior of the rectory thus: "The parsonage consisted of three rooms in front on the ground floor, the best parlour, the common parlour, and the kitchen; behind there were Mr. Austen's study, the back kitchen and the stairs; above them were seven bedrooms and three attics. The rooms were low-pitched but not otherwise bad, and compared with the usual style of such buildings it might be considered a very good house."[6] This description can be supplemented with more precise details concerning the interior of the rectory from Jane's early letters. Like the walls of Barton Cottage in *Sense and Sensibility,* which were hung with Elinor Dashwood's drawings, some of the walls were adorned with drawings by Jane's artistically gifted sister, Cassandra. Jane also mentions "paintings on tin," "Scriptoral pieces," a "Battle piece" and "French agricultural Prints."[7] As for the furnishings, if the Hepplewhite-style bureau-bookcase and two graceful mahogany chairs (now at Chawton Cottage, but known to have been at Steventon in Jane's time) are any indication, the rectory was comfortably furnished.

The most important room in the house as far as Jane Austen was concerned was the one she referred to in her letters as the "Dressing Room"—a second floor, blue-wallpapered room with blue-striped curtains at the windows adjoining the one in which she and Cassandra slept. It was there that Jane kept her square pianoforte, her still-existing portable mahogany writing desk, which her father presumably presented to her as a nineteenth-birthday present in 1794, and her favorite books. In this room, around 1787, her first literary attempts began soon after she had returned from Mrs. La Tournelle's Abbey School in Reading.[8]

By 1787, when Jane was twelve, she was already exhibiting a precocity that was encouraged by her family. Her father, an Oxford graduate and an excellent classical scholar who augmented his clerical income by taking in pupils, was undoubtedly her first instructor, not only in English grammar and history but probably in French. The volume from which she began studying French when she was eight is still extant and bears the inscription, "Miss Jane Austen, 5th Decr. 1783," on one of its endpapers. It contains what are probably Jane's earliest known signatures, and includes two childish scrawls, "Mothers angry fathers gone out" and "I wish I had done," apparently scribbled by her during her inattentive moments.[9] Jane also may have received instruction from her father in the rudiments of Latin grammar, particularly the Eton Latin Grammar from which she included a quotation in a letter to her sister on January 24, 1809. Meanwhile, she had the run of the rectory library, a collection of more than five hundred volumes that was supplemented from time to time with contemporary fiction, poetry, history, and essays borrowed from circulating libraries.

Jane's mother, a niece of Dr. Theophilus Leigh, for more than half a century Master of Balliol College, Oxford, and Vice Chancellor of Oxford University, would certainly have assisted in her talented daughter's education. A witty woman, Mrs. Austen was remembered as a person who "united strong common sense with a lively imagination, and often expressed herself, both in writing and in conversation, with epigrammatic force and point."[10] Jane's ability as a writer apparently came from her mother's side of the family. Mrs. Austen was a clever rhymer and lively letter writer, while two of her Leigh cousins were also literary. The first, Cassandra Cooke, the wife of Jane Austen's godfather, the Rev. Samuel Cooke, vicar of Great Bookham in Surrey, was the author of a novel, *Battleridge, an historical tale founded on facts,* published in 1799.[11] The second, Miss Elizabeth Leigh, wrote a "History of the Leigh Family of Adlestrop, Glostershire [*sic*]" in 1788.[12] This still unpublished work contains many lively pen portraits of Jane Austen's maternal relations, notably a reference to the Steventon rectory family of Jane Austen's childhood in which Mrs. Austen is described as "the wife of the truly respectable Mr. Austen" and the mother of "eight children—James, George, Edward, Henry, Francis, Charles, Cassandra and Jane." To this Miss Leigh added: "With his sons (all promising to make figures in life) Mr. Austen educates a few youths of chosen friends and acquaintances. When among this liberal society the simplicity, hospitality, and taste which commonly prevail in different families among the delightful valleys of Switzerland ever recur to my memory."[13]

Jane Austen's education and literary attempts were also encouraged by two of her elder brothers, James and Henry. James, a precocious boy, had matriculated at St. John's College, Oxford, when he was fourteen. He is credited with having a large share in directing his younger sister's early reading and fostering her taste. Like his mother, James wrote verse. Those of his poems that have survived, ranging from the light-hearted prologues and epilogues written for amateur theatrical performances at Steventon, to the more serious verses of his later years, indicate he was deeply religious, a lover of natural scenery (a taste he shared with Jane), and widely read. Henry, who was more worldly minded, shared his literary taste, his enthusiasm for the theater and the fine arts, and his clever conversation with Jane. It was a rewarding camaraderie that continued throughout her lifetime.

Henry also helped his brother James found a weekly periodical called *The Loiterer,* the first issue of which was printed at Oxford in 1789, when Jane was thirteen.[14] The separate issues, which were collected and published in two volumes after the last one appeared in March 1790, contained, among other things, several clever satirical novellas written by James and Henry, which were similar to, but more sophisticated than, those Jane was then attempting to write. Jane herself may have been the author of a witty letter signed "Sophia Sentiment" that appeared in the ninth issue of *The Loiterer* (March 28, 1789). Although there is no certainty she wrote the letter, it has been suggested it not only contains personal observations she could have gathered when she was a schoolgirl in Oxford in the spring of 1783 but reflects her known reading tastes between then and 1789.[15]

Still another home influence was Jane Austen's only sister, Cassandra, almost three years older than herself, whose interest in and encouragement of Jane's literary activities continued throughout her younger sister's lifetime. From their earliest childhood, Jane and her sister were devoted companions. Their niece Anna Lefroy recalled they ". . . were everything to each other. They seemed to lead a life to themselves within the general family life which was shared only by each other. I will not say their *true,* but their *full,* feelings and opinions were known only to themselves."[16] Cassandra and Jane attended the same schools and read (and usually admired) the same books. When Jane began to write, Cassandra was her first reader. Four of Jane's juvenilia were dedicated to Cassandra: *The Beautifull* (*sic*) *Cassandra, Catharine or The Bower, Ode To Pity,* and *The History of England* ("By a partial, prejudiced, & ignorant Historian").[17] Jane's assault on English history was illustrated by her older sister with thirteen witty watercolor portraits of the monarchs Jane treated so cavalierly. Characteristically, Cassandra depicted Jane's favorite, Mary, Queen of Scots, as a beautiful blue-eyed charmer, while Elizabeth I, whom Jane did not like, was portrayed as a sharp-eyed, pointed-chinned virago, with a forest of plumes waving from her elaborate coiffure and several wilted roses stuck in her bosom.

The unique position Jane's father held in his parish also contributed to her social development. As his wealthy cousins, the Knights of Godmersham, Kent, who owned most of the land in Steventon parish, never lived there, Jane's father came to be regarded as their local representative. His status was strengthened by two other factors. First, as a recognized scholar from a long-established and respectable Kentish family, he was undoubtedly the best-educated man in the community. Second, his wife's aristocratic and academic connections enabled his family to move in the best social circles in the neighborhood, thereby introducing Jane Austen at an early age to the milieu she later depicted with authority in her mature fiction.[18]

The North Hampshire nobility of Jane Austen's time was represented by the Dukes of Bolton of Hackwood Park near Basingstoke: Lord Dorchester (the former Sir Guy Carleton of American Revolutionary War fame) of Kempshott Park near Steventon, and Lord Portsmouth of Hurstbourne Park, a vast estate to the west of Steventon. Jane Austen would have known of the social activities that took place in these great houses mostly from hearsay, since as far as is known she was familiarly acquainted with but one member of the local aristocracy—Lord Portsmouth, who, as a boy, had been a pupil of her father.[19] As a gesture of his continued friendship the Austens were always invited to the ball he gave annually on the anniversary of his first marriage. Jane was occasionally invited by Lady Dorchester to attend balls at Kempshott Park. She also frequently met all of these notables at monthly dancing assemblies during the winter months at either the Town Hall or the Angel Inn in Basingstoke.

In the main, however, Jane's intimate Hampshire friends were restricted to the landed gentry, the clergy and other members of what was then termed the "middling class of society." It should also be noted that the people with whom Jane Austen associated during her formative years were for the most part forthright eighteenth-century folk, untouched by the primness that later characterized their Victorian counterparts.

"They [i.e., the Austens] were not rich & the people around with whom they chiefly mixed, were not at all high bred, or in short anything more than *mediocre* & *they* of course tho' superior in *Mental powers & cultivation* were on the same level as far as *refinement* goes," Jane's snobbish niece, Lady Knatchbull, wrote many years later.[20] But Lady Knatchbull missed the point, for Jane Austen and her family and its associates were an integral part of the robust England that produced Hogarth, Rowlandson, Fielding, Richardson, and Samuel Johnson.

Among the local landed gentry with whom Jane and her family were on intimate terms were the Chutes of The Vyne[21] and the

Portals of Laverstoke House.[22] The Vyne is a magnificent country house near Basingstoke dating from the time of Henry VIII with later Georgian additions made by John Chute (1701-76). It was owned in Jane's time by William John Chute, who was almost constantly a member of Parliament from 1790 to 1820. Unlike the earlier John Chute, who liked to entertain Horace Walpole and other artistic friends in his handsome home crammed with the spoils of the Grand Tour, William John Chute (like Sir John Middleton in *Sense and Sensibility*) was a robust outdoor man with a passion for fox hunting.[23] This enthusiasm was shared by Jane's brothers, and there are several mentions of Chute and his younger clerical bachelor brother Tom in Jane Austen's early letters.

Laverstoke House, the home of the Portal family, provided Jane with the name of Joseph Bonomi, the architect mentioned in *Sense and Sensibility* who was responsible for the country house plans the insufferable Robert Ferrars flung into the fire. In 1759, the Portals, a wealthy family of Huguenot ancestry who owned the mill that manufactured the paper for the notes issued by the Bank of England, acquired the original Laverstoke House. This was inherited in 1793 by Harry Portal, an intimate friend of the Austens. He rented the old house to others and built the present Laverstoke House on a more elevated site from designs by Bonomi, then a fashionable Italian-born London architect.[24] As the neoclassical style was a novelty in North Hampshire, the new house was much discussed locally and Bonomi's name became more or less a household word. In that manner Jane Austen acquired a suitably impressive (and authentic) architect's name to use in *Sense and Sensibility,* which was begun in its present form in November 1797, when Laverstoke House was nearing completion.

Apart from the Chutes and the Portals, Jane Austen's intimate acquaintances during her Steventon days were the Lefroys of Ashe, the Digweeds of Steventon Manor, the Harwoods of Deane House, the Bramstons of Oakley Hall, the Lyfords of Basingstoke and the Terrys of Dummer House. In May 1783, the Rev. Isaac Peter George Lefroy, "an excellent man, of courtly manners, who knew the world, and had mixed in it,"[25] became the rector of Ashe. His wife, Anne, took an immediate fancy to Jane Austen, then seven who reciprocated "her enthusiastic eagerness of disposition."[26] From 1783 until 1801, when Jane moved from Steventon to Bath, she was an intimate friend of Mrs. Lefroy, whose surviving portrait reveals she was a beautiful woman. Mrs. Lefroy proved to be a trusted counselor to her young friend, gave her the run of the Ashe rectory library, in which the current fiction of the day (including the Gothic novels of Mrs. Ann Radcliffe) was well represented, and encouraged her burgeoning literary efforts.

In describing Mrs. Lefroy, who was twenty-five years older than Jane, Sir Egerton Brydges, the author and genealogist, wrote: "My eldest sister was fourteen years and a half older than me: she had an exquisite taste for poetry, and could almost repeat the chief English poets by heart, especially Milton, Pope, Collins, Gray, and the poetical passages of Shakespeare. . . . My sister was the most amiable and eloquent woman I ever knew, and was universally beloved and admired. She was a great reader, and her rapidity of apprehension was like lightning. She wrote elegant and flowing verses on occasional subjects with great ease. She was fond of society, and was the life of every party into which she entered."[27]

Other frequenters of Steventon rectory were the Digweeds, who had rented Steventon Manor from the Knights of Godmersham for many years. Hugh Digweed, the tenant in Jane's time, was the father of a large family of sons. One of them, Harry Digweed, who was possibly one of Jane's admirers rather than a casual friend, was referred to by her in an early letter as "my dear Harry."[28] The Harwoods of still-existing Deane House were an old Hampshire family. The squire in Jane's day was John Harwood, a bluff country character of the type Fielding depicted earlier as Squire Allworthy in *Tom Jones*. Jane was also fond of walking to Oakley Hall to call on Wither Bramston and his wife and Bramston's eccentric maiden sister who was known by the courtesy title of "Mrs. Augusta Bramston."[29] Bramston was famous for his porter (which Jane relished), while his wife was fond of making "transparencies" to decorate her windows, a hobby Jane recalled years later when she described three similar artistic efforts as adornments of Fanny Price's East Room at Mansfield Park. Later, when Jane had become a published author, Mrs. Augusta Bramston did not greatly admire her former neighbor's literary productions. She thought *Sense and Sensibility* and *Pride and Prejudice* were "downright nonsense," but expected to like *Mansfield Park* better, yet having finished the first volume "flattered herself she had got through the worst."[30]

Jane's other Steventon-area friends included the Terrys of Dummer House, another large family. Stephen Terry, a dancing partner of Jane's in her youth, left a memoir that contains revealing highlights of the Steventon of her girlhood.[31] Another was John Lyford of Basingstoke, a surgeon and male midwife, who not only was the Austens' medical consultant, but possibly attended Mrs. Austen at the time of Jane's birth.[32] He was a relation of Giles King Lyford, Jane's doctor in Winchester at the time of her death. Still another neighbor and friend was James Holder, the bachelor tenant of nearby Ashe Park. He shared his newspapers (then prohibitively expensive) with the Austens, thereby enabling Jane to keep abreast of the activities of her two naval brothers through the columns devoted to the long war with France. Holder, who was twenty-eight years older than Jane, was the unsuspecting villain in a bit of nonsense she included in one of her last letters to Cassandra from Steventon:

> Your unfortunate sister was betrayed last Thursday into a situation of the utmost cruelty. I arrived at Ashe Parke before the party from Deane, and was shut up in the drawing room with Mr. Holder alone for ten minutes. I had some thoughts of insisting on the housekeeper or Mary Corbett being sent for, and nothing could prevail on me to move two steps from the door, on the lock of which I kept one hand constantly fixed. We met nobody but ourselves, played *vingt-un,* and were very cross.[33]

Jane Austen's most notable and longest-lasting younger Steventon friends, however, were the Lloyd and the Bigg sisters. In January 1789, when Jane was thirteen, the widowed Mrs. Martha Lloyd rented the vacant rectory at Deane from Jane's father.[34] Mrs. Lloyd was the mother of three daughters. Martha, the eldest and Jane's favorite, who was nine years her senior, later lived with Mrs. Austen and her daughters in Bath, Southampton, and Chawton, and ultimately became the second wife of Jane's brother, Sir Francis Austen. Eliza Lloyd married the Rev. Fulwar-Craven Fowle, vicar of Kintbury in Berkshire; and Mary Lloyd married Jane's elder brother James after the death of his first wife and became the mother of the Rev. James Edward Austen-Leigh, Jane's first biographer. Mrs. Lloyd and two of her daughters, Martha and Mary, continued to live at Deane until January 1792, when they moved to Ibthorpe, eighteen miles northwest of Steventon. It was to Martha that Jane dedicated the first of her juvenilia, *Frederic & Elfrida,* ". . . for your late generosity to me in finishing my muslin Cloak."[35] Jane was fond of Mary Lloyd during the earlier years of their friendship, but later modified her feelings as Mary developed into a grasping and manipulative woman.

The same year Mrs. Lloyd moved into Deane rectory, Lovelace Bigg, a wealthy widower, inherited Manydown Park, an estate northeast of Steventon, from the last member of the Wither family.[36] He then changed his surname to Bigg-Wither and moved to Manydown with his two sons and six daughters. Although Lovelace Bigg-Wither and his sons took the hyphenated surname, his daughters did not. The elder son died in 1794, at which time the second son, Harris, became his father's heir. It was Harris Bigg-Wither who proposed marriage to Jane Austen in December 1802; he was at first accepted, but almost immediately rejected. Even so, her refusal did not alter her friendly relationship with his father and sisters, for she was a guest at Manydown on several occasions after 1802.

Closer to Jane than Harris Bigg-Wither, however, were three of his sisters, Elizabeth, Catherine, and Alethea Bigg, who were Jane Austen's lifelong friends. Elizabeth married the Rev. William Heathcote and after his death lived in the Cathedral Close in Winchester. It was she who arranged for the lodgings in Mrs. David's house on College Street, in Winchester, where Jane Austen died. Catherine married the Rev. Herbert Hill, an uncle of the poet Robert Southey and rector of Streatham in Surrey, where Jane visited them in 1811 and possibly again in 1814. Alethea, who was two years younger than Jane, lived with her sister Elizabeth in Winchester. But she was not there at the time of Jane Austen's death, having "frisked off like half England, into Switzerland," according to the last letter Jane wrote from Chawton.[37]

The relative security of Jane Austen's Steventon world was shattered late in 1800 when she returned home from a visit to Ibthorpe and learned that her father had decided to appoint his eldest son, James, as his deputy and move to Bath with her mother, Cassandra, and herself. Jane was reluctant to sever her long-established personal relationships, whose loss could never be compensated by the casual acquaintances and meaningless bustle of a town whose population consisted largely of invalids, staid elderly people such as her maternal uncle James Leigh-Perrot and his imperious wife, and giddy seasonal pleasure seekers. For almost a century, Bath had been a vast national finishing school where those on the fringes of aristocracy—the minor clergy, country gentry, and wealthy tradesmen and their families—had come to learn urbanity from the nobility. By 1800, however, the latter as well as the middling levels of society were leaving Bath for more fashionable seaside places such as Brighton. Meanwhile the lovely little terraced city was being taken over by social climbers, snobs, and *nouveaux riches*.

As an aspiring although as yet unpublished novelist, Jane Austen presumably sensed that the meaningless social obligations of Bath would leave her little time for writing. This intuition was subsequently confirmed by her sharply diminished literary activity during the five years she was an unwilling resident of Bath. As a dependent as well as a dutiful daughter, however, there was nothing to do but make the best of what she felt was an unhappy decision.

Fortunately, Jane's friend, Martha Lloyd, had accompanied her back from Ibthorpe and was there to console her in her dejection. It was also fortunate that Cassandra Austen was at Godmersham when the decision to move to Bath was made, thereby providing Jane with another sympathetic outlet for her grief over their father's hasty decision. Considering the closeness of the two sisters, it is logical to surmise that Jane shared her sorrow with Cassandra in her letters, knowing the latter would respect the confidentiality of her bitterness. If that happened, it is not surprising that there are no letters remaining from Jane from the time she learned of the proposed move until the beginning of 1801—the anguish she presumably expressed in them doubtlessly caused Cassandra to destroy them, if not at that time, then at least later, when she burned the greater part of her sister's correspondence before her own death. That communications were exchanged during the difficult period is evident by Jane's letter of January 3, 1801, the first surviving one to Cassandra after almost a month's silence, which begins: "As you have by this time received my last letter, it is fit that I should begin another . . ."[38]

Jane Austen shared Horace Walpole's dictum "They may say what they will, but it does one ten times more good to leave Bath than to go to it." Even so, the elegant Georgian city beside the Bristol

Avon was one of the architectural wonders of western Europe at the time Jane became a resident. Rebuilt during the eighteenth century with golden-toned stone not yet blackened by two centuries of damp and soot, it had classically balanced streets, squares, and crescents that rose in orderly regularity on a series of steep hills surrounding the site of Aquae Solis, the original Roman town to which rich rheumatics from the Continent had been attracted by the healing waters as early as the first century A.D.

Jane and her mother arrived there in the late afternoon of May 4, 1801. The following day she wrote to Cassandra: "The first view of Bath in fine weather does not answer my expectations; I think I see more distinctly through rain. The sun was got behind everything, and the appearance of the place from the top of Kingsdown was all vapour, shadow, smoke, and confusion."[39]

After the arrival of Cassandra and her father, and several fruitless attempts to secure a house, this advertisement in the *Bath Chronicle* for May 21, 1801, solved their problem of accommodation: "The lease of No. 4 Sydney Place, 3 years and a quarter of which are unexpired at Midsummer. The situation is desirable, the Rent very low, and the Landlord is bound by Contract to paint the first two floors this summer. A premium will therefore be expected. Apply Messrs. Weston and Foreman, Cornwall Buildings, Bath."[40]

This terraced house, one of a row of substantial residences dating from 1799, was ideal for several reasons. It was located at the far end of Great Pulteney Street in the new Bathwick area of the city and was a considerable distance from the Paragon, where their relations the Leigh-Perrots lived, an area the Austens were determined to avoid. The house was also near the recently opened Sydney Gardens, the same place Jane had mentioned in a letter to Cassandra written from Steventon in January 1801: "It would be very pleasant to be near Sidney [*sic*] Gardens!—We might go into the Labyrinth every day."[41]

Once the lease was signed, the Austens set out for a summer holiday in Devonshire, returning to Bath in October. It was while living in Sydney Place that Jane Austen made the final revision of *Susan* (i.e., *Northanger Abbey*), originally written in 1798-99, which she sold to Crosby & Son of London in 1803 for ten pounds, although it was not published at that time. It was also in Bath that she began her unfinished novel, *The Watsons*—the paper on which it is written is watermarked 1803. But Bath was not conducive to literary activity for Jane for several reasons. During the time she lived in Sydney Place her blighted romance with an unknown suitor in the West Country reputedly took place. Also during the same period she accepted and then turned down Harris Bigg-Wither's proposal of marriage in December 1802. It is therefore no wonder her creativity suffered.

The lease for the Sydney Place house expired in August 1804 when Jane and her parents were at Lyme Regis. While there, her mother received a letter from Mrs. Leigh-Perrot in Bath mentioning the new tenants of the Sydney Place house. In commenting on her aunt's imparted information in a letter to Cassandra, Jane said: "The Coles have got their infamous plate upon our door."[42] Presumably Mrs. Leigh-Perrot had also included rumors concerning the elegance of the household furnishings of the new occupants. Taking the word "plate" as her inspiration, Jane added dryly: "I dare say *that* makes a great deal of the massy plate so much talked of."[43]

When the Austens returned to Bath on October 25, 1804, they took a six-month lease on No. 27 Green Park Buildings, which was in another row of terraced houses on the opposite side of the city nearer to the river and within easy walking distance of the open country. It was there, on December 16, 1804, that Jane celebrated her twenty-ninth birthday, but the memory of it was marred by the death of her longtime friend, Mrs. Anne Lefroy of Ashe, who died after falling from her horse. Jane's father died a little over a month later, on January 21, 1805, after a brief illness.

Following his death, Mrs. Austen and her daughters remained at the Green Park address until March 25, 1805, when they moved into furnished lodgings at No. 25 Gay Street. This is a steeply sloping thoroughfare extending northward from the heart of Bath to John Wood the Elder's elegant residential circle known as the Circus, which Matthew Bramble in *Humphrey Clinker* described as ". . . a pretty bauble, constructed for show, and looks like Vespasian's amphitheatre [i.e., the Colosseum in Rome] turned outside in." How long the Austens remained in Gay Street is not known, but by early 1806 they had moved into other furnished lodgings in Trim Street. Interestingly, it was an address Cassandra Austen had wished to avoid for some unknown reason when the move from Steventon to Bath was first proposed.[44]

While living there, Mrs. Austen, her daughters, and their friend Martha Lloyd agreed to set up housekeeping with Jane's brother Francis and move to Southampton after his marriage later that year. Mrs. Austen had been reluctant to leave Bath because her gouty brother James Leigh-Perrot lived there most of the year to take advantage of the medicinal waters. Even as late as April 1806 she was still hoping to move from Trim Street into other furnished lodgings in Bath.[45] Less than two months later, however, she had agreed to join forces with her son Francis and move to Southampton. On July 2, 1806, Mrs. Austen and her daughters left Bath for Clifton, a small spa near Bristol, before setting out for visits to Gloucestershire, Warwickshire, and Staffordshire, after which they had agreed to meet Francis Austen and his bride and Martha Lloyd at Steventon. Later, Jane was to write to Cassandra from Godmersham: "It will be two years tomorrow since we left Bath for Clifton, with what happy feelings of Escape."[46]

Jane Austen's later distaste for Bath is difficult to reconcile with her using it as the background for parts of *Northanger Abbey* and *Persuasion*. Although Jane was never the naïve young girl she depicted Catherine Morland as being in *Northanger Abbey,* she shared Catherine's enthusiasm for the gaieties of Bath during her own earlier visits, which, by their very nature, were in marked contrast to the quiet routine to which she was accustomed at Steventon. Even then Jane's gift of satirical objectivity never blinded her to the ephemeral nature of the place. By the time she wrote *Persuasion,* however, Jane presumably regarded her early enthusiasm concerning Bath less favorably and projected her later distaste onto Anne Elliot, whose feelings concerning the frivolity of Bath reflected Jane's observations. But Jane did not have to wait until she wrote *Persuasion* to voice this attitude. On April 8, 1805, when she was still living in Bath, she wrote to Cassandra: "This morning we have been to see Miss Chamberlayne look hot on horseback.—Seven years & four months ago we went to the same Ridinghouse to see Miss Lefroy's performance!—What a different set are we now moving in! But seven years I suppose are enough to change every pore in one's skin, & every feeling of one's mind."[47]

When Mrs. Austen and her daughters arrived at Steventon from their summer rambles on October 4, 1806, they found Francis Austen and his bride and Martha Lloyd awaiting them.[48] Six days later the combined party left for Southampton. Situated on a peninsula between the mouths of the rivers Test and Itchen, Southampton was then a fashionable watering place, with a population of around eight thousand, to which people came for the benefits of the newly prescribed cure of sea bathing. Jane was already familiar with the town from her early school days in 1783 and at least one other visit ten years later, and although it was not her beloved Steventon, it was in her native Hampshire. At first the Austens contented themselves with furnished lodgings, during which time Jane paid calls with her brother Francis on his naval and civilian acquaintances in the area. Jane felt the cultivation of these people, many of whom were well-to-do, might prove embarrassing as far as reciprocal hospitality was concerned, but her subsequent letters reveal her fears were groundless, for many of the friends she acquired between 1806 and 1809 made her stay in Southampton a pleasant one, although unproductive for writing.

By February 1807 the Austens had decided to give up their temporary quarters and move into a large, old-fashioned house in Castle Square that was overshadowed by a multitowered sham Gothic castle that had recently been built on the site of the Norman Keep of Southampton Castle by the second Marquis of Lansdowne.[49] This fantastic edifice towered over the house into which they moved in March 1807. Jane's letters provide many pleasant domestic details concerning the place she called home for the next two years. For the first time since leaving Steventon the Austens had an adequate garden at Castle Square, and preparations were made to develop it properly. Jane reminded Cassandra to bring back a good collection of flower seed from Godmersham, "particularly Mignionette," while a gardener (who later turned out to be drunken and shiftless) was hired to put the beds and borders in order. While new plants were being bought, Jane insisted on including two of her favorites. "I could not do without a Syringa, for the sake of Cowper's Line," she told Cassandra, adding: "We talk also of a Laburnum."[50]

Fortunately, a contemporary watercolor of Jane Austen's Southampton home has been preserved, for the house has long since disappeared, although a brief description remains in the recollections of James Edward Austen-Leigh.[51] After describing it as "a commodious old-fashioned house in a corner of Castle Square," he added: "My grandmother's house had a pleasant garden, bounded on one side by the old city walls; the top of this wall was sufficiently wide to afford a pleasant walk, with an extensive view, easily accessible to ladies by steps. This must have been a part of the identical walls which witnessed the embarkation of Henry V. before the battle of Agincourt . . . "[52]

Jane Austen's fifteen surviving letters from her Southampton years are much more cheerful than the remaining ones written earlier from Bath. Two pages from an account book she kept for 1807 have also fortunately survived, throwing additional light on her daily routine during that particular year. One of the entries contradicts the statements of earlier biographers that she was without a piano from the time she left Steventon until she moved to Chawton. According to one of the entries in Jane's neat hand she paid the sum of two pounds, thirteen shillings, and sixpence for the rental of a "Piano Forte" for 1807.[53]

The account book also lists various other incidental expenses: £8 14s. 9d. for washing, £3 17s. 6d. for letters and parcels, 13s. 9d. for servants, £3 10s. 3d. for charity, £6 4s. 4d. for presents, £1 2s. 10d. for an unspecified journey, 17s. 9d. for water parties and plays, 11s. for pew rent, and £13 19s. 3d. for clothes and pocket money, making a total of £42 4s. 8d. These, and a few other incidentals, brought Jane's expenses for 1807 to £44 10s. 6d. Since the record shows she had £50 15s. on hand at the beginning of the year, she was left with £6 4s. 6d. with which to begin 1808. It would therefore seem Jane Austen was allowed £50 a year from the small annual family income for her private expenses.

Apparently the Austens regarded their stay in Southampton as only temporary, for there are indications in Jane's early letters from 1808 that her mother was contemplating a move elsewhere. On October 24, 1808, in a letter to her sister, Jane for the first time mentioned the possibility of the family's removal to Chawton. There has been much speculation among Jane Austen's biographers as to why her wealthy brother Edward did not provide a home earlier for his mother and sisters. Apparently there was nothing suitable at Edward's disposal prior to 1808, but in that year an event took place that finally enabled him to offer his mother and sisters a comfortable home in Chawton. Early in February Edward's steward and bailiff, Bridger Seward, died and was buried at Chawton on February 10,

1808, thereby freeing the house in which he had lived.[54] As the lease on the Castle Square house was due to expire at the end of March 1809, Mrs. Austen, after having Jane make inquiries concerning the kitchen garden attached to the Cottage (as the house in Chawton was then called),[55] accepted her son's offer, specifying that Seward's widow must be out of the house by midsummer 1809.[56] On January 30, 1809, in a letter to Cassandra, Jane commented: "She (Mrs. Austen) hopes you will not omit begging Mrs. Seward to get the Garden cropped for us—supposing she leaves the House too early, to make the Garden an object to herself."[57]

While Jane and Cassandra were making arrangements for the furnishing of their new house at Chawton, Mrs. Austen did her part by providing suitable silver for the dining parlor. Jane commented to Cassandra: "My mother has been lately adding to her possessions in plate—a whole tablespoon and a whole dessert spoon, and six whole teaspoons—which make our sideboard border on the magnificent. They were mostly of the produce of old or useless silver."[58] Then, after imparting the further intelligence that "a silver tea-ladle is also added," Jane shared her anticipated joys by exclaiming: "Yes, yes, we *will* have a pianoforte, as good a one as can be got for thirty guineas, and I will practise country dances, that we may have some amusement for our nephews and nieces, when we have the pleasures of their company."[59]

The second and most productive period of Jane Austen's literary career began at the age of thirty-three when she arrived with her mother and sister at their new Chawton home on July 9, 1809.[60] Unlike her urbane contemporary, the Rev. Sydney Smith, who once declared, "I have no relish for the country, it is a kind of healthy grave,"[61] Jane rejoiced in her return to a rural environment. Her first surviving letter from Chawton is a set of doggerel verses written to her brother Francis on July 26, 1809, on the occasion of the birth of his first son, Francis William Austen, born fourteen days earlier in Alton, a little over a mile from Chawton. By that time Francis was on the high seas, having sailed in the *St. Albans* in May of the same year at the head of a convoy of East Indiamen bound for Canton, China.[62] Jane's poem is mainly devoted to the birth of Francis's son, but ends with a witty description of her new home:

As for ourselves, we're very well;
As unaffected prose will tell.—
Cassandra's pen will paint our state,
The many comforts that await
Our Chawton home, how much we find
Already in it, to our mind;
And how convinced, that when complete
It will all other Houses beat
That ever have been made or mended,
With rooms concise, or rooms distended.[63]

Built during the late seventeenth century, the plain brick house, now owned by the Jane Austen Society, stands at the junction of the former London main roads from Winchester and Portsmouth, the fork of which was occupied in Jane's time by a shallow pond.[64] Originally used as a posting inn and alehouse, the property later was occupied by the stewards of Chawton Great House. Jane's niece Caroline, who knew "the Cottage" well as a child, has left the best description of it as it was in Jane's time:

> The front door opened on the road, a very narrow enclosure of each side protected the house from the possible shock of any run-away vehicle—A good sized entrance, and two parlours called dining and drawing room, made the length of the house; all intended originally to look on the road—but the large drawing room window was blocked-up and turned into a bookcase when Mrs. Austen took possession and another was opened at the side, which gave to view only turf and trees—a high wooden fence shut out the road (the Winchester road it was) all the length of the little domain, and trees were planted inside to form a shrubbery walk—which carried round the enclosure, gave a very sufficient space for exercise. . . . There was besides a good kitchen garden, large court and many out-buildings, not much occupied—and all this affluence of space was very delightful to children, and I have no doubt added considerably to the pleasure of a visit—[65]

Turning to the interior, Caroline continued:

> Everything indoors and *out* was well kept—the house was well furnished, and it was altogether a comfortable and ladylike establishment, tho' I believe the means which supported it, were

> but small. . . . The house was quite as good as the generality of Parsonage houses then—and much in the same old style—the ceilings low and roughly finished—*some* bedrooms very small—*none* very large but in number sufficient to accommodate the inmates, and several guests. . . . The dining room could not be made to look anywhere but on the road—and there my grandmother often sat for an hour or two in the morning, with her work or her writing—cheered by its sunny aspect and by the stirring scene it afforded her. . . . I believe the close vicinity of the road was really no more an evil to her than it was to her grandchildren. Collyer's daily coach with six horses was a sight to see! and most delightful was it to a child to have the awful stillness of night so frequently broken by the noise of passing carriages, which seemed sometimes, even to shake the bed.[66]

Concerning Jane Austen's domestic activities at Chawton, Caroline Austen recalled:

> At 9 o'clock she made breakfast—*that* was *her* part of the household work—The tea and sugar stores were under *her* charge—*and* the wine—Aunt Cassandra did all the rest—for my Grandmother suffered herself to be superseded by her daughters *before* I can remember; and soon *after*, she ceased even to sit at the head of the table. . . . I don't believe Aunt Jane observed any particular method in parcelling out her day but I think she generally sat in the drawing room till luncheon: when visitors were there, chiefly at work. . . . After luncheon, my Aunts generally walked out—sometimes they went to Alton for shopping—Often, one or the other of them, to the Great House—as it was then called—when a brother was inhabiting it, to make a visit—or if the house [i.e., Chawton Great House] were standing empty they liked to stroll around the grounds—sometimes to Chawton Park—a noble beech wood, just within a walk—but sometimes, but that was rarely, to call on a neighbour—They had no carriage, and their visitings did not extend far—there were a few families living in the village—but no great intimacy was kept up with any of them—they were upon *friendly* but rather *distant* terms with all.[67]

These are pleasant and enlightening details as far as Jane Austen's last home are concerned. But the important thing about the house at Chawton is that it was there her genius finally reached fruition. The six novels she either revised or wrote there are among the treasures of the English-speaking world.

CHAPTER

3

Beaux and a Blighted Romance

The question of why Jane Austen chose to remain single will never be answered with any degree of certainty. By sifting the evidence that has survived, however, it is possible to suggest at least four plausible reasons why she eventually chose celibacy rather than subject herself to the uncertain risks of matrimony.

The first surmise is fairly obvious. Young women of Jane's social class whose fathers were unable to provide them with dowries stood little or no chance of attracting suitable husbands in the materialistic marriage market of her day. Jane's father's combined stipend from his parishes of Steventon and Deane never amounted to more than six hundred pounds a year. Although that was sufficient, when combined with the extra income he derived from taking in pupils, to keep his family in comfort, little remained to set aside marriage portions for his two daughters.

Apparently Cassandra's fiancé, the Rev. Thomas Fowle, who had been one of her father's pupils, loved her sufficiently to disregard her dowerless state when they became engaged around 1792.[1] In any event he left her a legacy of one thousand pounds as a token of his unmaterialistic affection when he died of yellow fever in San

Domingo in 1797. Cassandra, who from then on gave up any idea of marrying, invested her inheritance carefully, and the income from the principal relieved her from actual want for the rest of her life. Jane was not so fortunate, for until she became a published author in 1811, she was totally dependent on her family.

Jane's close attachment to Cassandra could also have been a second and major factor in her deciding to remain single. From their earliest years they had developed such a strong bond of affection for one another that Jane's nephew and first biographer emphasized this closeness in the *Memoir* thus:

> Their sisterly affection for each other could scarcely be exceeded. Perhaps it began on Jane's side with the feeling of deference natural to a loving child toward a kind elder sister. . . . They lived in the same house, shared the same bed-room, till separated by death. They were not exactly alike. Cassandra's was the colder and calmer disposition; she was always prudent and well judging, but with less outward demonstration of feeling and less sunniness of temper than Jane possessed. It was remarked that "Cassandra had the *merit* of having a temper always under command, but that Jane had the *happiness* of a temper that never required to be commanded."[2]

Jane's mother put it more succinctly when she remarked, "If Cassandra were going to have her head cut off, Jane would insist on sharing her fate."[3] It would therefore seem that even though Jane might have received offers of marriage during her early womanhood (and only one is definitely known to have taken place), she could never have regarded any of her suitors as a substitute for the sister whose innermost thoughts were inextricably woven with her own.

A third possible reason for Jane's remaining single, and one that can be documented from her letters, was her almost lifelong squeamishness concerning pregnancy and the other perils that accompanied what she called "mothering."[4] This might have been because she lost two of her sisters-in-law in childbed. In any event, in December 1798, when her brother James's second wife was expecting her first child, Jane confided to Cassandra: "Mary does not manage matters in such a way as to make me want to lay in myself."[5] Later, in February 1801, after a visit to the home of the Rev. Henry Dyson, rector of Baugherst, Hampshire, Jane reported further: "The house seemed to have all the comforts of little children, dirt & litter. Mr. Dyson as usual looked wild, & Mrs. Dyson as usual looked big."[6] Still later, in 1808, when referring to the wife of a business partner of her brother Henry, she wrote: "Mrs. Tilson's remembrance gratifies me, & I will use her patterns if I can; but poor Woman! how can she be honestly breeding again?"[7] Six months before her death, Jane prescribed "the simple regimen of separate rooms"[8] for the wife of a Kentish acquaintance who was already the mother of "numerous issue." Also, in the same year, she reacted angrily to the frequent pregnancies of her niece Anna Lefroy: "Poor Animal, she will be worn out before she is thirty . . . "[9]

Finally, Jane's cleverness and her uncanny ability to see through shams—qualities most men studiously avoided when choosing a wife—could have caused prospective suitors to shy away from her even if they were willing to reconcile themselves to her dowerless position. From 1796, when her surviving letters begin, until she left Steventon in 1801, her correspondence bristles with indications that she did not suffer fools gladly and that she was fully capable of uttering unvarnished truths that would have put many admirers to flight. This frankness gradually took on a kinder aspect as she grew older, but even her later letters reveal it would have been an uncomfortable experience for any pretentious individual to have been subjected to her penetrating observations. As usual, Jane summed up the situation perfectly in *Northanger Abbey,* which was written in 1798-99, when, as still a flirtatious but already objective young woman, she was already only too aware of the slim chance of matrimony that awaited anyone of her sex who was capable of giving a suitor an inferiority complex. "Where people wish to attach," Jane wrote, apparently from experience, "they should always be ignorant. To come with a well-informed mind, is to come with an inability of administering to the vanity of others, which a sensible person would always wish to avoid. A woman especially, if she have the misfortune of knowing any thing, should conceal it as well as she can."[10]

By the time Jane Austen made her debut in the autumn of 1792 at the age of seventeen at a ball at Enham House near Andover, she had already established herself in the North Hampshire area as a flirtatious young woman of spirit, delighting in lively and sometimes intimidating badinage. There is no way of knowing who her

Steventon area admirers were until 1796, when her surviving letters begin. From the ensuing letters, however, it is possible to follow her temporary infatuations and more serious romantic attachments there and elsewhere with a fair degree of certainty.

As far as can now be ascertained, the first man for whom Jane Austen had a passing fancy was Edward Taylor (1774-1843), the eldest son of the Rev. Edward Taylor of Bifrons, Kent, an Elizabethan manor house that had been rebuilt in 1767 as an elegant Georgian mansion.[11] Taylor, who was a year younger than Jane, was a distant relation of Sir Brook Bridges III of Goodnestone, whose daughter, Elizabeth, had married Jane's brother Edward in 1791. Jane apparently met Taylor three years later when she and Cassandra were visiting Edward at Rowling, his small country house near Canterbury. Except for two brief mentions of Taylor in Jane's early letters, little is known concerning this infatuation. In 1796, when she was again at Rowling, she accompanied her sister-in-law, Elizabeth Austen, on a visit to Nackington, another Kentish estate, at which time she wrote Cassandra: "We went by Bifrons, & I contemplated with a melancholy pleasure, the abode of Him, on whom I once fondly doated."[12] But Jane's partiality for Taylor never materialized into anything more than a pleasurable acquaintance, for in 1800, when her sister reported the rumor of his engagement from Godmersham, Jane commented, "I hope it is true that Edward Taylor is to marry his cousin Charlotte. Those beautiful dark eyes will then adorn another Generation at least in all their purity."[13]

Contrary to Jane's hopes, however, Taylor did not marry "his cousin Charlotte," a daughter of his maternal uncle Thomas Watkinson Payler of Kent. Instead, in September 1802, he married Louisa, the only child of the Rev. J. C. Beckington of Bourne, Kent. Taylor later was a member of Parliament for Canterbury from 1807 to 1812.

Neither history nor family tradition has preserved Edward Taylor's reaction to Jane Austen's fondness for him. However, her letters are fairly explicit concerning a long-standing admiration for her by the Rev. Edward Bridges (1779-1825), her other identifiable Kentish beau.[14] Bridges was the fifth son of Sir Brook Bridges III of Goodnestone, Kent, and a younger brother of the wife of Jane's brother Edward.

Jane probably met Bridges in 1794, during her first known visit to East Kent. By 1796, when she was again her brother Edward's guest at Rowling, she was on intimate enough terms with Bridges to be his partner when they opened an impromptu dance at Goodnestone.[15] Shortly thereafter, Bridges matriculated at Emmanuel College, Cambridge, from which he received his master of arts degree in 1808. Meanwhile, by 1798, Bridges had become friendly enough with Jane to playfully refer to her as "t'other Miss Austen."[16] Later, in August 1805, Jane and Bridges were houseguests of his mother at Goodnestone Farm, from which Jane reported to Cassandra: "It is impossible to do justice to the hospitality of his attentions toward me, he made a point of ordering toasted cheese for supper entirely on my account."[17]

Ten years later, either before or after Bridges was ordained an Anglican priest, he apparently mustered up enough courage to propose to Jane and was turned down, or was checked before he got around to asking for her hand in marriage. Her refusal or rebuff apparently left no hard feelings, for when Jane encountered Bridges on a visit to Mrs. Thomas Knight in Canterbury in June 1808, she made it a point to comment on his "unaltered manners" to her in a letter to Cassandra.[18] Later, in October of the same year, Jane obliquely referred to Bridges's apparent desire to marry her when she wrote to her sister at Godmersham: "I wish you may be able to accept Lady Bridges's invitation, tho' *I* could not her son Edward's."[19]

Bridges was not long in seeking consolation elsewhere, however, for in 1809 he married Harriet Foote, a daughter of John Foote of Lombard Street, London. One year later he became the vicar of Lenham, Kent, a living he held, among others, until his death in 1825. His marriage was apparently not a happy one, for in commenting on his wife in September 1813, Jane wrote pointedly: "She is a poor Honey—the sort of woman who gives me the idea of being determined never to be well—& who likes her spasms & nervousness & the consequence they give her, better than anything else."[20] As for Bridges, Jane added this additional brief comment one month later: "We have had another of Edward Bridges' Sunday visits. I think the pleasantest part of his married life must be the dinners, and breakfasts, and luncheons, and billiards that he gets in this way at Gm. [i.e., Godmersham] Poor wretch! he is quite the dregs of the family as to luck."[21]

As for Jane Austen's Steventon-area admirers, only five have been identified with any certainty. The first was Harry Digweed, the second son of Hugh Digweed of Steventon Manor, the estate that adjoined the grounds of Jane's birthplace.[22] Little is known concerning Digweed except that propinquity had thrown Jane and himself together from childhood. By 1798, however, Jane referred to Digweed affectionately in a letter to her sister written from the Bull and George Inn at Dartford, where she and her parents were staying on their way back to Steventon from Godmersham. At that time Jane's mahogany lap desk and dressing boxes had been separated by mistake from the Austens' other luggage and "put into a chaise which was just packing off as we came in, and were driven away toward Gravesend in their way to the West Indies." This gave Jane an uneasy half hour, for she continued: "No part of my property could have been such a prize before, for in my writing-box was all my worldly wealth, £7, and *my dear Harry's* [italics mine] deputation. Mr. Nottley immediately dispatched a man and horse after the chaise, and in half an hour's time I had the pleasure of being rich as ever; they were got about two or three miles off."[23] The "deputation" mentioned by Jane in connection with her "dear Harry" was presumably permission to shoot game on the Steventon estate granted by Jane's brother Edward. Tradition reports that one of the reasons Jane's father decided to move from Steventon to Bath was because his imperious sister-in-law, Mrs. Leigh-Perrot, suspected "a romantic attachment between Jane and a Digweed man"—probably Harry.[24] In any event, the affair (if such it was) came to naught, for in March 1808, Digweed married Jane Terry of Dummer House, one of Jane's friends, whose peculiarities of expression became the source of great amusement to Jane during her Chawton years.[25]

Charles Fowle (1771-1806) was also one of Jane's early admirers.[26] The fourth son of the Rev. Thomas Fowle, vicar of Kintbury, Berkshire, Fowle was also a first cousin of Martha Lloyd, Jane's intimate friend. A pupil of Jane's father in his youth, Fowle had become intimate enough with Jane by 1796 to be commissioned to buy silk stockings for her, a luxury she later discovered she could ill afford. Fowle made the purchase anyway, causing Jane to comment to Cassandra: "What a good-for-nothing fellow Charles is to bespeak the stockings! I hope he will be too hot for the rest of his life for it!"[27]

Again, this attachment came to nothing, although Jane and Fowle remained good friends until his untimely death. Four years after the silk-stocking episode, Fowle was admitted to Lincoln's Inn in London to study for the bar. In 1799, he married Honoria Townsend of Newbury, Berkshire, and began practicing as a barrister there. He also took an active part in the home defense crises of 1799 and 1804-05, when Napoleon threatened to invade England. Late in 1805, Fowle's health broke down very suddenly; Jane wrote Cassandra that he had gone to Bath for treatment. He died in February 1806, at which time his obituary in the Reading *Mercury*, besides identifying him as a "Barrister-at-Law," added that he was the "Major Commandant of the Hungerford Volunteer Infantry."

Besides Harry Digweed and Charles Fowle, Jane Austen is also believed to have had at least three other local admirers during her young womanhood. These were an unidentifiable "Mr. Heartley,"[28] John Willing Warren (1771-?1830)[29] and the Rev. Charles Powlett (1763-1835).[30] Jane stigmatized Warren, a son of Peter Warren of London, as being "ugly,"[31] but he more than made up for his homeliness by being agreeable. After matriculating at St. John's College, Oxford, in February 1786, Warren became an undergraduate friend of Jane's brothers James and Henry. He also contributed to *The Loiterer*.

Warren, who frequently stayed at Steventon rectory during Jane's earlier years, was elected a Fellow of Oriel College, Oxford, in 1791 after having won the English Essay Prize a year earlier for his paper on "General Knowledge, its real nature and advantages to be derived from it." Choosing the law as his profession, Warren was called to the bar in London in 1798, two years after Jane had archly referred to his "indifference to me" in a letter to her sister.[32] Later, Warren was named a Charity Commissioner—a person of good and sound behavior appointed by the Lord Chancellor to investigate and correct any breaches of charitable trust within a specified county.

Jane's relations with him did not end when Warren settled in London, for in March 1814, when she was staying with her brother Henry in Henrietta Street, Covent Garden, she wrote to Cassandra: "John Warren and his wife are to dine here, and to name their own day in the next fortnight," to which she added the ambiguous comment, "I do not expect them to come."[33]

Of the Rev. Charles Powlett, Jane's fifth Steventon-area admirer, a great deal is known. He was the son of Navy Lt. Percy Powlett—one of the three illegitimate sons of Charles Powlett, third Duke of Bolton of Hackwood Park, Hampshire, and Lavinia Fenton, the original Polly Peacham in John Gay's *Beggar's Opera* (1728)—and received his early education at Charterhouse and Westminster schools in London. Later he matriculated at Trinity College, Cambridge. In the meantime, because of his aristocratic connections, he spent a great deal of his time at Hackwood Park, where he ran with a fast set and incurred sizable debts.

Six years before he appeared in Jane Austen's letters, he became the rector of Winslade, Hampshire, where he lived with his widowed and indulgent mother, who was described in his obituary as having been a Dover lady not entirely of her husband's own sphere of connections. In 1796, Powlett became the rector of Itchen Stoke, also in Hampshire, a post he held until 1817, the year of Jane Austen's death.

Described in his obituary as having been a diminutive person whose "limbs were not well formed," Powlett made the mistake of trying to kiss Jane at a ball in January 1796, at which time he was rebuffed.[34] Evidently he took the hint, for later in the same year he married Anne Temple, a daughter of the Rev. William Johnston Temple, vicar at St. Gluvias, Cornwall and an intimate friend of James Boswell, Samuel Johnson's biographer.

Jane Austen was not particularly taken with Powlett's bride, for in December 1798, she referred to her as having been "discovered to be everything that the Neighbourhood could wish her, silly & cross as well as extravagant."[35] Later, in January 1801, when Jane dined in the company of the Powletts at Deane rectory, she added: "Mrs. Powlett was at once expensively & nakedly dress'd; we have had the satisfaction of estimating her Lace & her Muslin; & she said too little to afford us much other amusement."[36]

Powlett subsequently became a chaplain in ordinary to the Prince Regent, and the additional debts he incurred while associating with the raffish Carlton House set necessitated his leaving England to avoid his creditors. He died in Brussels in 1834 at the age of sixty-nine.

All five of these early and presumably casual flirtations of Jane Austen's are shadowy, however, in comparison with a romantic episode that took place when she was twenty-one. At the time of

Jane's first surviving letter, dated January 9, 1796, Cassandra Austen was away from home on an extended visit to the Fowle family at Kintbury in Berkshire. Meanwhile, a young Irishman had arrived at Ashe rectory near Steventon for a Christmas visit to his aunt and uncle, and a flirtation had developed between Jane Austen and him. The young man was Thomas Langlois Lefroy (later chief justice of Ireland), the eldest son of Colonel Anthony Peter Lefroy of Limerick, who was himself the elder brother of the Rev. Isaac Peter George Lefroy, rector of Ashe.[37]

Tom, as he was familiarly called, was a month younger than Jane Austen. Born in Ireland in January 1776, he outlived her by fifty-two years. He matriculated at Trinity College, Dublin, in 1790, when he was thirteen, and after taking numerous prizes and medals, received his Bachelor of Arts degree in 1795.

In the meantime he had been admitted in October 1793 to Lincoln's Inn in London, where he kept only eight terms, then the required number for students who meant to be called to the Irish Bar. While in England, Tom was under the protection of a paternal great-uncle, Benjamin Langlois, a former secretary of the British embassy in Vienna as well as a former member of Parliament.

Since Langlois was a frequent visitor to Ashe rectory it is likely that he was responsible for Tom's visit to Hampshire for the Christmas season of 1795-96. In any event, Tom did not remain there long, for shortly after January 15, 1796, he returned to London, from which he set out later for Ireland, and was called to the Irish Bar the next year. In 1799 he married Mary, the only daughter of Jeffrey Paul of Silver Spring, Wexford. Mary's only brother, who died young, was Tom's closest friend at Trinity College, a relationship that "led to visits at that gentleman's family residence, and to a tender attachment between himself and Miss Paul, and subsequently to their marriage."[38]

Jane was undoubtedly attracted by the attentions of the handsome, well-educated, young Irishman, while he, in turn, was temporarily captivated by her good looks, vivacity, and intelligence. In the meantime, Mrs. Lefroy and her husband (and presumably old Benjamin Langlois), began to regard with alarm the flirtation between Tom, who still had to make his way in the world, and dowerless Jane Austen. During the early part of January 1796, someone reported the flirtation to Cassandra Austen at Kintbury, and she hastened to admonish her younger sister to be careful not to give cause for gossip.

To this warning, after having attended a ball at which Tom was present, Jane replied archly:

> You scold me so much in the nice long letter which I have this moment received from you, that I am almost afraid to tell you how my Irish friend and I behaved. Imagine to yourself everything most profligate and shocking in the way of dancing and sitting down together. I *can* expose myself, however, only *once more,* because he leaves the country soon after next Friday, on which we *are* to have a dance at Ashe after all. He is a very gentlemanlike, good looking, pleasant young man, I assure you. But as to our having ever met, except at the three last balls, I cannot say much; for he is so excessively laughed at about me at Ashe, that he is ashamed of coming to Steventon, and ran away when we called on Mrs. Lefroy a few days ago.[39]

Later in the same letter Jane reported that Tom, wearing a white coat, had turned up in the meantime at Steventon rectory, adding: "He is a very great admirer of Tom Jones, and therefore wears the same coloured clothes, I imagine, which *he* did when he was wounded."[40] Jane's reference was to a passage in Fielding's novel which said: "As soon as the sergeant was departed, Jones rose from his bed, and dressed himself entirely, putting on even his coat, which, as its color was white, showed very visibly the streams of blood which flowed down it."[41] Actually, as a descendant of Tom Lefroy has suggested, his ancestor's morning coat was possibly made of banin, a fine light-colored Irish tweed, that would have appeared singular in England where black or blue cloth was then customary.[42]

In a letter still anticipating the proposed ball at Ashe rectory, Jane continued airily: "I look forward with great impatience to it, as I rather expect to receive an offer from my friend in the course of the evening. I shall refuse him, however, unless he promises to give away his white coat."[43] Still later, she added: "I mean to confine myself in future to Mr. Tom Lefroy, for whom I do not care sixpence."[44] By then, however, the flirtation had developed to the stage where another of her admirers, John Willing Warren, who was then staying at Steventon rectory, had drawn a likeness of Tom for her and had "delivered it to me without a sigh."[45] Finally, when the day of the Ashe ball arrived, Jane wrote to Cassandra:

"At length the day is come on which I am to flirt my last with Tom Lefroy, and when you receive this it will be over. My tears flow as I write at the melancholy idea."[46]

But that was not the end of the affair, casual though it might have been, for although Tom left Hampshire shortly afterward, Jane continued to take an interest in his activities. In a letter written in November 1798, after Mrs. Lefroy had called at Steventon rectory, Jane reported to Cassandra: "I was enough alone to hear all that was interesting, which you will easily credit when I tell you that of her nephew she said nothing at all, and of her friend [i.e., the Rev. Samuel Blackall, a later admirer of Jane] very little. She did not mention the name of the former to *me,* and I was too proud to make any enquiries; but on my father's afterwards asking where he was, I learnt that he was gone back to London in his way to Ireland, where he is called to the Bar and means to practice."[47]

Long after Jane Austen's death the family of Captain Anthony Lefroy [i.e., Tom's younger brother], who was barrack master at York for many years, circulated the report that Tom, who was by then chief justice of Ireland, had jilted Jane. But this tale was groundless, as shown by a letter that Jane's niece Caroline Austen wrote in April 1869 to her brother, who was then writing the *Memoir:*

> I think I need not warn *you* against raking up that old story of the still living Chief Justice. That there was something to it, is true—but nothing out of the common way (as *I* believe). Nothing to call ill usage, and no very serious sorrow endured. The *York* Lefroys got up a very strong version of it all, and spread their own notions in the family—but they were for years very angry with their kinsman [i.e., Chief Justice Lefroy], and rather delighted in a proof as *they* thought, of his early heartlessness. I have *my* story from my Mother, who was near at the time. It was a disappointment, but Mrs. Lefroy sent the gentleman off at the end of a *very* few weeks, that no more mischief might be done. If *his* love had continued for a few more years, he *might* have sought her out again—as he was *then* making enough to marry on—but who can wonder that he did *not?* He was settled in Ireland, and he married an Irish lady, who certainly *had* the convenience of *money*—there was *no* engagement, and never *had* been.[48]

But it remained for the chief justice himself to have the last word. When, shortly before his death in 1869, he was questioned concerning his brief affair with Jane by a nephew, the latter afterward recorded: "He did not state in what her fascination consisted, but he said in so many words that he was in love with her, although he qualified his confession by saying it was a boyish love."[49]

The Rev. Samuel Blackall was Jane Austen's last-known admirer before she left Steventon in 1801. Born in Devonshire in 1770, Blackall was a great-grandson of Offspring Blackall, bishop of Exeter from 1707 until his death in 1716, and an older brother of Dr. John Blackall, the celebrated early-nineteenth-century British diagnostician.[50] Described by a contemporary as "a tall, overpowering personage,"[51] Blackall matriculated at Emmanuel College, Cambridge, in 1787, was elected a Scholar the following year, and graduated in 1791. Three years later he was ordained priest, was elected a Fellow, and became a tutor of the college. Meanwhile, he coveted the desirable college-controlled living of North Cadbury in Somerset, then worth a clear eight hundred pounds a year. As the incumbent at that time did not die until 1812, however, Blackall had to take a long view of the situation and remain a bachelor. Otherwise he would have lost his Fellowship.

This was the situation when he was a guest of the Lefroys at Ashe rectory in the winter of 1797, at which time he met Jane Austen, who appreciated his cultivated if somewhat pompous attitude. In November 1798 Jane included the following in a letter to Cassandra after a visit from Mrs. Lefroy at Steventon rectory:

> She showed me a letter which she had received from her friend [i.e., Blackall] a few weeks ago (in answer to one written by her to recommend a nephew of Mrs. Russell to his notice at Cambridge), towards the end of which was a sentence to this effect: "I am very sorry to hear of Mrs. Austen's illness. It would give me particular pleasure to have an opportunity of improving my acquaintance with that family—with the hope of creating to myself a nearer interest. But at present I cannot indulge any expectation of it." This is rational enough; there is less love and more sense in it than sometimes appeared before, and I am very well satisfied. It will all go on exceedingly well, and decline away in a very reasonable manner. There seems no likelihood of his coming into Hampshire this Christmas, and it is therefore most probable that our indifference will soon be mutual, unless his regard, which appeared to spring from knowing nothing of me at first, is best supported by never seeing me. . . . Mrs. Lefroy made no remarks on the letter,

> nor did she indeed say anything about him as relative to me. Perhaps she thinks she has said too much already.[52]

The last sentence is significant, for it could mean that Mrs. Lefroy had tried to interest Jane in Blackall, suggesting that his prospects of gaining the valuable Somerset living made him worth waiting for as a husband. Even so, the next mention of Blackall in Jane's correspondence occurs in a letter written to her brother, Francis, in July 1813, which shows that her Cambridge admirer remained a bachelor until he received the living he coveted. Having presumably forgotten Jane Austen, he felt free to marry Susannah Lewis, a daughter of James Lewis of Clifton, formerly of Jamaica (and not of Antigua as Jane mentioned in her letter). The relevant passage reads:

> I wonder whether you happened to see Mr. Blackall's marriage in the Papers last Jany. *We* did. He was married at Clifton to a Miss Lewis, whose Father had been late of Antigua. I should very much like to know what sort of Woman she is. He was a piece of Perfection, noisy Perfection himself which I always recollect with regard.—We had noticed a few months before his succeeding to a College Living, the very Living which we remembered his talking of & wishing for; an exceeding good one, Great Cadbury [*sic*] in Somersetshire.—I would wish Miss Lewis to be of a silent turn & rather ignorant, but naturally intelligent & wishing to learn;—fond of cold veal pies, green tea in the afternoon, & a green window blind at night.[53]

By the time of Jane Austen's encounter with the Rev. Samuel Blackall, Steventon rectory had ceased to be the lively household that it had been during her girlhood. By 1798, Jane's elder brothers (with the exception of the mentally retarded George, who was looked after elsewhere) had married and set up homes of their own, while her two naval brothers were almost constantly at sea in the long struggle with France. Jane's father had ceased to take in private pupils, and her mother was in uncertain health. Cassandra's engagement to the Rev. Thomas Fowle had ended tragically when he died of yellow fever in 1797, and although there are hints in Jane's early letters that indicate that her parents and even she had not despaired of Cassandra's marrying someone else, Cassandra apparently did not consider it. As for Jane, she had reached the age where, to quote her own words, she was not "very much in request" as a dancing partner.[54] By 1800, Jane's father had turned sixty-nine, while her mother was sixty-one, both ages considered old at that time. Mounting inflation and taxes brought on by the long war with France, as well as a succession of rigorous winters (the one of 1798 being the coldest in the memory of anyone then living), may well have contributed to Jane's father's sudden decision to retire to Bath with his wife and two daughters. When the decision was made late in 1800, Cassandra was twenty-seven and Jane was twenty-five. Since both were still unmarried their father may well have felt that his daughters stood a better chance of obtaining suitable husbands in Bath than in the rural area in which they had grown to maturity.

Before settling in their new Bath home, however, Jane accompanied her parents and sister to the seaside villages of Sidmouth and Colyton, while the following summer they visited Dawlish and Teignmouth, two other seaside places. Presumably plans for these visits had been formulated before the Austens left Steventon, for in a letter written in January 1801, Jane anticipated: ". . . spending future summers by the Sea. . . "[55] Even so, it was on one of these visits, between 1801 and the autumn of 1804, that Jane Austen reputedly fell in love.

Unlike Jane's brief flirtation with Tom Lefroy, which can be documented with a fair degree of accuracy, the accounts of what Jane's niece Caroline Austen referred to as her aunt's "nameless and dateless" seaside romance are beset with contradictions. All accounts originating with members of the family of the second and third generation from Jane Austen agree that she met and presumably fell in love with a charming young man staying at one of these seaside places. After that the discrepancies begin. The first account was set down late in the nineteenth century by Mrs. Louisa Langlois Bellas, a daughter of Jane Austen's niece Anna Lefroy, who could have imparted some of the information:

> The Austens with their two daughters were once at Teignmouth, the date of that visit was not later than 1802, but besides this they were once travelling in Devonshire, moving about from place to place, and I think that tour was before they left Steventon in 1801, perhaps as early as 1798 or 1799.

> It was while they were so travelling [*sic*], according to Aunt Cassandra's account many years afterwards, that they somehow made acquaintance with a gentleman of the name of Blackall. He and Aunt Jane mutually attracted each other, and such was his charm that even Aunt Cassandra thought him worthy of her sister. They parted on the understanding that he was to come to Steventon, but instead came I know not how long after a letter from his brother to say that he was dead. There is no record of Jane's affliction, but I think this attachment must have been very deep. Aunt Cassandra herself had so warm a regard for him that some years after her sister's death, she took a good deal of trouble to find out and see again his brother.[56]

There are three glaring errors in Mrs. Bellas's account. First, Jane Austen was unlikely to have been in Devon in either 1798 or 1799, for documentary evidence shows that she, in the company of her parents and sister, visited her brother Edward in Kent during the summer of 1798, and remained there until October. Her surviving letters reveal that she was with her parents at Steventon for the rest of the year. The second error, claiming that she met "a gentleman by the name of Blackall" while at the seaside in 1798 or 1799, is also disproved by the fact that the Rev. Samuel Blackall was in Hampshire as a guest of the Lefroys at Ashe during the winter of 1797, as already mentioned above. Jane's letters also show she was still at Steventon during the earlier part of 1799, and that from May to June she and her mother accompanied the Edward Austens to Bath, after which Jane returned with Edward to East Kent.[57]

Mrs. Bellas later modified what she had written, for when Jane Austen's letters were first published by her great-nephew, Lord Brabourne, in 1884, she wrote the following note in her copy of the book, thereby bringing her former account more into line with what is actually believed to have happened between 1801 and 1804. Where she had acquired her updated information or learned that Jane's suitor was a young clergyman, is not known. The revised account reads:

> In the summer of 1801 the father, mother and daughters made a tour in Devonshire. They went to Teignmouth, Starcross, Sidmouth etc. I believe it was at the last place named that they made acquaintance with a young clergyman when visiting his

> brother, who was one of the doctors of the town. He and Jane fell in love with each other, and when the Austens left he asked to be allowed to join them again further on in their tour, and the permission was given. But instead of his arriving as expected, they received a letter announcing his death. In Aunt Cassandra's memory he lived as one of the most charming persons she had known, worthy even in her eyes of Aunt Jane.[58]

The third account was recorded by Mrs. John Hubback, born Catherine Anne Austen, a daughter of Jane's brother Francis. Mrs. Hubback also made the same mistake as Mrs. Bellas in stating that Jane's seaside suitor was named Blackall, although she did not kill him off as early as Mrs. Bellas did, but rather kept him alive long enough for Cassandra to visit him "in '32 or thereabouts." This visit was possible, for the Samuel Blackall who was associated with Jane Austen at Steventon in 1797 was still alive at North Cadbury in 1832 and did not die until 1842. Although he did not have a brother named Edward, the clergyman that Cassandra actually visited around 1832 was apparently the one she remembered from her Steventon days. Mrs. Hubback's account reads:

> If ever she *was* in love it was with Dr. Blackall (I think that was the name) whom they met at some watering-place, shortly before they settled at Chawton. There is no doubt she admired him extremely, and perhaps regretted parting, . . . I do not think Dr. Blackall died until long afterwards. If I do not mistake there were two brothers, one of whom was called Mr. Edward B— and I never heard of what became of him. The other, the Dr., Aunt Cassandra met with again long afterwards when she made an excursion to the Wye in company with Uncle Charles, two of his daughters and my sister Cassandra. My cousin Cassie Austen, the only survivor of that party, could I have no doubt tell when and how they met—I only remember that my Aunt found him stout, red-faced and middle-aged—very different from their youthful hero. It must have been in '32 or thereabouts, and I believe he died soon afterwards.[59]

In view of the confusion apparent in both Mrs. Bellas's and Mrs. Hubback's accounts it is fortunate that there was at least one member of the Austen family who set down two versions of Jane's seaside romance that seem to come as close as is now possible to ascertain what actually happened in Devonshire. The writer was

Jane's niece Caroline Austen, whose reminiscences concerning her aunt are notable for their acuteness and accuracy. When Caroline's brother was collecting material for the *Memoir,* she sent him this account of Jane's romance:

> During the few years my grandfather lived at Bath, he went in the summer with his wife and daughters to *some* sea-side. They were in Devonshire, and in Wales—and in Devonshire an acquaintance was made with some very charming man—I never heard Aunt Cassandra speak of anyone else with such admiration—she had no doubt that a mutual attachment was in progress between him and her sister. They parted—but he made it plain that he would seek them out again—and shortly afterwards he died. My Aunt told me this in the late years of her own life, and it was quite new to me then—but all this, being nameless and dateless, cannot I know serve any purpose of yours—and it brings no contradiction to your theory that Aunt Jane never *had* any attachment that overclouded her happiness, for long. *This* had not gone far enough to leave misery behind.[60]

Using this letter and his own recollections of what he had heard from other unspecified sources, Caroline's brother gave this account in the *Memoir:*

> There is one passage of romance in her history with which I am imperfectly acquainted, and to which I am unable to assign name, or date, or place, though I have it on sufficient authority. Many years after her death, some circumstances induced her sister Cassandra to break through her habitual reticence, and to speak of it. She said that, while staying at some seaside place, they became acquainted with a gentleman, whose charm of person, mind and manners was such that Cassandra thought him worthy to possess and likely to win her sister's love. When they parted, he expressed his intention of soon seeing them again; and Cassandra felt no doubt as to his motives. But they never again met. Within a short time they heard of his sudden death. I believe that, if Jane ever loved, it was this unnamed gentleman; but the acquaintance had been short, and I am unable to say whether her feelings were of such a nature as to affect her happiness.[61]

After the publication of the *Memoir,* Caroline Austen was induced to set down an expanded account of what she recalled concerning Jane's seaside romance. It is the fullest and the most factual account available:

> All that I know is this. At Newtown Aunt Cassandra was staying with us when we made the acquaintance of a certain Mr. Henry Eldridge of the Engineers. He was very pleasing and very good looking. My Aunt was much struck with him, and *I* was struck by her commendation as she rarely admired anyone. Afterwards she spoke of him as one so unusually gifted with all that was agreeable, and said he had reminded her strongly of a gentleman whom they had met one Summer when they were by the sea (I think she said in Devonshire) who had seemed greatly attracted by my Aunt Jane. That when they parted (I imagine he was a visitor there also, but his family might have lived near) he was urgent to know where they would be the next summer, implying or perhaps saying that he should be there also wherever it might be. I can only say the impression left on Aunt Cassandra's mind was that he had fallen in love with Aunt Jane. Soon afterwards they heard of his death. I am sure she thought him worthy of her sister from the way she recalled his memory, and also that she did not doubt either that he would have been a successful suitor.[62]

As a contrast to Caroline Austen's plausible narrative of Jane Austen's seaside romance, it may be appropriate here to insert an alternative fanciful theory advanced by Constance Pilgrim.[63] She maintains that Jane Austen's unknown seaside lover was none other than Captain John Wordsworth, a younger brother of William Wordsworth, the poet. Miss Pilgrim even gives the date 1797 as the year in which Jane Austen supposedly met Wordsworth, as well as identifying Lyme Regis as the place where the romance presumably took place. Her theory was based on the fact that William and Dorothy Wordsworth lived at Racedown Lodge, a house in the Dorset hills midway between Lyme Regis and Crewkerne, from 1795 to 1798, during which time Captain Wordsworth visited his brother and sister before their removal to the Lake District in 1799. How the meeting between Jane Austen and Captain Wordsworth took place is not explained. His movements are well documented, however, and there is no mention of any seaside romance.[64]

Jane Austen's activities during 1797 are also well known, and rule out any visit to Lyme Regis at that time. Jane's presence at Steventon during the earlier part of that year was imperative in order to support her sister, who had just received the news of the death of her fiancé in San Domingo. It became Jane's duty to inform members of her family by letter of the tragedy, a fact borne out by a letter written by her cousin, Eliza de Feuillide, in May 1797. In this Eliza mentioned that she had just received a letter from Jane telling her that everyone at Steventon was "in great affliction . . . for the death of Mr. Fowle, the gentleman to whom our cousin Cassandra was engaged."[65] Later in 1797 Jane accompanied her mother and sister to Bath, where they remained with the Leigh-Perrots until just before Christmas.

As for Captain John Wordsworth, ample contemporary evidence shows that he was at first greatly attached to Mary Hutchinson, who eventually married his brother, the poet, in 1802. After that he turned his attentions to Mary's sister, Sara, and would have married her had he not been lost when his ship, the *Earl of Abergavenny,* foundered in a storm off Portland Bill in February 1805. The writings of William Wordsworth also indicate his younger brother's long-standing devotion to Sara Hutchinson, which Samuel Taylor Coleridge confirmed in a letter written in 1808, in which he said: "Had Captain Wordsworth lived, I had high hopes of seeing her [i.e., Sara Hutchinson] blessedly married as well as prosperously."[66]

Still another imaginative account of Jane Austen's romance was put forward by Sir Francis Doyle during the late nineteenth century.[67] He related a story that he had been told by Miss Ursula Mayow, who claimed she had heard it thirty or forty years previously from a niece of Jane Austen's, whom Miss Mayow did not further identify. This version of Jane's romance claimed that she and her father and Cassandra visited the Continent during the short-lived Peace of Amiens in 1802-03 and included Switzerland in their itinerary. While there they supposedly met a young naval officer who fell in love with Jane, who returned his affection. Later, when the Austens left for Chamonix by the regular road, their friend took a different and more rugged route over the mountains. When the Austens reached Chamonix they waited for the young man but he never arrived. Finally they learned that he had overtaxed his strength and had died of brain fever on the way.

Doyle's tale has no basis for several reasons. First, no continental trip by the Austens, including a stay in Switzerland, could have been made without leaving some record of their stay behind. Second, Jane's father, with an annual income of only six hundred pounds to support himself, his wife, and his daughters, could hardly have afforded so expensive a journey. Nor is he likely to have left his wife behind and traveled only with his daughters. And third, Jane's own correspondence shows that she was at Dawlish in South Devon in the summer of 1802.

The last man with whom Jane Austen is known to have been emotionally involved, and the only one definitely known to have made her a proposal of marriage, was Harris Bigg-Wither of Manydown Park near Steventon.[68] Jane had known him since 1789, when his father, Lovelace Bigg, had inherited the Hampshire properties of the Withers of Manydown, at which time he took the additional name of Wither.

Harris was eight years old and Jane was fourteen when his father took up residence at Manydown. Harris appears for the first time in her correspondence ten years later, when she dined with him and his father at Deane rectory, the home of her elder brother the Rev. James Austen.[69] Shortly thereafter, Harris's father suffered from a serious illness (from which he later recovered). While he was ill, Jane commented sardonically: "Poor man! — I mean Mr. Wither — his life is so useful, his character so respectable and worthy, that I really believe there was a good deal of sincerity in the general concern expressed on his account."[70] Harris, who had developed into an oversized young man, whose awkwardness was further exaggerated by taciturnity, an inhibiting stutter, and a stubbornness that caused his father a good deal of grief,[71] is also mentioned in Jane's early letters as having suffered from poor health.[72] But nothing in her references indicated that there were any tender feelings between herself and the heir of Manydown.

Fortunately, a pocket diary kept by Mary Austen, James Austen's wife, provides an exact chronicle of what happened at the time: Harris proposed to Jane, was accepted, then quickly rejected.[73] On September 1, 1802, Jane and Cassandra arrived from Bath at Steventon, where they stayed until September 3, at which time they set out for Godmersham to visit their brother Edward and his family. On October 28 they returned to Steventon and remained until November 25, when they went on to Manydown. A little over a week later, on December 3, 1802, the Manydown carriage arrived unexpectedly at Steventon rectory, bringing Jane and Cassandra and Catherine and Alethea Bigg, all in a state of extreme agitation. After tearful farewells, the Bigg sisters were driven back to Manydown, while Jane and Cassandra, without giving any explanation, insisted that their brother James take them back to Bath the next day. Since James did not have a curate, the request was difficult, as it allowed him little time to find someone to take his Sunday duties. Nevertheless, and contrary to their usual thoughtfulness, Jane and Cassandra were insistent, and the next morning James and his sisters left Steventon rectory for Bath. Eventually the story was revealed. On Thursday evening, December 2, 1802, Harris Bigg-Wither, then aged twenty-one, proposed to Jane and was accepted. After presumably sharing the news with Cassandra, however, Jane apparently began to reconsider the proposal and the next morning withdrew her consent, after which she and Cassandra left immediately for Steventon.

Many years later, Jane's niece Catherine Hubback, who had been permitted by her Aunt Cassandra to read some of Jane's letters before they were destroyed, wrote: "I gathered from the letters that it was in a momentary fit of self-delusion that Aunt Jane accepted Mr. Wither's proposal, and that when it was all settled eventually, and the negative decisively given she was much relieved. I think the affair vexed her a good deal, but I am sure she had no attachment to him."[74] But the pertinent commentary on the Bigg-Wither affair was made by Caroline Austen, who was well acquainted with the story from her mother, Mrs. James Austen. Caroline wrote:

> I conjecture that the advantages he could offer, and her gratitude for his love, and her long friendship with his family, induced my aunt to decide that she would marry him when he should ask her, but that having accepted him she found she was miserable. To be sure, she should not have said "Yes" overnight; but I have always respected her for her courage in cancelling that "Yes" the next morning; all worldly advantages would have been to her; and she was of an age to know this quite well (she was nearly twenty-seven). My Aunts had very small fortunes; and on their father's death, they and their mother would be, they were aware, but poorly off. I believe most young women so circumstanced would have gone on trusting to love after marriage.[75]

As for Harris Bigg-Wither, like Mr. Collins, he looked elsewhere. Two years after his proposal to Jane Austen was rejected, he married an heiress, Anne Howe Frith of Carisbrooke, Isle of Wight, who bore him five sons and five daughters.[76] Meanwhile, his rejection by Jane did not damage her relationship with his father and sisters for they remained Jane's close friends until her death.

As far as is known, the Bigg-Wither episode was Jane Austen's last emotional entanglement. Except for a playful suggestion made by Mrs. Thomas Knight, Edward Austen's adoptive mother, that Jane might consider the Rev. John Rawstorne Papillon, the rector of Chawton, as a prospective husband once she had moved there from Southampton, she had apparently given up all thoughts of ever marrying. Even then, Jane treated Mrs. Knight's suggestion in a bantering manner, for when Cassandra conveyed it to her sister in a letter from Kent, Jane replied: "I am very much obliged to Mrs. Knight for such a proof of the interest she takes in me—& she may depend upon it, that I *will* marry Mr. Papillon, whatever may be his reluctance or my own.—I owe her much more than such a trifling sacrifice."[77] Needless to say, Jane Austen never considered "fidgety" John Rawstorne Papillon as a husband,[78] for by the time she arrived at Chawton she was ready to begin her second and most creative literary period. To quote Catherine Hubback further: ". . . she always said her books were her children, and supplied her sufficient interest for happiness; and some of her letters, triumphing over the married women of her acquaintance,. and rejoicing in her own freedom from care were most amusing."[79]

CHAPTER

4

Jane Austen and the Events of Her Time

Hostile critics have never forgiven Jane Austen for having limited the scope of her novels to "pictures of domestic life in country villages,"[1] rather than broadening her literary canvas to include the historical events of her time. For instance, in 1913 Frederick Harrison, the English positivist philosopher, wrote to Thomas Hardy, the novelist, describing Jane as "a rather heartless little cynic . . . penning satirettes about her neighbors whilst the Dynasts were tearing the world to pieces, & consigning millions to their graves."[2] This carping observation is typical of complaints made over the years by those who cannot excuse Jane for the almost complete absence from her writings of anything relating to the French Revolution, the Napoleonic wars, or other current events.

In leveling these criticisms, however, Jane's detractors have unwittingly betrayed the ineptitude of their own accusations. Even Shakespeare, whom Jane Austen's censors would likely hesitate to reprove, was guilty of the same offense, if it can be so termed. Although Shakespeare lived in one of the most exciting periods of English history, there is no mention in any of his works of the Spanish Armada, the almost continuous wars in the Low Countries during his lifetime, the trial and execution of Mary, Queen of Scots, or the circumnavigation of the globe by Sir Francis Drake, to name only a few of the highlights of the Elizabethan Age.

It is worth noting that most of the popular literature of Jane Austen's time can be classified as escapist. As one writer has expressed it:

> Not till the nineteenth century had well advanced did the Napoleonic campaigns or the picturesque adventures of aristocratic émigrés find a place in fiction. Scott wrote of the France of Louis XI, not of that of Louis XVI. Mrs. Radcliffe and her numerous imitators placed their heroines in dilapidated castles, but castles in Cloud-Cuckoo Land, not in the war zones. Miss Edgeworth described Irish peasantry, not their counterparts in the rebellion fomented by our Government in La Vendee. Byron's imagination was excited by the fate of a fifteenth century Venetian Doge, not by the greater tragedy of the last to bear that office, to whom a young French general came as a declared Attila. Coleridge's Ancient Mariner shot a harmless bird, not a French sailor.[3]

From childhood Jane Austen was familiar with what was happening in the great world beyond the boundaries of Steventon Parish. The Hampsons of Taplow in Buckinghamshire, Jane's paternal grandmother's family, were involved in the colonial affairs of Jamaica,[4] while her father acted from 1760 as trustee for a plantation in Antigua.[5] This connection, and the Hampsons' colonial activities, presumably gave Jane sufficient background for Sir Thomas Bertram's visit to his West Indian plantations in *Mansfield Park*. Another connection with the great world was Jane Austen's paternal great-aunt, Mrs. Jane Payne, who was a woman of the bedchamber to the Princess Augusta of Saxe-Gotha from the time of the latter's marriage in 1736 to Frederick Louis, Prince of Wales, until 1767.[6] A more important link with the world outside Steventon rectory, however, was Jane's paternal aunt, Mrs. Philadelphia Hancock, who lived in India from 1752 to 1765. It was no doubt through her that Jane became familiar with Indian affairs and cuisine, both of which are reflected in her juvenilia.[7]

Jane was also a near neighbor during her early years of at least three men who were intimately connected with the American Revolution. The first was Henry Hulton of Clanville Lodge, a few miles west of Steventon, who was the first commissioner of customs for the American colonies from 1767 to 1775.[8] Hulton was involved in the Boston Tea Party of 1773 and was still at his post in Boston two years later at the time of the battles of Concord, Lexington, and Bunker Hill. It is possible that Jane's elder brother James was acquainted with Hulton and imparted the latter's recollections to the rectory household. This is given credence by a reference in an essay James wrote for *The Loiterer*, in which he said: ". . . my old acquaintance Capt. Prolix would think me a brute did I not express myself highly delighted with the account of the battle of Bunker's [*sic*] Hill, though he well knows I have not heard it on the most moderate computation less than two hundred times."[9]

Jane's second possible source of information concerning the war in America could have been Lord Dorchester, the former Sir Guy Carleton, who lived at nearby Kempshott Park from 1786 to 1803.[10] Lord Dorchester was responsible for the repulse of the American forces at Quebec in 1776. He served as the British commander in chief for America from 1781 to 1783 before retiring to Hampshire, where Jane is known to have attended balls given in his home. An even more likely source of information was General Edward Mathew, a close connection of Jane's family, who lived a few miles from Steventon.[11] Mathew, of the Coldstream Guard, had fought with distinction throughout the American Revolution and was later governor and commander in chief of the West Indies in 1782-83. His daughter Anne became the first wife of Jane's eldest brother, James, in 1792.

The most far-reaching worldly event that influenced Jane, however, occurred in France in 1781, when her cousin, Eliza Hancock, who had lived on the Continent since 1777, married Jean-François Capot de Feuillide, a captain of dragoons in the queen's regiment. Although none of the letters Eliza wrote to Jane's family at that time have survived, others written by her to another member of her family in England dating from the same period are still extant.[12] If these are similar to those she sent to Steventon rectory, Jane Austen, a highly intelligent child, undoubtedly reveled in the glimpses of the glittering world of prerevolutionary France her sophisticated cousin imparted. Moreover, Eliza's letters, written after she had fled to England after the outbreak of the French Revolution, reveal that she was not only keenly interested in politics, but possibly shared her reflections with her bright young cousin.

Jane Austen's horizons were additionally enlarged in or around 1783, when her third brother, Edward, was adopted by his wealthy and childless distant paternal cousin, Thomas Knight II of Godmersham,

Kent. Edward, then sixteen, had been a favorite of Knight and his wife since he was a child. As he was destined for the role of a cultured country gentleman, his adoptive parents sent him on the Grand Tour between 1786 and 1788 rather than to Oxford. Edward is known to have spent a year at Dresden, where he received marked attentions at the Saxon Court.[13] Later he extended his tour at least as far south as Rome, where he had his portrait painted when he was twenty-one.

The same period was also notable for a national incident that unquestionably left a vivid impression on the Steventon household. This was the impeachment and trial of Warren Hastings, which began in 1788, when Jane was twelve, and concluded in 1795 with Hastings's acquittal. Hastings had earlier sent his only son, George, to England from India in 1761, entrusting him to Jane's father for his education. According to family history, the child died at the age of six. But that did not decrease the friendship between the Austens and Hastings, for a copy of the latter's translation of some of the odes of Horace was kept by Jane's father in the rectory schoolroom at Steventon for his pupils to emulate.[14] Later, when Hastings was pronounced not guilty of corruption and cruelty during his administration in India, Jane's favorite brother, Henry, wrote him a letter of congratulation.[15]

In 1786, when Jane was ten, her brother Francis entered the Royal Naval Academy at Portsmouth a few days before his twelfth birthday, thereby broadening her interest in national affairs even further.[16] Two years later he left the Academy to serve, first as a volunteer and later as a midshipman and lieutenant, in the king's ships in the East Indies. He remained there until 1793, when he returned to England to serve on the home station and later in the Mediterranean, the Atlantic, and the Baltic. Francis Austen's duties aboard the *Perseverance,* one of the vessels of the East Indian squadron, coincided with the period in which Jane Austen's earliest juvenilia were written, two of which, *Jack & Alice* and *The Adventures of Mr. Harley,* were dedicated to him. Later, in her *History of England,* completed when she was almost sixteen, Jane compared her brother with Sir Francis Drake, foretelling a brilliant career for him. The prediction came true, for he ended his days at the age of ninety-one as Sir Francis William Austen, Admiral of the Fleet.

Francis was followed at the Academy in 1791, when Jane was fifteen, by his twelve-year-old younger brother, Charles, who remained there until 1794.[17] In that year he left to serve as a midshipman in the Royal Navy, a career that subsequently included service not only on the home station but in the Mediterranean and the Atlantic and Indian oceans as well. Meanwhile, the French Revolution had erupted, followed by the execution of Louis XVI and France's declaration of war on Great Britain in 1793. From then on, with the exception of the short breathing space provided by the Peace of Amiens in 1802-03, Jane Austen's naval brothers were actively engaged in the war at sea. During that time, as a devoted sister, she not only corresponded with them regularly and read their letters from their far-flung battle stations with avidity, she also followed their careers in the published *Navy Lists* with even more interest than the Musgrove sisters in *Persuasion.* Jane followed this routine until Napoleon was banished to St. Helena in 1815, for according to her niece Caroline Austen: "She wrote very fully to her Brothers when they were at sea."[18] The greater part of the correspondence exchanged between Jane Austen and her naval brothers has unfortunately not survived. In any event, there can be no doubt that Jane became well informed concerning matters relating to the Royal Navy of her time, a knowledge she used later in depicting William Price and the naval establishment at Portsmouth in *Mansfield Park* and in portraying Captain Wentworth, Admiral and Mrs. Croft, and the other naval characters in *Persuasion.*

With two brothers already in the king's service, Jane Austen gained another military connection in 1793 when her brother Henry became a lieutenant in the Oxfordshire Militia.[19] Henry, who later was promoted to adjutant and paymaster of the regiment, continued to serve until 1801, and besides having regular duties in England, he was stationed for a time in Ireland. His regiment was typical of the county militia units raised primarily for home defense and stationed in country towns that Jane Austen referred to in *Pride and Prejudice.* Later, many of these military companies were transferred to a great camp assembled on the South Downs at Brighton, where they remained from 1794 through 1796 to discourage threats of a French invasion. As far as is known, Jane Austen never visited Brighton Camp, but she was familiar enough with what went on there to use the site as the background for the elopement of Lydia Bennet and George Wickham in *Pride and Prejudice.* It is also worth noting that this pivotal episode in Jane's novel was prefigured in an essay written by her brother

James and published in *The Loiterer*, in which he described a similar situation thus: "Great, however, was my surprise to find on my arrival, the whole house was in confusion, and still greater to hear that Miss had, that very morning, eloped with a young officer, who had been some time quartered at a neighboring town."[20]

Although none of the Austens lost their lives in the long war with France, the deaths of two other persons closely connected with them were the cause of great affliction. The first occurred in February 1794, when Jane's cousin Eliza's husband was guillotined in Paris during the Reign of Terror on a trumped-up charge when he tried to help a friend who had been accused of conspiring against the French Republic.[21] Eliza had earlier come to England and it is not known where she was staying when she received the news of her husband's death. But her strong attachment to Jane's father makes it likely that sooner or later she sought the sympathy of his family at Steventon. More important was the effect the tragedy had on the passionately English eighteen-year-old Jane; for from then on she heartily detested the French.[22]

The other casualty was the Rev. Thomas Fowle, to whom Jane's sister, Cassandra, had become engaged around 1792. Fowle had accompanied his kinsman, Lord Craven, commanding officer of The Buffs, as a private chaplain when Craven's regiment was ordered to the West Indies as a part of a military operation to reduce the French Sugar Islands.[23] Fowle's death from yellow fever in San Domingo in February 1797 was such a blow to Cassandra Austen that she never afterward entertained the idea of marriage. This decision, in light of the well-documented lifelong intimacy that existed between herself and her younger sister, might also have ultimately influenced Jane to remain single.

By 1797, the year Jane began *First Impressions* (later transformed into *Pride and Prejudice*), her midshipman brother Charles had participated in the capture of the French frigate *La Tribune* in home waters after a running fight of several hours. Later, he was made a lieutenant after distinguishing himself when he assisted in driving a Dutch line-of-battle ship into Helvoetsluys following Admiral Duncan's victory over the Dutch at Camperdown. Still later, when Charles was fortunate enough to return home for a brief visit, Jane and her family were amused to see he had left off powdering his hair, having had it cropped short like most of the young naval officers of the day for convenience on shipboard.[24]

Subsequently, Charles served in the Mediterranean, where he assisted in making prizes of several privateers. One of these, the *Scipio,* surrendered during a violent gale. Charles put off from his own vessel in an open boat with only four men and, after boarding the *Scipio,* held it until reinforcements arrived the next day. For this daring action, Charles received a special commendation as well as a share in the prize, which he promptly used to buy a handsome topaz cross and gold chain for each of his sisters, a generosity that presumably served Jane later as the genesis for the amber cross episode in *Mansfield Park.*[25]

As for Francis Austen, his naval career at that period had included service in the *Lark,* one of the squadron that brought the Princess Caroline of Brunswick to England for her unfortunate marriage to the Prince of Wales. After that he was assigned to vessels engaged in the blockading of Cadiz during the period of Napoleon's Egyptian campaign and Nelson's victory over the French fleet at the Battle of the Nile. Later, Francis achieved distinction in the Mediterranean by capturing *La Ligurienne,* a splendid new brig that was to have followed Napoleon to Egypt; the capture and burning of a Turkish line-of-battle ship on the coast of Egypt; and the delivery of an important naval dispatch from Lord St. Vincent at Gibraltar to Lord Nelson, then at Palermo.[26]

Many of these exploits were known to Jane Austen and her family from newspapers long before her brothers' letters recounting them reached Steventon. Meanwhile, Jane kept up her naval brothers' spirits by writing them informative letters and assisting in making and dispatching items that would increase their creature comforts on shipboard. One of her letters in particular gives an intimate glimpse of the period when the families of naval officers contributed to the personal foodstuffs that they took along to augment the scanty fare aboard the king's ships. Jane wrote to Cassandra: "My father furnishes him [i.e., Charles] with a pig from Cheesedown; it is already killed and cut up, but is not to weigh more than nine stones; the season is too far advanced to get him a larger one. My mother means to pay herself for the salt and the trouble of ordering it to be cured by the sparibs [*sic*], the souse, and the lard."[27]

By the time of the Peace of Amiens in March 1802, Jane Austen had moved with her parents and sister to Bath. The cessation of hostilities brought her naval brothers ashore for the time being.

The peace was responsible, however, for an adventure experienced by Jane's brother Henry and his wife, Eliza, the former Madame de Feuillide. Early in 1803, they went to France, presumably to try to salvage anything that remained from the estate of Eliza's first husband. Their visit was abruptly ended when Napoleon revoked the peace in May 1803, at which time hundreds of British tourists were unable to leave France. Henry and Eliza were more fortunate, however, for according to family tradition, Eliza effected their escape by relegating her husband to the role of an invalid in the back of their traveling carriage, while she, with her mastery of French, took over and gave the orders for fresh horses at the posting stations on their way northward from Paris to the unspecified port from which they eventually escaped to England.[28]

With the renewal of hostilities, Jane's naval brothers again reported for active duty that continued throughout the remainder of the war. Charles Austen resumed his duties aboard the *Endymion,* where he remained until 1804, when he was transferred to the North American station to assist in preventing neutrals from trading with France, an activity in which he was engaged until the year before the outbreak of war between the United States and Great Britain in 1812.

Francis Austen's assignments were even more interesting. The resumption of hostilities with France, headed by the man the British were by then calling "The Corsican Ogre," also engendered a fear that England would be invaded. This was no idle fancy, for Napoleon had concentrated the Grand Army in the French maritime provinces, where he caused the Bayeux Tapestry to be paraded in public to arouse enthusiasm for what he thought would be a triumphant crossing of the English Channel.[29] But the British were not so easily intimidated. Although they still put their trust in the Channel fleet to turn back the flat-bottomed barges in which Napoleon hoped to transport his troops during favorable weather, another measure was taken to establish a second line of defense. This was the creation of the Sea Fencibles, a home guard to be called into action should the French succeed in landing on the Kent or Sussex beaches. One of these groups, the North Foreland unit, with headquarters at Ramsgate, Kent, was commanded by Francis Austen in 1803-04. It was at Ramsgate during that time that Sir Egerton Brydges encountered Jane Austen, who had presumably driven over from Godmersham to visit her brother. In recalling the event, Brydges wrote: "The last time I think that I saw her was at Ramsgate in 1803: perhaps she was then about twenty-seven years old. Even then I did not know that she was addicted to literary composition."[30]

The anticipated invasion never took place and Francis Austen again went to sea in one of the vessels engaged in blockading the northern French ports. It was during that time that Napoleon proclaimed himself the Emperor of France. This caused Francis to comment dryly in an account he was then writing of Boulogne: "The inhabitants are French, subjects to Napoleon the First, lately exalted to the Imperial dignity by the unanimous suffrages of himself and his creatures."[31] Early in 1805, Francis was transferred to the *Canopus* and assigned to the squadron blockading the combined French and Spanish fleets then bottled up in the harbor of Cadiz. Francis had every hope of taking part in the inevitable forthcoming battle (i.e., Trafalgar), but shortly before it took place, his ship, among others, was dispatched by Lord Nelson to Gibraltar for supplies. In that way Francis missed the Battle of Trafalgar on October 21, 1805, a stroke of fate that caused him great mental anguish.[32]

Francis was present in February of the next year at the Battle of San Domingo, where he had the pleasure of giving a "three-decker a tickling which knocked all *his sticks* away."[33] This engagement, the details of which were presumably imparted to Jane in one of his letters, provided her with the fact that Captain Wentworth, the hero of *Persuasion,* was "made commander in consequence of the action off St. Domingo." In a letter written by Jane's mother in April 1806 she mentioned she had lately received a letter from her nephew, the Rev. Edward Cooper, who had written "to congratulate us on Frank's Victory and safety."[34]

Eighteen months after the death of her father in 1805, Jane Austen accompanied her mother, her sister, Martha Lloyd, and her brother Francis, who had recently married, to Southampton, where they lived until early 1809. Francis apparently chose Southampton because of its proximity to Portsmouth and the naval anchorage at Spithead, for after having assumed the command of the *St. Albans* in 1807 he continued to be based in that area until late in 1810. As Southampton and Portsmouth were then hives of wartime naval activity as well as the temporary residence of many of Francis's naval friends, Jane Austen was able to come into closer contact with the stirring events of the war; and this is reflected in several of her letters dating from her Southampton years. Her interest was further stimulated in 1808 when she was staying at Godmersham, at which time Francis Austen arrived in the Downs after having convoyed a fleet of merchantmen to St. Helena. Earlier, on June 20, 1808, he had made the following entry in the log of the *St. Albans:* "Exchanged numbers with the *Raven* brig. The brig is from off Lisbon. The French have taken possession of Spain. The Spanish Royal Family are prisoners in France."[35] This matter-of-fact entry recorded the beginning of the Peninsular War in Spain and Portugal, during which Wellington, as the head of the British, Spanish, and Portuguese armies, slowly drove the French back across the Pyrenees, thereby contributing to Napoleon's first abdication in 1814. Less than a month later, Francis convoyed a fleet of troopships to Portugal, where, on August 21, 1808, he watched the Battle of Vimeiro, the first engagement of the Peninsular War, through his telescope from the deck of the *St. Albans.*[36]

In the meantime, Jane Austen had become so incensed over the trial of a popular British naval officer that she vented her anger by writing a series of spirited verses in his defense. These were occasioned by the court-martial and reprimanding of Sir Home Popham in April 1807 for having withdrawn his squadron from the Cape of Good Hope without orders. Popham's case, which he argued ably himself, won him a great deal of sympathy, and his career was hardly affected, for he was made a rear admiral in 1814 and became a Companion of the Bath the next year. Before that took place, however, Jane Austen championed Popham as follows:

Of a Ministry pitiful, angry [and?] mean,
A gallant commander the victim is seen.
For promptitude, vigour, success, does he stand
Condemn'd to receive a severe reprimand!
To his foes I could wish a resemblance in fate:
That they, too, may suffer themselves, soon or late,
The injustice they warrant. But vain is my spite,
They *cannot* so *suffer who never do right.*[37]

Two years later, a letter of Jane's contained a significant political reference. In January 1809 a rumor had circulated in Southampton that George III's mental condition had deteriorated so badly that a regency was imminent. But, as Jane expressed it, the report "seems to have been heard of only here." To this she added: ". . . my most political correspondents make no mention of it. Unlucky that I should have wasted so much reflection on the subject."[38] This reveals, despite the assertions of her hostile critics, that Jane Austen was very much interested in the events of her day.

Jane Austen's letters from Southampton also contain significant references to the Peninsular War, then in its earlier stages. On January 10, 1809, she told Cassandra: "The 'St. Albans' perhaps may soon be off to help bring home what may remain by this time of our poor army, whose state seems dreadfully critical."[39] Jane was referring to the British troops under Sir John Moore, who had advanced into Spain from Portugal to threaten Napoleon's invading army. Moore was forced to retreat through the mountains of northern Spain in the dead of winter to Corunna, where he rallied his demoralized men and succeeded in evacuating most of them before he was mortally wounded. The news did not take long to reach England, for the vessel bearing the dispatch was blown northward by a raging southwester.[40] As Francis Austen was in charge of the disembarkation of Moore's troops at Spithead, he presumably communicated the details of the defeat at Corunna to Jane. In any event, on January 30, 1809, she commented on them to Cassandra: "I wish Sir John had united something of the Christian with the Hero in his death.—Thank Heavens! We have had no one to care for particularly among the Troops—no one in fact nearer to us than Sir John himself."[41]

The exact meaning of Jane's statement is obscure, as no relationship between her family and that of Sir John Moore can be traced, but her indictment of Sir John's inability to include "something of the Christian with the Hero in his death" needs clarification as it has subjected her to the charge of priggishness. The best explanation of her ambiguous reflection was offered by the late Sir Charles Oman, Professor of Modern History at Oxford: "What Jane was thinking of with regard to Sir John's deathbed—of which a rather full narrative survives—was that he is reported to have said nothing about God and the other World, but a great deal about public opinion in England, and his hope that it would acquit him; as well as some messages to Lady Hester Stanhope and other friends in London. I think she was hinting that it was not a very 'Christian' end, and that her words have no further meaning."[42]

In the meantime, Francis Austen and his wife had moved from Southampton to Portsmouth, and it was presumably during Jane's occasional visits to them that she became familiar with the bustling naval town, its dockyards, and the anchorage at Spithead, a knowledge that stood her in good stead when she wrote *Mansfield Park.* With the Francis Austens' departure from Southampton, Jane's mother began to search for smaller accommodation for her daughters and herself. After considering several locations she decided to move to Chawton in Hampshire, where her son Edward had offered to provide her with a permanent home. After moving to Chawton, Jane completely revised *Sense and Sensibility,* begun at Steventon in 1797; the final version was published in November 1811. In order to be available for the correcting of the proofs of *Sense and Sensibility,* Jane went to London in April 1811, staying with her brother Henry and his wife. By that time he was a partner in a flourishing banking business, lived in a handsome house on Sloane Street, and was on intimate terms with many people of consequence, notable among whom was the well-known political leader Sir Francis Burdett, the champion of the raffish wife of the Prince Regent. Henry's wife, Eliza, also had a wide acquaintance among the titled French emigrés, and one of these, the Comte d'Antraigues, a secret agent for Russia, entertained the Henry Austens and Jane during her 1811 visit to London.[43] Meanwhile, Jane had been witnessing changes on the national scene. Late in 1810, soon after celebrating the fiftieth anniversary of his reign, George III had become permanently deranged. His condition led to the Prince of Wales being created Prince Regent, a position he continued to hold until his father's death in 1820.

After the publication of *Sense and Sensibility,* Jane Austen concentrated on the final revision of *First Impressions,* written at Steventon in 1796-97, which she renamed *Pride and Prejudice.* It was published in 1813, the year after the United States declared war on Great Britain. The conflict was primarily brought on because of the unlawful capture or search of American merchantmen trading with France or her colonies by the British and the impressment of American seamen. Jane's brother Charles, serving on the North American station, had been engaged in these practices since 1804. By 1810, at least four thousand American sailors had been seized by the British, and the United States retaliated by canceling trade relations with England. The British responded by blockading American ports. That action led to a declaration of war by the United States in June 1812, followed by a series of brilliant American naval victories that seriously embarrassed Great Britain. These incidents, or an unspecified one in particular, were presumably in Jane Austen's mind when she caused Tom Bertram in *Mansfield Park* to declare: "A strange business, this in America, Dr. Grant! What is your opinion? I always come to you to know what I am to think of public matters."[44]

Three months after she had begun *Mansfield Park* in February 1811, Jane Austen made another comment on the war in Europe in a letter to her sister. Writing on May 31, 1811, she exclaimed: "How horrible it is to have so many people killed!—And what a blessing that one cares for none of them!"[45] Jane's reference was to the latest news from Spain, where the Peninsular War had continued for three years. Jane has been reproached by some critics for the seemingly callous statement expressed in the latter part of her comment. The censure is not valid, however, for with two brothers who had been on active service since the outbreak of the war with France, she was well acquainted with the enormity of the conflict that had turned the relatively stable world of her younger days into a turmoil that could only be viewed with detachment in order to preserve one's sanity. Jane's remark is therefore apparently only an outmoded way of saying she was thankful she was not personally acquainted with any of those who were listed as casualties.

While *Mansfield Park* was being written, Francis Austen took command of the *Elephant,* attached to the North Sea fleet. Later, when war broke out between the United States and Great Britain, he captured the *Swordfish,* an American privateer operating out of Boston. Still later, when *Mansfield Park* was in its unrevised state, Jane wrote to Francis in July 1813: "And by the bye—shall you object to my mentioning the Elephant in it, & two or three other of your old Ships. I *have* done it, but it shall not stay, to make you angry.—They are only just mentioned."[46] In expressing her envy of her brother's good fortune in being able to visit Sweden on his tour of duty in the Baltic, Jane added: "Your Profession has it's [*sic*] douceurs to recompense for some of its Privations;—to an enquiring & observing Mind like yours, such douceurs must be considerable.—Gustavas-Vasa, & Charles 12th, & Christina, & Linneus [*sic*]—do their Ghosts rise up before you?"[47] Then, to show Francis she was following his progress in the Baltic (presumably by referring to an atlas), she added: ". . . I have always fancied it [i.e., Sweden] more like England than many Countries;—& according to the Map, many of the names have a strong resemblance to the English."[48] It is passages like this that tantalizingly reveal fleeting glimpses of an entirely different Jane Austen from the one mirrored in her chatty letters to her sister.

Charles Austen returned to England in 1811 from the North American station in the *Cleopatra* (another ship mentioned by Jane Austen in *Mansfield Park*). At that time he became the Flag Captain aboard the *Namur* at the Nore anchorage at the mouth of the Thames. His duties included the regulation of all men recruited for the navy in the Thames and eastern ports, and also the task of manning the warships fitted out in the Thames and Medway, an activity that frequently necessitated the use of press gangs. It is not known if Jane Austen ever discussed the latter practice with Charles, but we do know she did receive information from him concerning education aboard the king's ships that she apparently drew on later when she came to write the "poor Dick Musgrove" episode in *Persuasion*.

When Jane was paying her last visit to Godmersham in 1813, she was joined by Charles and his wife and daughters. At that time she presumably queried him about the naval schoolmaster for she told Cassandra, concerning a young naval friend: "I have made Charles furnish me with something to say about Young Kendall.—He is going on very well. When he first joined the Namur, my Br [i.e., brother] did not find him forward enough to be what they call put in the Office, & therefore placed him under the Schoolmaster, but he is very much improved, & goes into the Office now every afternoon—still attending School in the morng [*sic*]."[49]

By the time this was written, the tide had begun to turn against Napoleon. Out of the army of 550,000 men who had set out on the Russian campaign in 1812, only 20,000 had survived. This disaster was followed in 1813 by Napoleon's defeats at Leipzig and the Battle of the Nations, after which the formerly all-powerful emperor withdrew to the west bank of the Rhine. Meanwhile, the war in Spain had ended in defeat for the French. All of this caused Jane Austen to share in the national euphoria over the turn of events by adding a personal note of her own. Writing to Cassandra from Godmersham on November 6, 1813, she exclaimed: "What weather! & what news!"[50] After five years of bloody fighting in Spain and Portugal, Wellington's army was about to cross the Pyrenees into France, while the Allied armies were also closing in on Napoleon. The days of the First Empire were numbered, and it is no wonder that Jane added: "I hope you derive full share of enjoyment from each."[51]

As the long war with France was finally drawing to a close there was tremendous rejoicing. Late in March 1814, the triumphant Allies entered Paris, and Napoleon abdicated unconditionally at Fontainebleau in April and was banished to Elba. Louis XVIII, who had grown old and obese in exile in England, returned to the throne of his fathers, and was followed by so many British visitors one of the popular songs of the day declared: "All the world's in Paris."[52] Still later in the year London was *en fête* for the visit of the Allied Sovereigns, headed by the Emperor Alexander I of Russia and his ally, the King of Prussia, who arrived in England with their retainers and other dignitaries in June 1814 to celebrate the downfall of Napoleon.

Jane Austen apparently was delighted to be at Chawton at that time, far removed from the tumultuous welcome accorded the visiting worthies, for she was busily engaged in writing *Emma.* Even so, Jane's letters contain brief references to the month-long festivities, which were highlighted by the repeated rudeness the emperor and his disagreeable sister, the Grand Duchess of Oldenburg, exhibited throughout their stay, although their official host, the Prince Regent, did everything in his power to make the occasion an ostentatiously memorable one.[53]

As Cassandra was staying in London with Henry Austen, Jane cautioned her on June 14, 1814: "Take care of yourself, and do not be trampled to death running after the Emperor."[54] A spectacular naval review at Portsmouth had also been planned to highlight the Allied Sovereigns' visit, and Jane added: "The report in Alton yesterday was that they would certainly travel this road either to or from Portsmouth."[55] Contrary to Jane's expectations, however, the visiting sovereigns did not pass through Chawton either on their way to or from Portsmouth, but Jane's brother Francis was present at the review. In her next letter to Cassandra, Jane wrote: "I heard yesterday from Frank. When he began his letter he hoped to be here on Monday, but before it was ended he had been told that the naval review would not take place till Friday, which would probably occasion him some delay." To this she added: "I hope Fanny [her niece Fanny Knight] has seen the Emperor, and then I may fairly wish them all away."[56] Characteristically, Jane's mercurial brother Henry had managed to attend the grand ball at Burlington House given on June 20, 1814, by the members of White's, the fashionable London club, in honor of the emperor and the other visitors at a cost of nine thousand pounds,[57] causing Jane to exclaim: "Henry at White's! Oh, what a Henry!"[58]

More significant as far as Jane Austen's political views are concerned was a comment she made in a letter written to her friend Martha Lloyd in September 1814 on the war then in progress between the United States and Great Britain. In speaking of Henry, Jane wrote: "*His* view, and the view of those he mixes with, of Politics, is nor chearful [*sic*]—with regard to an American war I mean;—they consider it as certain [i.e., a further conflict in the future], and as what is to ruin us. The [Americans?] cannot be conquered, and we shall only be teaching them the skill in War which they may now want. We are to make them good Sailors and Soldiers, and g[ain?] nothing ourselves.—"[59]

In 1815, Francis Austen, who had returned home the year before from the Baltic, was made a Companion of the Order of the Bath. From then on he and his family lived for several years either at Chawton Great House, which had been lent him by his brother Edward, or at Alton, where he was readily available for consultation when Jane began her naval-oriented novel *Persuasion* in the summer or autumn of 1815.[60] Earlier, Charles Austen, who had grown restless at his post at the Nore, was appointed to the *Phoenix* in October 1814 and sailed for the Mediterranean. On the renewal of hostilities after Napoleon's escape from Elba late in February 1815, the *Phoenix* and two other vessels under Charles's command were sent in pursuit of a Neapolitan squadron supposedly in the Adriatic. After the surrender of Naples, Charles instigated a close blockade of Brindisi and was instrumental in persuading the castle and two of the enemy's largest frigates in the harbor to hoist the colors of the restored King of Naples, thereby gaining him a special commendation from the Admiralty.[61]

Meanwhile, on March 1, 1815, Napoleon had landed near Cannes, on the south coast of France and marched northward. By June he had raised an army composed largely of his former troops and was moving in a northeasterly direction from Paris toward Brussels, where Wellington and Blücher, the commanding officers of the British and Prussian forces, had their headquarters. Near there, at Waterloo, on June 18, 1815, Napoleon was defeated, and four days later he abdicated for the second and last time. As it was customary to decorate the mailcoaches and stagecoaches leaving London with flags and laurel branches in honor of a great victory, those that passed through Chawton on their way to Portsmouth and Southampton would certainly have been greeted by Jane Austen and her family with joyous relief, knowing the long war with France was finally over.

These historic events were on everyone's tongue when Jane began *Persuasion,* a simple love story, yet also a heartfelt personal tribute to the iron men and wooden ships that had thwarted Napoleon's ambition to turn Great Britain into another conquered province. As such, it was the closest that Jane ever came in her novels to becoming involved in national events. Even so, in writing about the navy in *Persuasion,* Jane was on firm ground. Once she had assigned it a prominent role in her story, she was fortunate in possessing a thorough knowledge of the king's ships and the men who commanded them, which she had acquired over the years from her two naval brothers. What is more, her last completed novel was also subtly infused with the intense interest in the events of her time that had preoccupied her thoughts from her earliest years onward.

CHAPTER

•5•

The Elegant Amenities

In the biographical notice that Henry Austen wrote of his sister as a preface to the posthumous publication of *Northanger Abbey* and *Persuasion* he said:

> In the present age it is hazardous to mention accomplishments. Our authoress would, probably, have been inferior to few in such acquirements, had she not been so superior to most in higher things. She had not only an excellent taste for drawing, but, in her earlier days, evinced great power of hand in the management of the pencil. Her own musical attainments she held very cheap. Twenty years ago they would have been thought more of, and twenty years hence many a parent will expect their daughters to be applauded for meaner performances. She was fond of dancing, and excelled in it.[1]

Although Henry Austen did not mention it in his biographical notice, Jane Austen was also keenly interested in the theater, both amateur and professional, and her lifelong preoccupation with drama, particularly the comedy of manners, undoubtedly influenced her as a writer.

The playacting episode in Jane Austen's *Mansfield Park* is the literary apotheosis of the rage for amateur theatricals that obsessed British society from the 1770s until the first part of the nineteenth century.[2] The craze did not reach Steventon rectory until 1782, when Jane was seven. Even so, there were two earlier British amateur theatricals of the kind that were performed at Steventon that should be noted. Before the death of the first Duke of Marlborough in 1722, several of his grandchildren, with the aid of a group of young officers, attempted to amuse the old hero by performing Dryden's *All for Love* and Addison's *Rosamund* in the Bow Window room at Blenheim. Later, in 1732, William Hogarth was commissioned by John Conduitt, Master of the Mint, to record a Lilliputian performance of Dryden's *Indian Emperor or The Conquest of Mexico* staged in London for the benefit of the children of George II.[3]

By the last quarter of the century, however, dramatic performances by youthful members of the family were on the wane, having been superseded by a craze for adult theatricals. As a result, temporary arrangements for playacting sprang up all over England, in places ranging from converted domestic outbuildings or large rooms in private dwellings that lent themselves to theatrical purposes to elaborate imitations of regular London playhouses. The most notable was erected at Wargrave in Berkshire in the late 1770s by the spendthrift Earl of Barrymore at a reputed cost of sixty thousand pounds. In the main, however, those who felt the urge to act had to fall back on converting large rooms in their homes into temporary theaters, an arrangement adopted by Fanny Burney's uncle at Barborne Lodge near Worcester, where a room seating not more than twenty people was provided with a curtained-off stage at one end, while the musicians who played for the performance took up their stations in an outside passage.[4] This arrangement was similar to the one planned for the performance of *Lovers' Vows* in *Mansfield Park,* which was terminated so dramatically by Sir Thomas Bertram's return from Antigua.

At Steventon rectory the dining parlor was used as a makeshift theater for the earlier productions.[5] Tradition also says the rector's barn was used on occasion as a temporary theater, but probably not until the Christmas theatricals of 1787. In a letter written in September of that year, Philadelphia Walter, a cousin of Jane Austen's, said: "My uncle's barn is fitting up quite like a theater, & all the young folks are to take their part."[6]

There is no record or tradition that Jane Austen ever acted in any of the Steventon theatricals, but there is a neighbor's testimony that she was endowed with histrionic ability. In writing of Sir William Heathcote of Hursley Park, Hampshire, the novelist Charlotte M. Yonge recalled: "His mother was Elizabeth, daughter of Lovelace Bigg-Wither of Manydown Park in the same county . . . and it may be interesting that her son remembered being at a Twelfth-day party where Jane Austen drew the character of Mrs. Candour, and assumed the part with great spirit."[7] That Jane Austen was able to breathe life into one of the wittiest roles in Sheridan's *The School for Scandal* on such short notice is an argument in favor of her having taken part in the Steventon theatricals of her girlhood.

The first play known to have been acted at Steventon was *Matilda,* a tragedy in five acts by Dr. Thomas Francklin, a friend of Dr. Samuel Johnson's and a fashionable London preacher of the type for whom Henry Crawford expressed his admiration in *Mansfield Park.*[8] Francklin's play was acted some time during 1782; Jane's elder brother, James, then seventeen and the poet of the family, wrote a prologue and an epilogue for the performance.[9] Two years later, when Jane was nine, Sheridan's *The Rivals* was acted at Steventon, also with a prologue and an epilogue written by James. As *The Rivals* requires eleven male and five female characters it is obvious that the Austens could hardly have mustered enough actors and actresses within the family circle to fill all the roles without resorting to a good deal of doubling of parts. Fortunately, there was at least one family in the neighborhood, the Lefroys of Ashe, that would have been willing to provide volunteers.

In 1783 the cultural horizons of the Steventon area were considerably broadened when the Rev. Isaac Peter George Lefroy, a well-educated clergyman, became the rector of neighboring Ashe.[10] Finding his parsonage house decidedly lacking in architectural distinction, he immediately mortgaged the living,[11] using the money raised to transform Ashe rectory into a charming late Georgian gentleman's country residence that soon became a focal point for generous and lively hospitality. In these endeavors, Lefroy was joined by his wife, Anne. Mr. and Mrs. Lefroy were sophisticated, with a knowledge of the London theater and a wide acquaintance of friends, so it is reasonable to assume that they not only would have offered their assistance with the performance of *The Rivals*, but would also have encouraged their family and friends to do likewise. Although this cannot be proved, the suggestion is given credence by the fact that Mrs. Lefroy's brother, Sir Egerton Brydges, the poet and antiquarian bibliographer, was connected later with at least one play produced at Steventon. Also, in those days before the blight of Evangelicalism had spread like a pall over England, it was perfectly consistent with the dignity of a clergyman or his wife to participate in amateur theatricals—witness Mrs. Grant's willingness to play the part of the Cottager's Wife in *Lovers' Vows* in *Mansfield Park*.

The 1787 theatrical activities at Steventon were the most notable of them all, made memorable by the presence of the Austens' worldly cousin, Eliza de Feuillide. Eliza, who had arrived in England from France the year before, had taken part in amateur theatricals since she was a child and had also acted in private theatricals staged by her aristocratic French friends.[12] In September 1787, when she and her cousin Philadelphia Walter were at Tunbridge Wells, she had requested that the comedies *Which Is the Man?* by Hannah Cowley, and *Bon Ton, or High Life Above Stairs*, by David Garrick, be presented at the local theater.[13] Later, Philadelphia Walter informed a brother in a letter that these two plays were to be given at Steventon that Christmas.[14] But that did not happen, for the play that was presented either in the barn or the dining parlor at Steventon on December 26-28, 1787, was the comedy *The Wonder: A Woman Keeps a Secret*, by Susannah Centlivre, for which James Austen also wrote a prologue and an epilogue.[15] His copy of the epilogue, inscribed "spoken by a Lady in the character of Violante," is a saucy declaration of independence of "Creation's fairest part" from the domination of "Creation's mighty Lords" and was presumably tailored to Eliza de Feuillide's specifications. As Eliza was one of the chief motivators in the 1787 Steventon theatricals, she would almost certainly have insisted on speaking James Austen's lively epilogue, which ends with the rhetorical flourish:

But thank our happy stars, those days are o'er,
And Woman holds a second place no more;
Now forced to quit their long held usurpation,
These Men all wise, the Lords of the Creation;

To our superior rule themselves submit.
Slaves to our charm, & vassals to our wit.[16]

Another epilogue was composed for the same play by Sir Egerton Brydges, and bears the inscription: "Intended to have been spoken in the character of Violante, at a private Theatre, in Hampshire, 1787."[17] Brydges had rented the vacant rectory at Deane from Jane Austen's father in 1786 in order to be near his sister at Ashe,[18] and his composing an epilogue for *The Wonder* suggests that he was actively involved in its production. If that is true, his personal participation in the Christmas theatricals of that year invites another possibility. By 1787, Brydges's brother-in-law, the rector of Ashe, had completed the addition to his rectory begun in 1783, consisting of a central hall on the ground floor with a library on the left side of the entrance, and a spacious drawing room and a dining parlor on the right. These rooms, which still exist today, are connected by a wide archway equipped with folding doors. When the latter are opened, a proscenium arch is created between the drawing room, which could have been used to seat the audience, and the dining parlor, which could have served as a temporary stage for playacting. Although there is no surviving evidence that these apartments were ever used for amateur theatricals, there are two reasons that suggest the possibility that they might have. First, the dining parlor at Steventon rectory was too small to accommodate many spectators, much less the actors themselves, while the rector's barn would have been too cold and drafty to serve as a theater during the winter. Second, Sir Egerton Brydges's proven interest in the amateur theatricals at Steventon as well as the well-authenticated intimacy that existed between the Austens and the Lefroys would have made the offer by the latter of using their two adjoining rooms at Ashe rectory as an alternate theater a welcome one.

Susannah Centlivre's comedy was followed by the presentation of three other plays at Steventon during 1788. The first was David Garrick's adaptation of John Fletcher's comedy *The Chances*.[19] As it called for a cast of fourteen male and four female characters, it is reasonable to assume that it was again a Steventon-area collaboration rather than a production put on exclusively by Jane Austen's family. Prologues written by James Austen for *The Chances* and the other two plays that followed it still exist, but if he matched them with epilogues the latter are no longer among his surviving papers. Garrick's adaptation of *The Chances* was "acted at Steventon in July 1788." It was followed shortly thereafter by another play, the title of which is now unknown, the prologue being merely described as for "a private Theatrical Exhibition at Steventon 1788."[20] The third play produced in the same year was the *Tragedy of Tom Thumb,* either in Henry Fielding's original version or Kane O'Hara's later adaptation and condensation.[21]

As far as is known the last two plays presented at Steventon were *The Sultan, or a Peep into the Seraglio,* a comedy by Isaac Bickerstaffe, and James Townley's farce, *High Life Below Stairs.*[22] No prologue or epilogue by James Austen for the latter has survived, but the epilogue he provided for Bickerstaffe's comedy, the plot of which has many resemblances to Mozart's *The Abduction from the Seraglio,* is dated 1790 and states it was "spoken by Miss Cooper as Roxalana."[23] This is confirmed in a letter by Eliza de Feuillide, written from Paris shortly thereafter, in which she said: "I suppose you have frequent accounts from Steventon, & that they have informed you of their theatrical performances, *The Sultan & High-Life below stairs.* Miss Cooper performed the part of *Roxalana & Henry the Sultan.*"[24]

The performances of Bickerstaffe's comedy and Townley's farce apparently rang down the curtain on the amateur theatricals at Steventon. There is a family legend, however, that claims Henry Austen and Eliza de Feuillide revived playacting there after her husband was guillotined in Paris in 1794, the outcome being that Henry became Eliza's second husband.[25] This tradition is questionable, however, for the movements of both Henry and Eliza, after her return to England, presumably during the early part of 1790, are well documented in the privately printed *Austen Papers 1704-1856,* in which there is no mention of private theatricals at Steventon or elsewhere after 1794.

As the Steventon theatricals took place between 1782 and 1790, they coincided with the period during which Jane Austen's juvenilia were written. It is therefore not surprising to discover three attempts at play writing among her youthful literary efforts. The first two, dating between 1787 and 1790, are *The Visit* and *The Mystery. The Visit,* one of the wittiest of Jane Austen's juvenilia and dedicated to her eldest brother, James, is the more interesting. The wording of the dedication is significant as it preserves the titles of either two of Jane's juvenile writings no longer in existence, or of two plays by James that have not survived. After the preamble, Jane's dedication reads: "The following Drama, which I humbly recommend to your Protection & Patronage, tho' inferior to the celebrated Comedies called 'The School for Jealousy' & 'The travelled Man,' will I hope afford some amusement to so respectable a *Curate* as yourself, which was the end in view when it was first composed by your Humble Servant the Author."[26] *The Visit* is notable for its lively dialogue and includes many farcical touches concerning a dinner visit to a Lord Fitzgerald's house by a party (one of them named Willoughby). By comparison, *The Mystery* is more routine, its chief significance being that Jane Austen undoubtedly drew her inspiration for its two whispering scenes from Sheridan's *The Critic,* then only recently produced in London.[27]

Although Jane Austen's *Love and Freindship* (*sic*), dating from her fourteenth year, is not a play, it contains a hint in its last paragraph that reveals her familiarity even at an early age with the London stage of her time. To wind up her story, Jane transformed two of her fictional characters into real actors: "Philander & Gustavas, after having raised their reputation by their Performances in the Theatrical Line in Edinburgh, removed to Covent Garden, where they still Exhibit under the assumed names of *Lewis & Quick.*"[28] The "assumed names" touch was a sly joke on Jane's part, for William Thomas ("Gentleman") Lewis and John Quick were both well-known actors who had played in the initial performance of Sheridan's *The Rivals* in 1775.[29]

There is still another theatrical reference in one of Jane Austen's prose writings dating from around 1792 that deserves to be mentioned. In *The Three Sisters,* in which she satirized the premarital scheming of three embryonic viragos named Mary, Georgiana, and Sophia Stanhope, Jane painted a lively scene during which Mary Stanhope, in making demands on her prospective husband, declared: "You must do nothing but give Balls & Masquerades. You must build a room on purpose & a Theatre to act Plays in. The first Play we have shall be *Which Is the Man,* and I will do Lady Bell Bloomer."[30] Jane's choice of that particular play by Mrs. Hannah Cowley is interesting as it was one of the plays proposed by her cousin Eliza for the 1787 Christmas season. Jane Austen apparently read the play when it was being considered for the 1787 theatricals at Steventon rectory when she was twelve, for twenty-nine years afterward, in thanking her nephew James Edward Austen for some pickled cucumbers that his father had sent from Steventon to Chawton and that she found "extremely good," she quoted a phrase ("tell him what you will") from Mrs. Cowley's play in conjunction with the gift.[31]

Jane Austen's third attempt at play writing is included under the heading of "Scraps" in *Volume the Second.* Dating from around 1793, the piece is called "The First Act of a Comedy" and concerns the adventures of a family en route to London. The highlight of the skit comes when Chloe, one of the characters, reads over a bill of fare at the inn where the family is staying, at which time she discovers that the only food available consists of "2 Ducks, a leg of beef, a stinking partridge, & a tart."[32] Taking this in her stride, Chloe settles for the leg of beef and the stinking partridge, after which she breaks into song, joined by a chorus of postilions in the best Gilbert and Sullivan manner.

These three juvenile attempts at play writing have been augmented recently to include a fourth and longer dramatic effort that has proved to be somewhat of a problem. After the performances of *The Sultan* and *High Life Below Stairs* at Steventon in 1790, it seems that Jane Austen wrote a five-act play, a dramatization of Samuel Richardson's *The History of Sir Charles Grandison.* Called *Sir Charles Grandison or the Happy Man,* the play, a free adaptation of episodes from Richardson's novel, is based on an attempt by the wicked Sir Hargrave Pollexfen to force a marriage on Harriet Byron, the heroine, who is rescued by Sir Charles Grandison and eventually becomes his wife. The play was long believed by Jane's collateral descendants to have been written down by Jane from the dictation of James Austen's daughter Anna (later Mrs. Benjamin Lefroy), who was frequently at Steventon rectory from the time of her mother's death in 1795 until her father's second marriage in 1797. This tradition, which never had been questioned until recently, was recorded by Fanny Lefroy, one of Anna's daughters, thus: "I have still in my possession, in Aunt Jane's writing, a drama my mother dictated to her, founded on *Sir Charles Grandison,* a book with which she was familiar at seven years old."[33]

This has recently been disputed by Brian Southam, who maintains that the earliest part of the manuscript was written by Jane

Austen before Anna was born in 1793, while the rest of the play was completed by Jane no later than 1800 when Anna was seven, the age at which Anna's daughter maintained that her mother dictated the play to her aunt. Although Anna is reputed to have been a very bright child, it is hard to believe that any seven-year-old could have been so familiar with a novel as complicated as *Sir Charles Grandison* as to be able to reduce its complexities of plot and characterization to a play. This is Southam's conclusion, for he dismisses the tradition of Anna's authorship by saying: "It is quite possible that during Anna's later visits to Steventon, between 1796 and 1800, Jane Austen was working intermittently on 'Grandison,' revising and continuing the early pages, with the young niece at her elbow, offering suggestions and even being allowed, as a special privilege, to write on the manuscript itself—inserting a word or two here and there, changing a phrase, bringing a character on stage. That, almost certainly, was the extent of Anna's contribution; and if we grace it with the name of collaboration, that is the sum of it."[34]

Although there is no evidence that Jane Austen attended a professional theatrical performance before 1799, when she was twenty-three, her novel, *Susan* (i.e., *Northanger Abbey*), written in 1798-99, indicates that she was already a devotee of "good hardened real acting,"[35] for it gives a lively account of her heroine's visit to the Theater Royal in Orchard Street, Bath. As Jane and her mother and sister were in Bath during the later part of 1797, her account of the evening at the theater in her novel could have stemmed from actual observations made during that particular visit. There was also a handsome theater in Winchester, fourteen miles from Jane's birthplace, to which she could have been taken as a child, but there is no evidence that this happened.[36] In 1799, however, when Jane Austen and her mother again visited Bath in the company of her brother Edward and his wife and their two eldest children, they attended a performance at the Theater Royal on the evening of June 20, 1799. Jane's letter to her sister at Steventon written the day before merely says: "The Play on Saturday is *I hope* to conclude our Gaieties here, for nothing but a lengthened stay will make it otherwise."[37]

The account in the *Bath Herald and Reporter* for June 29, 1799, however, reveals that Jane saw Kotzebue's drama *The Birth-Day* and the "pleasing spectacle of Blue Beard" on that occasion. In discussing the play the newspaper critic wrote:

> If the German Author has justly drawn down censure for the immorality of his productions for the stage, this may be considered as expiatory—this may be accepted as his *amende honourable;* it is certainly throughout unexceptionable, calculated to promote the best of interest of virtue, and the purest principles of benevolence; and though written in the style of Sterne, it possesses humour without a single broad Shandyism. It may not be amiss here to observe that mirth can certainly be excited on the stage, without having recourse to obscenity or profaneness—a custom which, to the disgrace of the age we live in, has been too much countenanced in theatric exhibitions, and from the applause the unthinking part of the audience gives to these disgraceful passages, it has occasioned *"the Clowns to speak even more than is set down for them.—" "'Tis villainous and should be reformed altogether."*[38]

Edward Austen might have chosen *The Birth-Day* and the "pleasing spectacle of Blue Beard" for an evening's entertainment because his two small children were members of the theater party. But it should be pointed out that Kotzebue's more sensational *Lovers' Vows,* which Coleridge said made its appeal by "a pathos not a whit more respectable than the maudlin tears of drunkenness,"[39] and which Jane Austen later selected to bring out the weaker characteristics of the participants in the Mansfield Park theatricals, was performed no fewer than six times in Bath when Jane lived there from 1801-06.[40] This suggests that she was quite familiar with the play long before she used it in *Mansfield Park.*

Jane Austen's mention of Mrs. Dorothy Jordan, the celebrated comic actress, in a letter written in January 1801 indicates the possibility that she had previously attended one or several of her performances at a London theater. On her way back to Hampshire, Cassandra, who had been visiting in Kent, had anticipated attending a play in London in which Mrs. Jordan was the star. Something happened to disappoint her, for Jane wrote: "You speak with such noble resignation of Mrs. Jordan & the Opera House that it would be an insult to suppose consolation required."[41] In a later letter, Jane continued in the same strain: "I dare say you will spend a very pleasant three weeks in town, I hope you will see everything worthy [of] notice, from the Opera House to Henry's office in Cleveland Court; and I shall expect you to lay in a stock of intelligence that may procure me amusement for a twelvemonth to come."[42]

Practically nothing is known concerning Jane Austen's theatrical activities while she was a resident of Bath between 1801 and 1806, other than that she was an admirer of the acting abilities of Robert William Elliston, a star of the Theater Royal in Orchard Street. Elliston later moved on to the London stage, where Jane again saw him perform. Jane was not alone in her admiration for him, for Byron said he could conceive nothing better than Elliston in gentlemanly comedy and some parts of tragedy. The only other comment suggesting that the Austens were occasional theatergoers while living in Bath is to be found in a letter written by Jane's mother in April 1806 to her daughter-in-law Mary Austen at Steventon, in which she said: "Cooke, I dare say, will have as full houses to-night & Saturday, as he had on Tuesday."[43] The actor referred to by Mrs. Austen was George Frederick Cooke, whose portrayals of Shakespeare's tragic characters and bouts with the bottle were equally famous.

There is little to indicate that Jane Austen attended the theater regularly while living in Southampton between 1806 and 1809. That she did attend an occasional performance is revealed by an item in her list of expenses for 1807, in which she noted that she had spent seventeen shillings and nine pence for water parties and plays during that year.[44] While living at Southampton, Jane also became friendly with a Mr. Valentine Fitzhugh, whose sister-in-law, Mrs. William Fitzhugh, was an ardent admirer of Mrs. Siddons and in the habit of encamping herself in the actress's dressing room wherever she was performing, in order to assist her celebrated friend with her makeup and dressing.[45] Unfortunately, Jane left no record of her conversations with Mrs. Fitzhugh's brother-in-law concerning the theater or otherwise, although she did recommend that he read Madame de Staël's new novel, *Corinne, or Italy.* In any event, conversation with Valentine Fitzhugh would have been difficult under any circumstances, for Jane recorded that he was so deaf that "he could not hear a cannon, were it fired close to him." But apparently this did not deter Jane, for "having no cannon at hand to make the experiment," she took this for granted, "and talked to him a little with my fingers, which was funny enough."[46]

Shortly before leaving Southampton, Jane wrote to Cassandra: "A larger circle of acquaintance & an increase of amusement is quite in character with our approaching removal," adding, "Yes—I mean to go to as many Balls as possible, that I may have a good bargain."[47] Meanwhile, in anticipation of a visit from one of her brothers, she said: ". . . we mean to take the opportunity of his help, to go one night to the play. Martha [Lloyd] ought to see the inside of the Theatre once while she lives in Southampton, & I think she will hardly wish to take a second view."[48]

Jane was speaking of the no longer existing French Street Theater, then mainly served by provincial companies, although the celebrated Mr. and Mrs. Charles Kemble played there for a few nights in August 1808.[49] Although Jane was fond of what she called "good hardened real acting" by professionals, there is no record that she attended the Kembles' performances. But her letter of November 20, 1808, indicates that she had taken a dislike to the French Street Theater either because of its dirtiness or the poor quality of its performances.

Jane mentioned only two of the London playhouses by name in her six novels. In *Sense and Sensibility,* Willoughby "ran against Sir John Middleton"[50] in the lobby of Drury Lane Theater, at which time he learned that Marianne Dashwood was seriously ill at Cleveland. And in *Pride and Prejudice,* the scatterbrained Lydia Bennet, in complete disregard of the shame that her scandalous behavior with Wickham had brought on her family, could only prattle: "To be sure London was rather thin, but however the Little Theatre was open."[51] There is only one other mention of playgoing in London in Jane's mature fiction and that is a vague reference to an "evening at one of the theatres" in *Pride and Prejudice,* at which time Elizabeth Bennet and her aunt, Mrs. Gardiner, talked over intimate family matters in what was presumably a theater box while the rest of the party watched the action on the stage. In *Emma* all of the action took place in the country, although Jane did use Astley's Equestrian Amphitheater in London, which she had visited in 1796, as the background for one of the turning points in her story. As for *Persuasion,* although Jane was familiar with the Theater Royal on Orchard Street in Bath, she included only a few vague references to it toward the end of her novel.

In real life, however, Jane Austen rarely missed an opportunity to visit the London theaters when she was staying with her banker brother, Henry, a keen theatergoer. Unfortunately there are no surviving letters to fill in the details of Jane's activities from July 26,

1809, until April 18, 1811. Starting at the latter date, however, a sufficient amount of correspondence exists to provide a fair estimate of her theatrical activities up to November 28, 1814, the last time she is known to have attended a performance.

In April 1811, Jane Austen went to London to be available for the proofreading of *Sense and Sensibility.* Shortly after her arrival, Shakespeare's *King John,* with Mrs. Siddons in the role of Constance, was announced for presentation at Covent Garden Theater for the evening of Saturday, April 20, 1811. As Jane expressed a desire to attend the performance, her brother Henry agreed to accompany her. A day before the event, however, the play was canceled, and Henry and Jane went instead to the Lyceum Theater, where they saw *The Hypocrite,* an adaptation by Isaac Bickerstaffe of Colley Cibber's version of Molière's *Tartuffe, ou l'Imposteur.* In telling her sister about it, Jane wrote: "We *did* go to the play after all on Saturday, we went to the Lyceum, & saw the Hypocrite, an old play taken from Moliere's *Tartuffe,* & were well entertained. Dowton & Mathews were the good actors. Mrs. Edwin was the Heroine—& her performance is just what it used to be,"[52] which indicates that Jane had been a theatergoer for some time. Then, having learned that Mrs. Siddons did appear after all at Covent Garden, although not on the night that she was originally scheduled to perform, Jane reported her disappointment with some heat: "I have no chance of seeing Mrs. Siddons.—She *did* act on Monday, but as Henry was told by the Boxkeeper that he did not think she would, the places & all thought of it, were given up. I should particularly have liked seeing her in Constance, & could swear at her with little effort for disappointing me.—"[53]

Two years later Jane Austen set out with her brother Edward and his family from Chawton for Godmersham, stopping on the way in London, where Jane and Edward's daughters stayed with Henry Austen in his quarters over his bank at No. 10 Henrietta Street, Covent Garden. On the night of September 14, 1813, the party went by coach to the Lyceum Theater, where they had a private box on the stage, and saw a skit entitled *The Boarding House; or Five Hours at Brighton,* a musical farce called the *Beehive,* and *Don Juan, or The Libertine Destroyed,* a pantomime based on Thomas Shadwell's *The Libertine.* Jane wrote to Cassandra: "They [i.e., her nieces] revelled last night in 'Don Juan,' whom we left in hell at half-past eleven. We had scaramouch and a ghost, and were delighted. I speak of *them; my* delight was very tranquil, and the rest of us were sober-minded."[54] Even so, the evening was apparently a success, for Jane told Cassandra that they "were at home again in about four hours and a half; had soup and wine and water, and then went to our holes."[55] Jane later reconsidered her earlier reflections on *Don Juan,* for she admitted: "I must say I have seen nobody on the stage who has been a more interesting character than that compound of cruelty and lust."[56]

The next night the party went to Covent Garden Theater where they had "very good places in the box next the stage box, front and second row; the three old ones [i.e., Jane and her brothers Henry and Edward] behind of course."[57] There they saw *The Clandestine Marriage* by George Colman the elder and *Midas: an English Burletta,* by Kane O'Hara. In telling Cassandra about it, Jane said: "The new Mr. Terry was Lord Ogleby, and Henry thinks he may do; but there was no acting more than moderate, and I was as much amused by the remembrances connected with 'Midas' as with any part of it,"[58] a suggestion that Jane had possibly seen *Midas* at an earlier date. Later, in recounting her recent theatergoing in London in a letter to her brother Francis, then at sea, she added: ". . . the Clandestine Marriage was the most respectable of the performances, the rest were singsong & trumpery . . . , but *I* wanted better acting.—There was no Actor worth naming.—I believe the Theatres are thought at a low ebb at the present."[59]

Jane had submitted to the ministrations of a fashionable hairdresser to prepare for her appearance at Covent Garden, and knowing that Cassandra would relish the details she obliged her thus: "Mr. Hall was very punctual yesterday, and curled me out at a great rate. I thought I looked hideous, and longed for a snug cap instead, but my companions silenced me by their admiration. I had only a bit of velvet round my head."[60]

Jane Austen's next known visit to the theater took place in March 1814 when she was again staying with her brother Henry in Henrietta Street during the negotiations for the publication of *Mansfield Park.* On that occasion she and Henry were joined by her brother Edward and his daughter Fanny, who had been staying at Bath. As Edmund Kean, then the latest theatrical sensation, had been electrifying London audiences since January of that year with his novel and dynamic interpretations of several of Shakespeare's more celebrated tragic roles, the party went to Drury Lane Theater on the evening of March 5 for a performance of *The Merchant of Venice* with Kean in the role of Shylock. Jane was greatly impressed and told Cassandra: "We were quite satisfied with Kean, I cannot imagine better acting; but the part was too short, & excepting him and Miss Smith, and *she* did not quite answer my expectations, the parts were ill filled & the Play heavy."[61] Later, in a further comment on Kean, Jane added: ". . . it appeared to me as if there were no fault in him anywhere, & in his scene with Tubal there was exquisite acting."[62]

The program that same night at Drury Lane also included Robert William Elliston, the actor Jane had admired during her Bath years, in an oriental "melodramatic spectacle" called *Illusion, or the Trances of Nourjahad.* Jane and her party left before it was over, however, for she told Cassandra: "We were too much tired to stay for the whole of Illusion [i.e., *Nourjahad*] which has 3 acts;—there is a great deal of finery & dancing in it, but I think little merit. Elliston was Nourjahad, but it is a solemn sort of part, not at all calculated for his powers. There was nothing of the *best Elliston* about him. I might not have known him, but for his voice."[63]

Jane Austen's second theatrical party on that particular visit took her to Covent Garden Theater on the evening of March 7, 1814, for a performance of Dr. Thomas Arne's opera *Artaxerxes,* with Catherine Stephens, the celebrated British soprano, in the role of Mandane; a farce, *The Devil to Pay,* by Charles Coffey; and a pantomime. Before setting out Jane wrote to Cassandra: "We are to see 'the Devil to pay' to night. I expect to be very much amused.—Excepting Miss Stephens, I daresay Artaxerxes will be very tiresome."[64] After returning to Henrietta Street, she added: "I was very tired of Artaxerxes, highly amused with the Farce, & in an inferior way with the Pantomime that followed."[65] Even though Jane Austen was bored on that occasion by *Artaxerxes,* she was fond of at least two of the selections from Arne's opera, for her music preserved at Chawton not only includes a piano arrangement of Mandane's brilliant aria "The Soldier Tir'd," which she heard Miss Stephens sing that evening, but also another arrangement for solo piano of the overture to the same opera, the latter being copied out in her elegant copperplate hand.[66]

Jane's last evening at the theater during that visit to London was a disappointment to her, even though Catherine Stephens was again the female star in Charles Dibdin's *The Farmer's Wife.* Jane had a cold, and although the party had a private box at Covent Garden, her report on the performance was on the querulous side. Writing to Cassandra on March 9, 1814, she said: "Well, we went to the Play again last night, & as we were out (a) great part of the morning too, shopping & seeing the Indian Jugglers, I am very glad to be quiet now till dressing time."[67] She added: "The Farmer's Wife is a Musical thing in 3 Acts, & as Edward was steady in not staying for anything more, we were at home before 10—Fanny and Mr. J. P. [i.e., John Plumptre, one of Fanny's admirers] are delighted with Miss S, & her merit in singing is I dare say very great; that she gave *me* no pleasure is no reflection upon her, nor I hope upon myself, being what Nature made me on that article. All that I am sensible of in Miss S. is, a pleasing person & no skill in acting."[68] This criticism suggests that although Jane Austen was fond of music in small doses, she was also in accord with Sir Isaac Newton, who "never was at more than one Opera. The first Act he heard with pleasure, the second stretch'd his patience, and the third act he ran away."[69]

Although Jane Austen mentioned the Indian Jugglers without further comment, they were at that time one of the most famous attractions of London. These extraordinary performers, who had been brought to England earlier from India, were exhibiting "their wonderful powers" daily at No. 87 Pall Mall, the admission fee being three shillings. In speaking of them, Ackerman's *Repository of Arts* for 1813 said:

> Scarcely was the arrival of these Indian artists announced, when the whole fashionable world were attracted to Pall-Mall, and the talk of the town was engrossed by the feats of these Eastern Jugglers. . . . Among the extraordinary instances of dexterity exhibited by these men, none appear more surprising than the rapidity with which they keep four brass balls in motion; delivering them from one hand to the other, the whole being in the air at the same time, with a velocity that eludes the vigilance of the human eye. . . . Indeed it is generally allowed by those who have witnessed the feats of these interesting strangers, that our own jugglers are far inferior in all their operations, whether with cups and balls, or other tricks or legerdemain.[70]

As far as is known, Jane Austen's last visit to the professional theater took place late in 1814, when she was again in London, staying with her brother Henry in Hans Place in order to confer with her publisher, Thomas Egerton, concerning a proposed second edition of *Mansfield Park.* On the night of November 28, 1814, Jane accompanied her brothers Edward and Henry and other friends to Covent Garden Theater for a performance of *Isabella,* a tragedy adapted by David Garrick from Thomas Southerne's *The Fatal Marriage or The Innocent Adultery* in which the celebrated actress Eliza O'Neill played the leading female role. In describing her reactions to the play, Jane wrote to her recently married niece, Anna Lefroy: "We were all at the Play last night, to see Miss O'neal [*sic*] in Isabella. I do not think she was quite equal to my expectation. I fancy I want something more than can be. Acting seldom satisfies me. I took two Pocket handkerchiefs but I had very little occasion for either. She is an elegant creature however & hugs Mr Young delightfully."[71] Later, in a letter to her niece Fanny Knight, Jane used Miss O'Neill's ardent style of acting to characterize the contrasting behavior shown by her brother Charles's eldest daughter during a recent visit. Jane wrote: "That puss Cassy, did not shew more pleasure in seeing me than her Sisters, but I expected no better;—she does not shine in the tender feelings. She will never be a Miss O'Neal [*sic*];—more in the Mrs. Siddons line."[72]

Jane Austen was presumably recalling her own earliest attempts at music making when she later described the eight-year-old Catherine Morland in *Northanger Abbey* as being "fond of tinkling the keys of the old forlorn spinet."[73] Unlike Catherine, however, who only "learnt a year," and who regarded the day on which the music master was dismissed as one of the happiest of her life, Jane's interest in music continued throughout her lifetime. Moreover, even though she never was able to throw "a whole party into raptures by a prelude on the pianoforte, of her own composition,"[74] she must have been an accomplished amateur performer if her music books are an indication of her abilities as a pianist.[75] By the time she was twenty she had her own "square" piano installed in the upstairs dressing room at Steventon rectory that she shared with Cassandra.[76]

Jane Austen's only known music master was George William Chard, an excellent musician who was assistant organist at Winchester Cathedral from 1787 to 1802 and full organist and choirmaster at the cathedral from 1802 until his death in 1849.[77] At the time Jane was his pupil in the 1790s and for many years thereafter, Chard augmented his regular salary by traveling around Hampshire giving private music lessons, a practice that resulted in this reminiscence concerning his occasional eccentric behavior:

> [Dr. Chard] altho' possessing a very nice feeling for music . . . was more attach'd to fly-fishing and hunting, for frequently, when on his journies to his scholars . . . if perchance he heard the hounds, "Tally-ho, 'tis the merry ton'd hour" says he, "Have at ye, go it my Pippins, over hill and dale into the adjoining Country" and with or without the brush of the Fox, wd. brush into the first Public house handy for brandy, pipes and backie, till sometimes breakfast was next morning waiting for his return, besides the many pupils that had been hard practicing (during his absence) the *Battle of Prague*. . . .[78]

This piece, composed by Franz Kotzwara, a Bohemian musician, was one of the earliest known piano sonatas purporting to describe a battle and was included in the repertoire of practically every amateur pianist for well over a century. Even as late as 1878 Mark Twain heard it played by an American lady tourist in a hotel in Lucerne. He commented: ". . . she turned on all the horrors of *The Battle of Prague,* that venerable shivaree, and waded chin deep in the blood of the slain."[79] Jane Austen presumably studied the piece under Chard's tutelage, since she had her copy bound up with other musical favorites in a volume still preserved at Chawton Cottage.[80]

Although she was fond of music, Jane Austen was apparently not partial to its more strident manifestations, such as the "overtures" (i.e., symphonies) of Haydn and Pleyel that were the highlights of an outdoor concert she attended in Bath in June 1799.[81] She wrote to Cassandra: "There is to be a grand gala on tuesday [*sic*] evening in Sydney Gardens;—a Concert, with Illuminations & fireworks;—to the latter Eliz: [i.e., her sister-in-law, Elizabeth Austen] & I look forward with pleasure, & even the Concert will have more than it's usual charm with me, as the gardens are large enough for me to get pretty well beyond the reach of its sound."[82] Even so, Jane's letters reveal that she occasionally attended concerts at the Upper Rooms at Bath when she lived there from 1801 to 1806. These were the annual subscriptions concerts directed by Venanzio Rauzzini that featured music of the highest quality.[83] Rauzzini, who had been a friend of Mozart, had been the musical director of Bath since 1780. Not only was he an excellent musician, but the concerts he directed were among the most prestigious musical events in England at that time.

Jane used her familiarity with Rauzzini's musical evenings in the chapter in *Persuasion* that brings all the principal characters together for a concert in the elegant Upper Rooms at Bath. Jane also added a dash of comedy to her description by including a fling at the noticeable characters who usually frequent such affairs by having Anne Elliot's friend, Mrs. Smith, comment afterwards: "The little Durands were there, I conclude, with their mouths open to catch the music; like unfledged sparrows ready to be fed."[84]

As usual, Jane Austen was chary with her comments on the music that she heard at these affairs, but her reticence could have been out of consideration for Cassandra's known lack of interest in music. Usually Jane concentrated on what she wore to a concert, and on one occasion in 1805 she was quite explicit. Being still in mourning for her father, she assured her sister that her gown had been embellished with the proper doleful decorations. In describing her appearance, Jane wrote: "You were very right in supposing I wore my crape sleeves to the Concert. I had them put in on the occasion; on my head I wore my crape & flowers, but I do not think it looked particularly well."[85]

Caroline Austen is responsible for a very pleasant word picture of her aunt's private music making after she moved to Chawton in 1809: "Aunt Jane began her day with music—for which I conclude she had a natural taste; as she thus kept it up—tho' she had no one to teach; was never induced (as I have heard) to play in company; and none of her family cared much for it. I suppose, that she might not trouble them, she chose her practicing time before breakfast—when she would have the room to herself—She practiced regularly every morning—She played very pretty tunes, *I* thought—and I liked to stand by her and listen to them; but the music (for I knew the books well in after years) would now be thought disgracefully easy—Much that she played was from manuscript, copied out by herself—and so neatly and correctly, that it was as easy to read as print—"[86]

In 1811, when Jane Austen was in London prior to the publication of *Sense and Sensibility,* she included in a letter to her sister a description of a musical party given by her worldly cousin, Eliza Austen, that is a real-life counterpart of the one at which Willoughby cruelly snubbed Marianne Dashwood: "Between the Songs were Lessons on the Harp, or Harp & Piano Forte together—& the Harp Player was Wiepart, whose name seems famous, tho' new to me.—There was one female singer, a short Miss Davis, all in blue, bringing up for the Public Line, whose voice was said to be very fine indeed; & all the Performers gave great satisfaction by doing what they were paid for, & giving themselves no airs."[87]

In 1813 Jane wrote to Cassandra after attending a grand musical event at Canterbury. Jane was in distinguished musical company that evening, for the leading soprano soloist, Mrs. Maria Dickons, had sung the role of the Countess in the first English performance of Mozart's *The Marriage of Figaro* one year earlier in London.[88] At Canterbury, Mrs. Dickons thrilled the connoisseurs present with the bravura aria "Oh Ye Priests," from Handel's *Jephtha* and Daniel Purcell's "Mad Bess," among other numbers, while the choral part of the evening consisted of selections from Haydn's *Creation.*[89] But Jane was silent about them all, confining her remarks on the event merely to approving the behavior of Lady Bridges: "for being in a hurry to have the Concert over & get away, & for getting away at last with a great deal of decision & promptness."[90]

Later, in 1815, when Jane was staying with her brother Henry in London prior to the publication of *Emma,* she again mentioned music in a letter to her sister. Jane's niece Fanny Knight was also a guest of Henry Austen at that time: ". . . then came the dinner & Mr. Haden who brought good Manners & clever conversation;—from 7 to 8 the Harp; at 8 Mrs. L. & Miss E. arrived—& for the rest of the eveng [*sic*] the Drawg-room [*sic*] was thus arranged, on the Sopha-side the two Ladies Henry & myself making the best of it, on the opposite side Fanny & Mr. Haden in two chairs (I *believe* at least they had *two* chairs) talking together uninterruptedly.—Fancy the scene!"[91]

Meanwhile, Jane and Mr. Haden had been debating the power of music, for she told Cassandra: "I have been listening to dreadful Insanity.—It is Mr. Haden's firm beleif [*sic*] that a person *not* musical is fit for every sort of Wickedness. I ventured to assert a little on the other side, but wished the cause in abler hands."[92] As Fanny had been having troubles with a dilatory harp instructor, Jane Austen took the opportunity to express her feelings concerning music masters in general: "Mr. Meyers gives his three Lessons a week—altering his days & his hours however just as he chuses, never very punctual, & never giving good Measure.—I have not Fanny's fondness for Masters, & Mr. Meyers does not give me any Longing after them. The truth is I think, they are all, at least Music Masters, made of too much consequence & allowed to take too many Liberties with their Scholar's time."[93]

Although Jane Austen was praised by her brother Henry for her "excellent taste in drawing,"[94] little is known about how this particular talent was developed. An entry in her father's bank account for 1784, however, suggests that she might have received instruction from John Claude Nattes (ca. 1765-1822), whose later watercolors of Bath are elegant depictions of the city in which Jane lived from 1801 to 1805.[95] The entry shows a payment of eleven pounds and nine shillings to a "Claude Nattes" for the year 1784, when Jane was nine. This suggests that Jane's father had hired Nattes to give drawing lessons to the rectory children, two of whom, Cassandra and Henry, are known to have been artistically gifted. In any event only two known examples of Jane's handiwork remain: the sketch of a lace pattern that she included in a letter to her sister from Bath in June 1799 and the painted embellishments on a needle case made for her niece Louisa Knight.[96] That other drawings by Jane also existed at one time is shown by one of her earlier letters, for in speaking of some sketches that she had sent to a nephew in November 1798, she commented to Cassandra: "I hope George was pleased with my designs. Perhaps they would have suited him as well had they been less elaborately finished; but an artist cannot do anything slovenly."[97]

As she grew older, Jane Austen apparently devoted less time to drawing and painting; her literary activities would have left little time for them. Nevertheless her letters from 1809 onward contain references to exhibitions that she visited when in London. In 1811, when she was staying with the Henry Austens while correcting the proofs of *Sense and Sensibility,* she took time off to visit William Bullock's Liverpool Museum at No. 22 Picadilly and the British Gallery in Pall Mall.[98] At the museum, which contained a popular collection of paintings, exotic stuffed animals, birds, and reptiles, Jane saw, among other things, a gigantic boa constrictor. An American tourist who visited the museum a week or so later reported: ". . . [it] makes the story of Laocoön quite possible."[99] The exhibition of works by contemporary painters at the British Gallery was on a higher aesthetic level. But Jane made no comment on what she saw at either place, other than to say, "I had some amusement at each, tho' my preference for Men & Women, always inclines me to attend more to the company than the sight."[100]

Later in 1813, when Jane was again in London, she was taken by her brother Henry to three exhibitions. The first was the annual showing of the Society of Painters in Oil and Water Colours at the Great Room at Spring Gardens. Jane's account reads:

> Henry and I went to the Exhibition in Spring Gardens. It is not thought a good collection, but I was very well pleased—particularly (pray tell Fanny) with a small portrait of Mrs. Bingley, excessively like her. I went in hopes of seeing her Sister, but there was no Mrs. Darcy;—perhaps however, I may find her in the Great Exhibition which we shall go to, if we have time;—I have no chance of her in the collection of Sir Joshua Reynold's Paintings which is now shewing in Pall Mall, & which we are also to visit.—Mrs. Bingley's is exactly herself, size, shaped face, features & sweetness; there never was a greater likeness. She is dressed in a white gown, with green ornaments, which convinces me of what I had always supposed, that green was a favourite colour with her. I dare say Mrs. D. will be in Yellow.[101]

Even though she searched for a portrait resembling Mrs. Darcy at the two other exhibitions, Jane was unable to locate one: "We have been both to the Exhibition & Sir J. Reynolds',—and I am disappointed, for there was nothing like Mrs. D. at either. I can only imagine that Mr. D. prizes any Picture of her too much to like it should be exposed to the public eye.—I can imagine he wd have that sort of feeling—that mixture of Love, Pride & Delicacy."[102] Jane might not have discovered any portrait resembling Elizabeth Darcy at the Great Exhibition at Somerset House or the retrospective showing of Sir Joshua Reynolds's pictures at the British Institution (formerly Boydell's Shakespeare Gallery) in Pall Mall, but she did see several well-known canvases at the latter that are still admired in American and British art galleries—Sir Joshua's famous painting of Mrs. Siddons as the Tragic Muse and his portrait of Mrs. Sheridan as St. Cecelia, as well as the likenesses of Dr. Charles Burney, Joseph Baretti, Samuel Johnson, and Oliver Goldsmith loaned by Mrs. Gabriel Piozzi (the former Mrs. Henry Thrale), the friend of Dr. Samuel Johnson.[103]

Still later in 1813, Jane Austen was so elated concerning a friend's praise for her novels that she playfully told Cassandra: "I do not despair of having my picture in the Exhibition at last—all white & red, with my Head on one Side; or perhaps I may marry Mr. D'arbley [*sic*]."[104] Jane was referring to Alexander d'Arblay, the nineteen-year-old son of the novelist Fanny Burney (Madame d'Arblay), who had been baptized soon after his birth by Jane's godfather, the Rev. Samuel Cooke, at Great Bookham Church, Surrey, in April 1795, while his parents were living at Camilla Cottage near Great Bookham vicarage.

As for Henry Austen's statement that Jane was "fond of dancing, and excelled in it,"[105] her early letters contain many witty and revealing references to the Hampshire balls that she attended and obviously enjoyed. Notable among these was a Christmas dance in 1798, after which she wrote to Cassandra: "There were twenty dances, and I danced them all, and without any fatigue. . . . I had not thought myself equal to it, but in cold weather and with few couples I fancy I could just as well dance for a week together as for half an hour."[106] That Jane was occasionally not as popular at a dance as she would have liked is also shown from a comment that she sent to her sister after attending a ball at Kempshott Park: "I do not think I was very much in request. People were rather apt not to ask me till they could not help it; one's consequence, you know, varies so much at times without any particular reason. There was one gentleman, an officer of the Cheshire, a very good-looking young man, who, I was told, wanted very much to be introduced to me; but as he did not want it quite enough to take much trouble in effecting it, we never could bring it about."[107]

On one occasion Jane got a little tipsy at a ball: "I believe I drank too much wine last night at Hurstbourne; I know not how else to account for the shaking of my hand today;—you will kindly make allowance therefore for any indistinctness of writing by attributing it to this venial Error."[108] In a later letter to her sister in 1813, she remarked philosophically: "By the bye, as I must leave off being young, I find many Douceurs in being a sort of Chaperon for I am put on the Sofa near the Fire & can drink as much wine as I like."[109]

CHAPTER

•6•

Jane Austen and the Prince Regent

One of the supreme ironies of English literature is the fact that Jane Austen was obliged by circumstances beyond her control to dedicate *Emma* to the Prince Regent, a man she heartily despised. According to her first biographer, Jane regarded Edmund Bertram and George Knightley as her fictional ideals of what she expected real gentlemen to be. Being a realist, however, she admitted that these creatures of her fancy were "very far from being what I know English gentlemen often are."[1] Meanwhile, with these standards in mind, she weighted the sybaritic First Gentleman of Europe in her exacting balance and found him wanting.

Jane's intense dislike of "Prinny," as he was familiarly referred to by his close associates, can be found in a letter written in February 1813 to her friend Martha Lloyd, in which she declared her hatred for him.[2] Even so, Jane's intense dislike for "Prince Florizel" (another of his nicknames) was not a sudden expression of revulsion on her part. From 1788 until 1795, while she and her family were living at Steventon, she was a near neighbor of the prince for varying periods, during which time her brother James was frequently the prince's companion in the hunting field. In that manner, and through neighborhood reports, Jane was in an excellent position to learn a great deal about the goings-on at Kempshott Park, the prince's nearby hunting lodge, from the time of his disastrous honeymoon until he finally left Hampshire when Jane was nineteen.

In 1783, when the prince came of age, he celebrated his release from having been "locked up in the Palace of Piety,"[3] as Horace Walpole referred to George III's staid household, by violently reacting in the traditional manner of his Hanoverian forebears. Scorning the Tory principles of his conservative father, the prince ardently supported the Whigs, his political mentor being Charles James Fox, the great Whig statesman and a notorious gambler. At the same time the prince set up Edmund Burke as his philosophical ideal, Richard Brinsley Sheridan as his literary guide, Lord Petersham (an arbiter of male fashion) as his adviser on clothes, Henry Angelo as his instructor in fisticuffs and the foil, and the brilliant but erratic last Lord Barrymore as his companion in practical joking.[4] The prince's liberal cronies did not stop there, however, for he also included Barrymore's three notorious brothers and their sister, popularly known as Hellgate, Newgate, Cripplegate, and Miss Billingsgate, as his instructors in the swearing line, while Lady Letitia Lade, a former mistress of "Sixteen String Jack," a highwayman who was hanged in the 1770s, took him on as an eager pupil in the art of fast and reckless driving.[5] After a succession of temporary liaisons, the volatile prince fell head over heels in love with the buxom and twice-widowed Mrs. Maria Fitzherbert, a Roman Catholic, whom he secretly and illegally married in 1785.

The prince's association with the Steventon area began in 1788 when he was a guest of the sixth Duke of Bolton at Hackwood Park, near Basingstoke.[6] Interestingly, as far as Jane Austen was concerned, her eldest brother, James, was well acquainted with Lord Bolton's family. In 1785 he fell in love with the duke's daughter, Lady Catherine Powlett, and wrote a flowery sonnet to her in which he renounced "the charms of Paphos' blooming grove" for the pleasure of seeing his latter-day Venus walk on Hampshire soil.[7] In the meantime, while the prince was a guest of Lady Catherine's father, he greatly admired Kempshott Park, a recently built country home near Steventon, and rented it for a seven-year period to be used as a hunting lodge. Shortly thereafter, Mrs. Fitzherbert was brought down to inspect the house, and it was she who superintended the laying out of the gardens and the decoration of the principal rooms.[8]

To quote one contemporary chronicler, the advent of the prince at Kempshott ". . . did not prove a boon to the neighborhood. The quiet old country squires were led into unwonted extravagance in order to keep pace with the Royal demands on their hospitality, they indulged in orgies at variance with their former habits, while their ladies were horrified at the company which H.R.H. preferred to their own."[9] This statement is supported by the memoirs of Stephen Terry, who lived at Dummer House at that time, only three miles from Steventon. Terry, a dancing partner of Jane Austen in her youth, an intimate of her family, and a keen rider to hounds, recalled:

> On the Prince coming to reside at Kempshott, and finding there some choice spirits worth his acquaintance he added his feather to their uniform and joined their *post-prandial* jollifications; but I think he went too far with the old country Squires; they were taught to know that a *request* from Royalty is an *order*, and in such a way a glass of wine sent to a guest is working double tides, so the dining at Kempshott was a matter of no little danger, and the equilibrium of the journey home seldom well regulated by either master or man.[10]

Terry's father was among those invited to the prince's riotous parties, and upon receiving his first summons he felt obliged to wear his best clothes. As the distance between Kempshott and Dummer House was not too great a walk, Terry's father returned home on foot. Unfortunately, he was tipsy and did not notice that a prankster, presumably attached to the royal household, had smeared tar on the stiles he had to cross, and it was only after he reached home that he discovered his fine clothes were in such a sorry condition that he could never again wear them in the presence of royalty.[11] Antics like this were soon the talk of the neighborhood, so Jane Austen could hardly have escaped hearing of some of the excesses that took place during the prince's frequent visits to the Steventon area.

Once Mrs. Fitzherbert's plans for the garden and furnishings of the house had been carried out, Kempshott became a country rendezvous for the prince's raffish cronies. One of these was Charles

James Fox, who was present at a festive hunt breakfast "booted and spurred but . . . so gouty that he could neither walk or ride."[12] Also, according to Terry's memoirs: "Later, less respectable friends of the Prince soon made their appearance, Lady Jersey, Lady Cunyngham [*sic*] and Mesdames Hodges and Sturt, joined the field in hunting costume to the no small scandal of the neighbourhood."[13] Terry added: "The Prince himself lived hard and drank deep. He was already ungainly and crippled with gout. Nanny Stevens, of Dummer, a stout, strong woman, was deputed to be his nurse, and even helped him out of his bath like a baby, while his lazy valet did nothing but brush his clothes and look on."[14]

More important, as far as Jane Austen was concerned, the prince's visits to Kempshott coincided with the first regency crisis of 1788-89, brought on by the insanity of George III. Although *Catharine or The Bower,* her first attempt at serious fiction, was dedicated in its unfinished state in 1792 to her sister, Cassandra, it contains evidence that portions of it date from a slightly earlier period. The original manuscript of the unfinished novel in Jane's notebook *Volume the Third* contains numerous emendations that are not included in the standard published version of *Catharine.* For example, two mentions of a "Regency Bonnet" are made but were later erased by Jane, who substituted the names of other articles of clothing in their places.[15] The original entries are still decipherable, however, and suggest that Jane was aware of the role her rakish neighbor, the Prince of Wales, was then playing in national politics.

To elucidate: At the time of George III's attack of mental illness in 1788-89, party feeling between the Whigs and the Tories mounted to fever pitch when it appeared that the Prince of Wales, who was supported by the Whigs, would become regent in the event that his father did not recover. "The Opposition," wrote one loyalist in castigating the Whigs, "have been taking inconceivable pains to spread the idea that the disorder is incurable." Still another Tory declared: "The acrimony is beyond anything that you can conceive. The ladies are, as usual, at the head of all animosity, and are distinguished by caps, ribbands, and other emblems of party." At that time, Regency caps and bonnets, such as those mentioned by Jane Austen in *Catharine,* sold briskly from seven guineas up and were described by one fashion writer as "a mountain of tumbled gauze, with three large feathers in front, tied together with a knot of ribbons on which was printed in gold letters *Honi soit qui mal y pense de la Regence.*"[16]

How Jane Austen learned about these partisan bonnets honoring the prince is not known, but it is possible that she either saw them being worn by some of his female guests when they were visiting in the Steventon neighborhood, or they were described to her by others who had closer knowledge of what went on at Kempshott. Jane's mention of "Regency Bonnets" in *Catharine* (bearing the dedication date of 1792) therefore indicates that her novel was actually begun around the time of or shortly before the regency crisis of 1788-89. Otherwise, she would hardly have mentioned that particular type of millinery in the original draft of *Catharine,* only to erase the reference later as the passing of the regency crisis had rendered that style of female adornment unfashionable.

Meanwhile, with the outbreak of the French Revolution in 1789, Kempshott was soon crammed with emigrés who were permitted to live there by the prince. It was during that period that a spectacular hunt was staged by their royal host for their enjoyment:

> For their amusement a grand stag-hunt was got up, and as the royal stables could not mount them all, ten post horses were sent for from Demezy's, at Hartford Bridge. The grotesque appearance of the foreigners astounded the Hampshire men, as the Frenchmen were equipped with long horns over their shoulders in the style of their native country. Prince William turned out on a pony, and, according to habit, soon fathomed a deep ditch. A hind that was not expected to run straight was selected, in order that the foreigners might have a better chance of cutting in. At least five hundred horsemen were present. The hind was uncarted at Kempshott Park, and very soon after the foreigners were seen straggling all over the country. This day nearly drove George Sharp mad, for whenever his hounds came to a check, the Frenchmen, thinking all game was alike, blew their horns three times—and put them on a hare. Out of all the number that started, scarcely fifty got in at the end. Rowlandson afterwards did a clever drawing of this curious hunt, which was signed and dated 1792.[17]

The high living at Kempshott reached its climax in 1795, when the prince, who had unwillingly and bigamously married his cousin Princess Caroline of Brunswick, "brought his ill-fated bride to the house where Mrs. Fitzherbert had reigned supreme."[18] Jane Austen undoubtedly took a personal interest in this episode as her brother Francis, as senior lieutenant in the *Lark,* had accompanied the naval squadron that had brought the princess from Cuxhaven to England earlier in the year.[19] After the ill-matched couple were married at St. James's Palace in London on April 8, 1795—at which time the bridegroom was so drunk he had to be held up by his equerry[20]—they went a few days later for a hectic honeymoon to Kempshott, where the prince's mistress, the insanely jealous Lady Jersey, who had mixed a heavy dose of Epsom salts in the princess's food on her wedding night, acted as the Princess Caroline's lady-in-waiting and was the only other woman present.

By that time, Kempshott was satirically referred to as "the Royal lion's den."[21] To relieve his boredom, the prince was reported to have paid too open attentions to Lady Jersey at the dinner table, while the princess retaliated by "ogling the men, puffing at their pipes, shrugging her saucy shoulders and using language of Brunswickian coarseness."[22] In describing the situation, Gilbert Elliot, first Lord Minto, wrote:

> It appears that they [i.e., the prince and princess] lived together two or three weeks at first, but not afterwards as man and wife. They went to Windsor two days after the marriage, and, after a few days' residence there, they went to Kempshott, where there was no woman but Lady Jersey, and the men very blackguard companions of the Prince's who were constantly drunk and filthy, sleeping and snoring in boots on the sofa, and in other respects, the scene was more like the Prince of Wales at Eastcheap than like any notions she [i.e., Princess Caroline] had acquired before of a gentleman.[23]

This account was written by a partisan of the princess, but it was hardly exaggerated, since Stephen Terry's memoirs state: "The Prince spent his honeymoon at Kempshott and he there introduced the Princess to the society of his gayest sporting friends and most fascinating female acquaintance. Lady Jersey was supposed to have promoted the interest of Caroline because she was so forbidding in appearance, and an unattractive spouse might render him more constant to a handsome mistress. I had an opportunity of hearing from our own servants all the extraordinary doings of Queen Caroline and her attendants at the time of their retired honeymoon at Kempshott."[24] But the prince did not remain in the Steventon area long after his disastrous honeymoon, for shortly thereafter, having "done irreparable damage to the morals of his neighbours," he gave up Kempshott in October 1795 and rented the Grange, a house in another part of the country, as a hunting lodge.[25]

By the time the prince appeared again in the Jane Austen chronicle, he had been created Regent in January 1811; *Sense and Sensibility* was published in November of the same year. A little over a year later the Regent unwittingly came into Jane's orbit again, for there is a possibility that in giving her first published novel that title, Jane not only added a pithy phrase to the English language but also provided the editor of a London newspaper with an eye-catching headline to a story that involved the Regent.[26] At the time of the death of the old Duchess of Brunswick in 1813, her granddaughter, the Princess Charlotte, the only child of the Regent and his by-then estranged wife, paid a visit of condolence to her mother after having supposedly received her father's permission to do so. The event was promptly noted in the *Morning Post,* to which the editor added a toadying tribute to the Regent: "This it must be allowed, was manly, generous. The young Princess felt and acknowledged it so; she threw her arms round the neck of her Royal Father, thanked him with all the fine sensibility that forms so distinguishing a characteristic of her nature, and departed, with a pious ejaculation to Heaven."

A less partisan reporter on the *Morning Chronicle* had learned the true story, however, which his newspaper printed on April 1, 1813, to discredit the flattery bestowed on the Regent in the *Morning Post*. Briefly, Princess Charlotte had requested permission of her father to visit her mother but was told she had better wait until after the old duchess's funeral. The disappointed princess fired off another letter to her father, which went unanswered. At that point she took matters into her own hands, and after deciding that "silence gives consent," went to her mother anyway. This court gossip was seized upon by the *Morning Chronicle* to embarrass its rival, the *Morning Post,* and after quoting the latter's earlier boot-licking account, followed it with the true story, heading the article: *Sense and Sensibility*.

This invites a question: Was the phrase *sense and sensibility* a commonly used saying, quotation, or title before Jane Austen used it, or was it an original antithetical title created by her expressly for her first published novel? Attractive as the latter theory is, it can never be proven, for although the *Morning Post* headline might have been inspired by the title of Jane's novel that was then widely read, she, in turn, could have lifted it from an already published source as the title of her first published novel. During the 1790s an essay headed *Sense and Sensibility* appeared in the *Lady's Monthly Magazine,* which had a wide circulation among the wives of the gentry and professional classes. Since Jane is known to have begun the conversion of her *Elinor and Marianne* into *Sense and Sensibility* in 1797, it is possible that she not only read but used the *Lady's Monthly Magazine* title for her rewritten novel since it so perfectly mirrored the characters of her two heroines.[27]

The Prince Regent was the chief subject of a letter when he was next mentioned by Jane Austen. On February 16, 1813, Jane wrote to her friend Martha Lloyd: "I suppose all the World is sitting in Judgment upon the Princess of Wales's Letter. Poor woman, I shall support her as long as I can, because she *is* a Woman, & because I hate her Husband—but I can hardly forgive her for calling herself 'attached and affectionate' to a Man whom she must detest . . . but if I must give up the Princess, I am resolved at least always to think that she would have been respectable, if the Prince had behaved only tolerably by her at first."[28]

The letter referred to by Jane Austen was the climax of a violent disagreement between the eccentric Princess of Wales and the Regent over the Princess Charlotte, who had been treated by her parents like a royal shuttlecock since her birth in 1796.[29] During her earlier years the young princess was permitted to visit her mother frequently, but in 1813, when Charlotte was seventeen, she was given an establishment of her own near Carlton House, her father's London residence, at which time her mother's visiting rights were spitefully suspended by the Regent. This infuriated the Princess of Wales, who enlisted the help of Henry Brougham, the brilliant, vain, and eccentric Whig politician, who composed a long letter of protest to the Regent that was sent over the Princess of Wales's signature to her husband on January 14, 1813, imploring that his visiting restrictions to the Princess Charlotte be lifted. The letter, which remained unopened and unread for the time being, shuttled backward and forward several times between Lord Liverpool, the prime minister, and the Princess of Wales, to no effect.

Finally, on the advice of Brougham, who prided himself on being the advocate of the Princess of Wales against the Regent—who had refused to revoke the restrictions even after the letter had finally been read to him—a copy of the letter was turned over to the *Morning Chronicle* and was published on February 10, 1813. This caused an uproar between the Regent's partisans and those who sided with his wife.

That Jane Austen took the part of the latter "because she *is* a Woman"[30] might suggest that she was an advocate of women's rights long before the phrase became a part of the English language. Even so, Jane's statement "because I hate her Husband,"[31] following her avowed support of the Princess of Wales, is one of the strongest statements to be found in her surviving correspondence. But she was not being singular in her hatred, for from 1812 until 1837, when Victoria became queen, the British royal family was held in almost universal contempt. Even so conservative a man as the Duke of Wellington referred to the Regent and his disreputable brother as "the damnedest millstones about the neck of any Government that can be imagined,"[32] while Shelley, in writing of George III and his male progeny, went even farther by describing the lot as:

An old, mad, blind despised and dying King,
Princes, the dregs of their dull race, who flow
Through public scorn—mud from a muddy spring—
Rulers who neither see nor feel nor know
But leech-like to their fainting country cling.[33]

It was reserved for Keats's friend Leigh Hunt and his brother, John, the editors of *The Examiner,* to pillory the Regent so severely in print that they were imprisoned for publicly expressing criticisms of the same nature that Jane Austen included in her letter to Martha Lloyd. The Hunts' diatribe was inspired by an article that appeared on March 12, 1812, in the *Morning Post,* which referred to the Regent thus: "You are *the glory of the People*—You are the *Maecenas of the Age*—Wherever you appear you *conquer all hearts,* wipe away tears, excite *desire and love* and win *beauty* towards you—You breathe *eloquence,* you inspire the Graces—you are an *Adonis* in loveliness. . . ."

This was too much for the Hunts. Ten days later they not only reprinted the fulsome flattery of the Regent, which had appeared in the *Morning Post,* in their own paper, but followed it with: "That this

Adonis in Loveliness *was a corpulent gentleman of fifty!* In short, that this delightful, blissful, wise, pleasurable, honourable, virtuous, true and immortal PRINCE was a *violator of his word, a libertine over head and ears in debt and disgrace, a despiser of domestic ties, the companion of gamblers and demireps, a man who has just closed half a century without one single claim on the gratitude of his country or the respect of posterity."* This blast earned Hunt and his brother two-year prison sentences and a fine amounting to several hundred pounds.[34]

Jane Austen was busily engaged at Chawton at writing *Emma,* which she had begun in January 1814, when the Regent again appeared in her letters. The Allied Sovereigns, headed by the Emperor Alexander I of Russia and his ally, the King of Prussia, had arrived in England with other foreign dignitaries early in June to celebrate the downfall of Napoleon. In honor of the occasion the Regent, who prided himself on the elegance of his address, had included a spectacular naval review at Portsmouth as part of the festivities. This caused Jane to comment in a letter to Cassandra: "I long to know what this bow of the Prince's will produce."[35] This was followed shortly afterward in another letter to her sister with a further disparaging remark concerning the Regent. Jane wrote: "Only think of the Marquis of Granby begin dead. I hope, if it please Heaven there should be another son, they will have better sponsors and less parade."[36] Jane was referring to the death of George John Frederick Manners, Marquis of Granby, the infant son of the Duke of Rutland, who had been baptized some months earlier with elaborate ceremony "by the Archbishop of Canterbury, in the presence of the whole of the nobility and gentry;"[37] at Belvoir Castle in Leicestershire. The fact that the male sponsors had been the Regent and his brother, the Duke of York, gives point to her observation.

Emma was completed on March 29, 1815, and negotiations were being made for its publication by John Murray, the London publisher. In order to be available when the time came to correct the proofs, Jane left Cassandra at home and went up to London on October 4, 1815, to stay with her brother Henry, but publication was temporarily delayed when Henry became critically ill. It therefore became necessary for Jane to remain in London to nurse her brother. This circumstance resulted in her being placed in the position of being forced to dedicate *Emma* to the very man she had despised for so long.

Although during his illness Henry Austen was nominally under the care of Charles Thomas Haden, the surgeon from the Chelsea and Brompton Dispensary,[38] it was deemed necessary to call in the best medical advice obtainable, a move commented on later by Caroline Austen:

> Two of the great Physicians of the day had attended my Uncle during his illness—I am not, at this distance of time, sufficiently sure *which* they were, as to give their names, but *one* of them had very intimate access to the Prince Regent, and continuing his visits during my Uncle's recovery, he told my Aunt one day, that the Prince was a great admirer of her novels; that he often read them, and had a set in each of his residences—That *he*, the physician had told his Royal Highness that Miss Austen was now in London, and that by the Prince's desire, Mr. Clarke, the Librarian of Carlton House, would speedily wait upon her—

Caroline Austen's narrative is more or less duplicated by the author of the *Memoir*, with the exception that he narrowed down Caroline's "two of the great Physicians of the day" to "one of the Prince Regent's physicians."[40]

This statement was in turn further elucidated in an unsigned article, titled "Jane Austen," which appeared in the *St. Paul's Magazine* for March 1870: "She [i.e., Jane Austen] was then nursing her brother Henry, who was very ill, in Hans Place, and the court physician, Sir Henry Halford, attended him. Through the physician the Prince Regent's approbation of her works was first made known to Jane Austen, and it is very probable that he carried anecdotes of the authoress to the prince in her vocation of nurse and sister which augmented the Regent's admiration."[41]

How the author of this article learned that Sir Henry Halford was Henry Austen's physician is not known. However, the information might have been supplied by the first Lord Brabourne, son of Jane Austen's niece Fanny Knight, who was a contemporary of the anonymous author of the article. It is a matter of record that Fanny Knight stayed at Hans Place with Jane Austen for several weeks during Henry Austen's illness.[42] Therefore, if Sir Henry Halford had been in attendance there during that time, the fact could easily have been imparted to Lord Brabourne by his mother in recounting the events of that time.

In any event, whichever doctor it was who treated Henry Austen and informed his royal master that Jane was then in London thereby set the stage for a Regency divertissement spiced with such exquisitely unintentional humor that it appears in retrospect as one of the more spirited creations of Jane Austen's fancy. The principal in this real-life comedy was the Rev. James Stanier Clarke,[43] a solemn Anglican clergyman whose character seems to have been a blending of the pomposity of Mr. Collins and the obsequiousness of Mr. Elton. Born in 1765 in Mahon, Minorca, where his father, the Rev. Edward Clarke, was the chaplain and secretary to the British governor, Clarke was the elder brother of Dr. Edward Clarke, the celebrated traveler, and a grandson of the Rev. William Clarke, chancellor of the diocese of Chichester and a well-known antiquary. James Stanier Clarke was also an alumnus of Tonbridge School, which Jane Austen's father had attended.[44]

Upon completing his education at St. John's College, Cambridge, Clarke took holy orders, after which he became the rector of Preston in Sussex, the first of two benefices that he held in plurality until his death. Clarke also became a naval chaplain, serving under the command of Captain John Willet Payne, who introduced him to the then Prince of Wales. He was appointed as the prince's domestic chaplain in 1799 and librarian of Carlton House in 1805. By the time he made Jane Austen's acquaintance Clarke was also a recognized author, particularly on naval subjects, His biography of Lord Nelson, written in conjunction with John McArthur, a former purser of the *Victory,* had been published in 1809, while the *Naval Gazette,* a monthly magazine of naval history, which he started with McArthur, had begun its twenty-year run.

Clarke's ostentatious pomposity kept him from being popular with many of his associates, however, and he seems to have been the constant butt of the jokes of the lively crowd that surrounded the Regent. On one occasion, when he was a guest of his patron, Lord Egremont, at Petworth House in Sussex, the Regent and the Duke of Cumberland, who were also staying there at that time, put an ass in his bed.[45] Such pranks did not seem to upset Clarke, for he continued on his obsequious course, becoming a Canon of Windsor and Deputy of the Closet to the King before his death in 1834 at Brighton.

Jane Austen's first encounter with Clarke took place in November 1815, when he called on her at Hans Place at the instigation of the

Regent, who had instructed him to invite her to visit Carlton House, the Regent's London residence, described by a contemporary as being "finer than anything in England and not inferior to Versailles or Saint Cloud."[46] Jane called there on November 13, 1815, at which time Clarke gave her a personally conducted tour of the library, which was "finished with open book-cases designed in the Gothic style,"[47] richly inlaid Buhl furniture, and ebony chairs "of the character of the time of Henry VIII,"[48] as well as some of the other ornately decorated adjoining rooms overlooking the garden.[49] The Regent himself was then at Beaudesert, the country estate of the Marquis of Anglesey in Staffordshire, for a partridge shoot.[50]

According to an account of Jane's visit to Carlton House, written many years later by Caroline Austen: "Mr. Clarke, speaking again of the Regent's admiration of her writing, declared himself charged to say, that if Miss Austen had any other novel forthcoming, she was quite at liberty to dedicate it to the Prince,"[51] a suggestion that must have taken Jane Austen aback. That she did not intend at first to comply with the suggestion is also apparent from Caroline Austen's further statement: "My Aunt made all proper acknowledgements at the moment, but had no intention of accepting the honor so offered—until she was avised [*sic*] by some of her friends that she must consider the permission as a command."[52]

Two days after having been dazzled by the splendors of Carlton House, Jane Austen wrote to Clarke:

> I must take the liberty of asking you a question. Among the many flattering attentions which I recd from you at Carlton House on Monday last, was the Information of my being at liberty to dedicate my future work to H. R. H. the P. R. without the necessity of any solicitation on my part. Such at least, I believed to be your words; but as I am very anxious to be quite certain of what was intended, I intreat you to have the goodness to inform me how such a Permission is to be understood, & whether it is incumbent on me to shew my sense of the Honour, by inscribing the Work now in the Press, to H. R. H.—I shd be equally concerned to appear neither Presumptuous or Ungrateful.—[53]

Clarke lost no time in replying to Jane's note and wrote the next day:

> It is certainly not *incumbent* on you to dedicate your work now in the Press to His Royal Highness: but if you wish to do the Regent

> that honour either now or at any future period, I am happy to send you that permission, which need not require any more trouble or solicitation on your Part. . . . Your late Works, Madam, and in particular Mansfield Park reflect the highest honour on your Genius & your Principles; in every new work your mind seems to increase its energy and powers of discrimination. The Regent has read & admired all your publications.

This was a handsome compliment, but Clarke could not complete his letter without succumbing to the temptation of including a thinly disguised bit of self promotion:

> Accept my sincere thanks for the pleasure your Volumes have given me: in the perusal of them I felt a great inclination to write & say so. And I also dear Madam wished to be allowed to ask you, to delineate in some future Work the Habits of Life and Character and enthusiasm of a Clergyman—who should pass his time between the metropolis & the Country—who should be something like Beatties Minstrel
>
> *Silent when glad, affectionate tho' shy*
> *And now his look was most demurely sad*
> *& now he laughd aloud yet none knew why—*
>
> Neither Goldsmith—nor La Fontaine in his Tableau de Famille—have in my mind quite delineated an English Clergyman, at least of the present day—Fond of, & entirely engaged in Literature—no man's Enemy but his own. Pray dear Madam think of these things.[54]

Jane Austen was busy correcting the proofs of *Emma* and it was not until almost a month later that she replied:

> My "Emma" is now so near publication that I feel it right to assure you of my not having forgotten your kind recommendation of an early copy for Carlton House, and that I have Mr. Murray's promise of its being sent to His Royal Highness, under cover to you, three days previous to the work being really out. I must make use of this opportunity to thank you, dear Sir, for the very high praise you bestow on my other novels. I am too vain to wish to convince you that you have praised them beyond their merits. My greatest anxiety at present is that this fourth work should not disgrace what was good in the others. But on this

point I will do myself justice to declare that, whatever may be my wishes for its success, I am very strongly haunted with the idea that to those readers who have preferred "Pride and Prejudice" it will appear inferior in wit, and to those who have preferred "Mansfield Park" very inferior in good sense. Such as it is, however, I hope you will do me a favour of accepting a copy. Mr. Murray will have directions for sending one.[55]

With the business part of her letter behind her, Jane Austen terminated her reply by presenting herself in an ironic light that was in direct contrast to Clarke's none-too-subtle self-admiration:

I am quite honoured by your thinking me capable of drawing such a clergyman as you gave the sketch of in your note of Nov. 16th. But I assure you I am *not.* The comic part of the character I might be equal to, but not the good, the enthusiastic, the literary. Such a man's conversation must at times be on subjects of science and philosophy, of which I know nothing; or at least be occasionally abundant in quotations and allusions which a woman who, like me, knows only her own mother tongue, and has read very little in that, would be totally without the power of giving. A classical education, or at any rate a very extensive acquaintance with English literature, ancient and modern, appears to me quite indispensable for the person who would do any justice to your clergyman; and I think I may boast myself to be, with all possible vanity, the most unlearned and uninformed female who ever dared to be an authoress.[56]

But Clarke was not to be put off, for a few days later, after thanking Jane for the copy of *Emma* that she had sent him, which he had "very much admired—there is so much nature—and excellent description of Character in every thing you describe,"[57] he reverted abruptly to the personal level, adding with obsequious eagerness:

Do let us have an English Clergyman after *your* fancy—much novelty may be introduced—shew dear Madam what good would be done if Tythes were taken away entirely, and describe him burying his own mother—as I did—because the High Priest of the Parish in which she died—did not pay her remains the respect he ought to do. I have never recovered the Shock—Carry your Clergyman to Sea as the Friend of some distinguished Naval Character about a Court—you can then bring forward like Le Sage many Scenes of Character & Interest.[58]

Clarke then told Jane Austen that he had instructed John Murray to send her what he deprecatingly called "two little Works I ventured to publish from being at Sea—Sermons which I wrote & preached on the Ocean—& the Edition which I published of Falconer's Shipwreck."[59] There is also a mention in the same letter of another of Clarke's works that undoubtedly would have been of greater interest to Jane, a great admirer of the Stuarts. Clarke added: "I hope to have the honour of sending you James the 2d when it reaches a second Ed:—as some few Notes may possibly be then added."[60] Clarke was referring to his biography of James II, compiled from the Stuart Papers, then in the library of Carlton House.

Clarke went even further and offered Jane his *pied-à-terre* for her future visits to London: "Pray, dear Madam, remember that besides My Cell at Carlton House, I have another which Dr. Barne procured for me at No: 37, Golden Square—where I often hide myself," he wrote. "There is a small Library there much at your Service—and if you can make the Cell render you any service as a sort of Half-way House, when you come to Town—I shall be most happy. There is a Maid Servant of mine always there."[61] This offer was apparently a trifle too intimate for Jane Austen, for there is no record of any further communication between Clarke and herself until March 27, 1816, after she had left London for Chawton.

On that date Clarke wrote to Jane from the Royal Pavilion at Brighton:

> I have to return you the thanks of His Royal Highness, the Prince Regent, for the handsome copy you sent him of your last excellent novel. Pray, dear Madam, soon write again and again. Lord St. Helens and many of the nobility, who have been staying here, paid you the just tribute of their praise. . . . The Prince Regent has just left us for London; and having been pleased to appoint me Chaplain and Private English Secretary to the Prince of Cobourg, I remain here with His Serene Highness and a select party until the marriage. Perhaps when you again appear in print you may chuse to dedicate your volumes to Prince Leopold: any historical romance, illustrative of the history of the august House of Cobourg, would just now be very interesting.[62]

As Prince Leopold of Saxe-Coburg had recently become engaged to the Princess Charlotte, the Regent's only child, Jane Austen apparently realized that her correspondent's appointment as a member of the royal couple's household could make him an even more importunate nuisance. With this in mind, she evidently determined to get rid of him once and for all. Her letter from Chawton, appropriately written on April Fools' Day, 1816, is worthy to stand beside the one written by her "dear Dr. Johnson"[63] to Lord Chesterfield as one of the major epistolary snubs in English literature. Jane wrote: "I am honoured by the Prince's thanks and very much obliged to yourself for the kind manner in which you mention the work. . . . Under every interesting circumstance which your own talents and literary labours have placed you in, or the favour of the Regent bestowed, you have my best wishes. Your recent appointments I hope are a step to something still better. In my opinion, the service of a court can hardly be too well paid, for immense must be the sacrifice of time and feeling required by it."[64]

With that behind her, Jane Austen then rang down the curtain on the comedy with a declaration of her own literary independence:

> You are very kind in your hints as to the sort of composition which might recommend me at present, and I am fully sensible that an historical romance, founded on the House of Saxe Cobourg, might be much more to the purpose of profit or popularity than such pictures of domestic life in country villages as I deal in. But I could no more write a romance than an epic poem, I could not sit seriously down to write a serious romance under any other motive than to save my life; and if it were indispensable for me to keep it up and never relax into laughing at myself or other people, I am sure I should be hung before I had finished the first chapter. No, I must keep to my own style and go on in my own way; and though I may never succeed again in that, I am convinced that I should totally fail in any other.[65]

An earlier letter to her sister, Cassandra, contains this ironic comment: "I hope you have told Martha [i.e., Martha Lloyd] of my first resolution of letting nobody know that I might dedicate, &c for fear of being obliged to do it—& that she is thoroughly convinced of my being influenced now by nothing by the most mercenary motives.—"[66] Later, however, when she realized the dedication was mandatory, Jane wrote to Murray: "The Title page must be Emma, Dedicated by Permission to H. R. H. The Prince Regent,"[67] presumably hoping that the brevity of the suggested phrase would be sufficient to fulfill the distasteful command. But Murray, being better acquainted with the dedicatory formalities, as well as realizing the honor that had been conferred on his new author, was quick to point out that Jane's suggestion was unsuitable and that the title page was not the proper place on which a dedication should appear. As a result the wording was expanded and moved to a separate page at the beginning of the first volume. It read: "To His Royal Highness The Prince Regent, This Work Is, By His Royal Highness's Permission, Most Respectfully Dedicated, By His Royal Highness's Dutiful and Obedient Humble Servant, The Author."[68] Jane took Murray's correction with good grace, for she wrote to him: "As to my direction about the title-page, it was arising from my ignorance only, and from my having never noticed the proper place for a dedication. I thank you for putting me right. Any deviation from what is usually done in such cases is the last thing I should wish for. I feel happy in having a friend to save me from the ill effect of my own blunder."[69]

Meanwhile, Jane Austen had debated the necessity of spending money on a handsome binding for the copy of *Emma* that she was obliged to send to the Regent. On December 2, 1815, she wrote to Cassandra: "It strikes me that I have no business to give the P. R. a Binding, but we will take Counsel upon the question."[70] In the end, however, Jane decided to go ahead with the embellishment of the Regent's copy, and the three-volume set of *Emma,* specially bound in scarlet leather, handsomely decorated with gold tooling, including the Prince of Wales's three feathers, and bearing the Carlton House bookplate, is now one of the treasures of the Royal Library at Windsor.[71]

CHAPTER

7

Jane Austen's Reading

Jane Austen was no bluestocking. Unlike Dr. Johnson's friend Mrs. Elizabeth Carter, she never combined pudding making with translating Epictetus.[1] Nor, unlike the celebrated Mrs. Elizabeth Montague, who is buried near her in Winchester Cathedral, did she ever aspire to queen it over London's intellectual and artistic elite in an elegant salon decorated with the plumage of thousands of exotic birds.[2] On the other hand, Jane was hardly "the most unlearned and uninformed female who ever dared to be an authoress,"[3] as she playfully described herself to the Prince Regent's librarian, the Rev. James Stanier Clarke. Rather, she was one of those natural geniuses who, having obtained the rudiments of a good education, went on to cultivate herself through a lifelong addiction to good reading.

Besides her well-educated parents, Jane was fortunate in having two elder brothers, James and Henry, who were Oxford men and well read both in the earlier English classics as well as in the literature of their time. It was they who guided their talented younger sister's literary tastes and who presumably introduced her to books and periodicals that were not included in her father's library. Jane had the additional good fortune of having the run of the library of the Rev. Isaac Peter George Lefroy, the rector of Ashe, whose wife, a minor poetess and a well-read woman, is known to have encouraged Jane's taste and abilities from her earliest childhood.

In speaking of Jane Austen's literary taste her brother Henry said:

> Her reading was very extensive in history and belle lettres; and her memory extremely tenacious. Her favorite moral writers were Johnson in prose, and Cowper in verse. It is difficult to say at what age she was not intimately acquainted with the merits and defects of the best essays and novels in the English language. Richardson's power of creating, and preserving the consistency of his characters, as particularly exemplified in "Sir Charles Grandison," gratified the natural discrimination of her mind, whilst her taste secured her from the errors of his prolix style and tedious narrative. She did not rank any work of Fielding quite so high. Without the slightest affectation she recoiled from every thing gross. Neither nature, wit, nor humour, could make her amends for so very low a scale of morals.[4]

This evaluation was written by Jane's brother soon after he entered the priesthood following the failure of his banking business. His prose style was never noted for liveliness, and his account of his sister's literary tastes is tinctured with evangelical piety. Even so, Jane Austen's letters and other contemporary records indicate that Henry Austen's account of his sister's reading habits was, in the main, perceptive, if somewhat sanctimonious. She was familiar with *Tom Jones* as well as with Matthew Gregory Lewis's notorious novel, *The Monk,* about which she registered no maidenly disapproval, and her letters reveal she read, and presumably enjoyed, the writings of Swift, Defoe, Sterne, and other equally frank, earlier British writers as well as those of her own time.

As far as can be ascertained, the first book Jane Austen is known to have read was the children's classic *The History of Goody Two Shoes,* dating from around 1780, her copy of which she later presented to her niece Anna Austen (later Mrs. Benjamin Lefroy).[5] But Jane's juvenilia, dating from between 1787, when she was eleven, and 1793, when she was seventeen, also contain references to eleven identifiable books, plays, or poetical works she read during that period. These include *The Arabian Nights Entertainment;* what she referred to as "Gilpin's Tour to the Highlands," by the Rev. William Gilpin;

plays by Shakespeare, Mrs. Hannah Cowley, and Nicholas Rowe; *Lectures on the Catechism of the Church of England,* by Archbishop Thomas Secker; the then popular novels of Charlotte Smith; and even Goethe's *The Sorrows of Werther.*[6]

Since it is also known that she began the study of French at the age of eight, it is therefore not surprising that she owned and read a still-extant twelve-volume set of Arnaud Berquin's *L'ami des enfans,* which she acquired in December 1787, as well as Berquin's three-volume set of *L'ami de l'adolescence,* which she added to her growing collection of books a few years later.[7] It is presumed that the two Berquin works were presents to Jane from her sophisticated cousin, Eliza, Madame de Feuillide, who is also reputed to have helped her to perfect her knowledge of French, introduced her to Italian, encouraged her musical abilities, and familiarized her with at least some of the fashionable French literature of the period.

Still another French author Jane Austen is known to have read in the original language was Madame de Genlis, whose *Les Veillées du Château* she mentioned in a letter written to her sister in November 1800.[8] Jane was also acquainted with the same author's works in English translation. In *Emma* she alludes to *Adelaide and Theodore,* one of Madame de Genlis's shorter stories,[9] and when she was living in Southampton in 1807 she attempted to read the same author's *Alphonsine: or Maternal Affection,* at which time she wrote Cassandra: "'Alphonsine' did not do. We were disgusted in twenty pages, as, independent of a bad translation, it has indelicacies which disgrace a pen hitherto so pure . . ."[10] Returning the novel to the circulating library, she exchanged it for *The Female Quixote; or The Adventures of Arabella,* by Dr. Johnson's friend Mrs. Charlotte Lenox. Jane had read the novel before, for she told her sister it ". . . now makes our evening amusement; to me a very high one, as I find the work quite equal to what I remembered it."[11]

Jane Austen's Steventon letters and her early and later writings also show she relished the works of Dr. Johnson: *Rasselas* and *The Idler* are mentioned in *Mansfield Park;* the *Dictionary of the English Language* is referred to in *Northanger Abbey;* and *A Journey to the Western Islands* was parodied by her in *Love and Freindship* (*sic*). Jane's letters also reveal that her father's library contained Boswell's *Life of Johnson* and *Journal of a Tour to the Hebrides,* as well as Mrs. Piozzi's *Letters to and from the late Samuel Johnson.* She is also known to have read *A Journey from London to Genoa and An Account of the Manners and Customs of Italy,* by Johnson's friend Joseph Baretti. Of equal importance was Jane Austen's acquaintance with the works of Oliver Goldsmith. Not only did she own his *An History of the earth and animated nature* in eight elegantly bound volumes, which were presented to her by her uncle James Leigh-Perrot,[12] but she is also known to have read a four-volume set of the same author's *The history of England, from the earliest times to the death of George II,* in which she made numerous marginal annotations when she was a girl. These scribblings, which amount to more than forty strongly opinionated entries, are particularly interesting in view of Jane's well-known loyalty to the Stuarts. In taking issue with Goldsmith's unfavorable estimate of them, Jane noted in one place: "A family who were always ill-used, BETRAYED OR NEGLECTED, whose virtues are seldom allowed, while their errors are never forgotten." It is interesting to note that when her nephew—her first biographer—discovered this sentiment scrawled in the margin of one of the pages of Goldsmith's history when he read the same book as a boy, he added: "Bravo, Aunt Jane! Just my opinion of the case."[13]

Although Jane Austen did not refer to it by title, and then only indirectly, there was another book she possessed during her childhood. Writing to her sister in October 1808, announcing the arrival of a new doctor at Southampton, she commented: "We have got a new Physician, a Dr. Percival, the son of a famous Dr. Percival of Manchester, who wrote moral tales for Edward to give to me."[14] This is a reference to *A Father's Instructions; consisting of Moral Tales, Fables, and Reflections, designed to promote the Love of Virtue,* a book that encouraged young readers in "the writing of tales and fables" to "better display the power of imagination" and the "happy talent of relating familiar and trivial occurances [*sic*] with ease and elegance."

Several other books Jane Austen is known to have owned while living at Steventon have fortunately survived.[15] These include a handsomely bound set of David Hume's *The History of England,* which she mentioned in *Northanger Abbey;* one of an eight-volume set of Addison and Steele's *The Spectator,* also mentioned in the same novel; William Hayley's poems and plays; an elegantly bound set of Ariosto's *Orlando Furioso* in an English translation; Isaac D'Israeli's *Curiosities of Literature;* John Bell's *Travels from St. Petersburg in Russia, to diverse parts of Asia;* and the poetical works of James Thomson.[16]

Jane is also known to have read *The History of England,* by Robert Henry, for she mentioned it amusingly in a letter to her friend Martha Lloyd written in November 1800, before she set out from Steventon to Ibthorpe to visit Martha and her mother:

> I am reading Henry's History of England, which I will repeat to you in any manner you may prefer, either in a loose, disultary [*sic*], unconnected strain, or dividing my recital as the Historian divides it himself, into seven parts, The Civil & Military—Religion—Constitution—Learning & Learned Men—Arts & Sciences—Commerce Coins & Shipping—& Manners; so that for every evening of the week there will be a different subject; The friday's [*sic*] lot, Commerce, Coin & Shipping, You will find the least entertaining; but the next Eveng:'s portion will make amends.—With such a provision on my part, and if you will do your's [*sic*] by repeating the French Grammar, & Mrs. Stent [a tiresome old woman who lived with the Lloyds] will now & then ejaculate some wonder about the Cocks & Hens, what can we want?[17]

Jane Austen's serious reading at Steventon also included the published sermons and *Lectures on Rhetoric and Belles Lettres,* by the fashionable Scottish preacher the Rev. Hugh Blair, which she mentioned in *Catharine or The Bower* and in *Northanger Abbey,* and the Rev. James Fordyce's *Sermons to Young Women,* which she introduced brilliantly for comic effect in *Pride and Prejudice.* Her main literary fare at that time, however, was novels, of which she was an omnivorous reader and many of which she mercilessly parodied in her juvenilia. Presumably the rectory library at Steventon was well stocked with the works of the earlier eighteenth century British novelists, but more recent fiction was borrowed from circulating libraries in Basingstoke and Winchester. Jane mentioned one Basingstoke lending library in a letter written to her sister in December 1798: "I have received a very civil note from Mrs. Martin requesting my name as a Subscriber to her Library which opens the 14th of January & my name, or rather Yours is accordingly given. My Mother finds the Money. . . . As an inducement to subscribe Mrs. Martin tells us that her Collection is not to consist only of Novels, but of every kind of Literature, &c. &c—She might have spared this pretention to *our* family, who are great Novel-readers & not ashamed of being so;—but it was necessary I suppose to the self-consequence of half her Subscribers.—"[18]

Although Jane Austen as a girl and a young woman undoubtedly read many of the wildly improbable novels that she later referred to as the "mere Trash of the common-Circulating Library," she was nevertheless a discriminating reader, and her views on literature appear in many of her letters and novels. Her admiration for Samuel Richardson's works has already been mentioned.[19] Her enthusiasm for the novels of Fanny Burney (later Madame d'Arblay) was also strong, so much so that Alexander Dyce, the Shakespearean scholar, made a note in his copy of *Northanger Abbey* and *Persuasion:* "Miss Austen (as her nephew told me) thought Madame D'Arblay the very best of English novelists, and she used to praise the character of Sir Hugh Tyrold in Camilla as extremely well drawn."[20] Jane was thoroughly familiar with Fanny Burney's *Evelina, Cecilia, Camilla,* and *The Wanderer,* all of which she mentioned in her letters. When *Camilla* came out in 1796, Jane was listed among the subscribers to the novel as "Miss J. Austen, Steventon," and her five-volume set is now in the Bodleian Library at Oxford.[21] Jane's copy of Robert Bage's *Hermsprong: or Man as he is not* also survives, and references in her writings show that she was familiar with *Columella,* by Richard Graves, *Arthur Fitz-Albini,* by Sir Egerton Brydges, and *The Children of the Abbey* and *Clermont,* by Regina Maria Roche.

Jane Austen was also particularly fond of the novels of Mrs. Ann Radcliffe, whose *Romance of the Forest,* and particularly *The Mysteries of Udolpho,* she satirized in *Northanger Abbey.*[22] She also mentioned Mrs. Radcliffe's *The Italian, or the Confessional of the Black Penitents* in the same novel and later referred to *The Romance of the Forest* in *Emma.* The copy of *The Italian* that was owned by Jane Austen's friend and mentor, Mrs. Anne Lefroy of Ashe, still survives and may perhaps have been the copy Jane read during her Steventon years.[23] Although Mrs. Radcliffe was the acknowledged queen of the Gothic novelists, there were hundreds of other writers of varying abilities who took advantage of the craze for "horrid mysteries" to turn out imitations of the works of the woman who was referred to by her contemporaries as "the great Enchantress."

In 1798, when Jane and her parents returned to Hampshire from a visit to Godmersham, they stopped on their way at the Bull and George in Dartford. To while away the evening, Jane's father amused himself by reading *The Midnight Bell,* a recently published

Gothic thriller.[24] This is one of the seven "horrid" novels Isabella Thorpe recommended for Catherine Morland's reading after she had finished Mrs. Radcliffe's *The Italian.* Jane's mention of *The Midnight Bell* is so casual it invites the speculation that she and Cassandra had already read most of the other titles on Isabella Thorpe's list: *The Castle of Wolfenbach, Clermont, The Mysterious Warning, The Necromancer or The Tale of the Black Forest, The Orphan of the Rhine,* and *Horrid Mysteries,* all of them published between 1793 and 1798 and greatly in demand at the circulating libraries.[25] In any event, the fact that Jane Austen mentioned the titles of these long-forgotten sensational works in *Susan* (i.e., *Northanger Abbey*), her novel then in progress, indicates the type of light literature she was fond of reading.

Once Jane Austen's father had decided to move to Bath in 1800, he evidently deemed it impractical to move his library, for on January 14, 1801, Jane wrote to her sister: "My father has got above 500 Volumes to dispose of; I want James to take them at a venture at half a guinea a volume."[26] Jane's small collection of books was also sold at the same time, and most of them were apparently bought by her eldest brother, for several of them are still in the possession of James Austen's descendents.[27] The few letters that have survived from Jane's Bath years (1801-06) are devoid of the mention of books of any kind, much less any Jane read and enjoyed while she lived there. It is logical, however, to surmise that the Austens, being great readers, took advantage of the many circulating libraries for which Bath was then famous.

Apparently the Austens continued borrowing books from lending libraries after they moved to Southampton in 1806, for books are mentioned again in Jane's letters from that place. In January 1809, she and her mother were enjoying a Gothic thriller, *Margiana; or Widdrington Fair,* a five-volume Minerva Press novel by Mrs. S. Sykes, which Jane described in a letter to Cassandra: "We are now in Margiana, and like it very well indeed. We are just going to set off for Northumberland to be shut up in Widdrington Tower, where there must be two or three sets of victims already immured under a very fine villain."[28] Later, when she was reading a recently published novel by Sydney Owenson (afterward Lady Morgan), she told Cassandra: "We have got *Ida of Athens* by Miss Owenson, which must be very clever, because it was written as the Authoress says, in three months.—We have only read the Preface yet; but her Irish Girl [an earlier novel by the same author] does not make me expect much.—If the warmth of her Language could affect the Body it might be worth reading in this weather." Since this quip was followed by: "Adieu—I must leave off to stir the fire . . . ," the point of Jane's witticism becomes plain.[29]

At about the same time Jane Austen also presumably read Hannah More's *Coelebs in Search of a Wife,* an Evangelical tale, but before doing so she wrote to Cassandra: "Of course I shall be delighted, when I read it, like other people, but till I do I dislike it."[30] Still another novel that she read and apparently enjoyed at that period was Madame de Staël's *Corinne, or Italy,*[31] which had achieved such instant success as well as notoriety when it was published in Paris in 1807 that Napoleon, who loathed the author, took the trouble to write an unfavorable review of the book in the *Moniteur.*[32] Yet another book Jane Austen read while living in Southampton, and apparently disliked heartily, was *Letters from England: by Don Manuel Alvarez Espriella,* a literary hoax critical of the manners and customs of the British that was not written by a Spaniard at all but by the English poet Robert Southey. Apparently Jane had some doubts concerning the Spanish origin of the author, for her comment as a true-blue Englishwoman was typical of her national loyalty. Writing to her sister in October 1808, she said: "We have got the 2d vol. of Espriella's Letters, & I read it aloud by candlelight. The Man describes well, but is horribly anti-english [*sic*]. He deserves to be the foreigner he assumes."[33]

Although a good deal of her time after moving to Chawton in 1809 was devoted to the revision of *Sense and Sensibility* and *Pride and Prejudice* for publication and the writing of *Mansfield Park, Emma,* and *Persuasion,* Jane Austen still found time for reading. The Austens subscribed to a local book society that furnished reading matter of all types to its patrons.[34] Unfortunately, very few of Jane's letters between July 1809 and January 1813 have survived so there is no way of knowing what she read during that period. From 1813 onward, however, there is sufficient evidence concerning her reading activities to indicate that she read a good many serious works as well as novels.

Among these were Sir John Carr's *Descriptive Travels in the Southern and Eastern Parts of Spain and the Balearic Isles, in the year*

1809, which she consulted for details concerning Gibraltar when writing *Mansfield Park;*[35] Sir Charles William Pasley's *Essays on the Military Police and Institutions of the British Empire,* the author of which, Jane told Cassandra, was ". . . the first soldier I ever sighed for";[36] the antislavery writings of Thomas Clarkson, the abolitionist;[37] Sir John Barrow's account of Lord Macartney's embassy to China, which she mentioned in *Mansfield Park;* and books by Claudius Buchanan dealing with the establishment of the Anglican Church in India. During that period Jane was also particularly fond of the sermons of the great eighteenth-century divine Thomas Sherlock[38] and managed to spare a pound or two from her small income to subscribe to the published sermons of the Rev. T. Jefferson of Tunbridge, Kent.[39] A revealing passage in one of her letters of the time indicates that she did not like large books, preferring those that could be easily handled. Writing to her sister at Manydown in February 1813, Jane said: "I have been applied to for information as to the oath taken in former times of Bell, Book, & Candle but have none to give. Perhaps you may be able to learn something of its origin & meaning at Manydown. Ladies who read those enormous great stupid thick quarto volumes which one always sees in the Breakfast parlour there, must be acquainted with everything in the world. I detest a quarto."[40]

At some time during this same period Jane Austen presumably became acquainted with the letters of the famous denizen of the court of Louis XIV whom Horace Walpole designated as "Notre Dame de Sévigné," for there is an oblique reference to Madame de Sévigné in one of Jane's letters written from Kent in 1813.[41] Her small library at Chawton may also have included either Debrett's *Baronetage of England* (1808) or an earlier *Baronetage* by Bentham (1801-05), for Jane was able to answer a query from her niece Anna Austen, who was writing a novel in 1814, by stating explicitly: "There is no such Title as Desborough—either among the Dukes, Marquisses, Earls, Viscounts or Barons."[42] Jane was also familiar with Sir William Dugdale's account of the nobility and baronets of England, published in 1682, for she mentioned it by name along with an unspecified Baronetage in *Persuasion.*[43]

For the most part, however, Jane Austen's recreational reading at Chawton, as it had been elsewhere, was devoted to novels. As her niece Anna Lefroy recalled:

> It was my amusement during one summer visit to procure novels from a circulating Library at Alton, & after running them over to relate the stories of them to Aunt Jane, it was *her* amusement also, as she sat over some needle work, work of charity I must observe in which I fear that I took no other part—& greatly we both enjoyed it & so did Aunt C. [i.e., Cassandra] assuredly & in her quiet way with one piece of nonsense leading to another she wd. exclaim How can you both be so foolish! & entreat us not to make her laugh so much.[44]

Jane, in turn, mentioned novels quite often in her letters to Anna, and in one of them she painted a delightfully comic scene based on the improbable actions of the heroine of *Self-Control,* a popular novel by Mary Brunton. Jane had tried for some time without success to get a copy of this best-seller, but once she did she was so struck by its absurdity that she wrote Anna in December 1814: "I will improve upon it [i.e., *Self-Control*]; my Heroine shall not merely be wafted down an American river in a boat by herself, she shall cross the Atlantic in the same way, & never stop till she reaches Gravesent [*sic*]."[45]

Jane Austen is also known to have read Eaton Stannard Barrett's *The Heroine, or Adventures of a Fair Romance Reader,* which she described as "a delightful burlesque, particularly on the Radcliffe style."[46] She was also particularly fond of the novels of Maria Edgeworth and declared in mock seriousness in another letter to Anna Lefroy: "I have made up my mind to like no Novels really, but Miss Edgeworth's, Yours & my own.—"[47] The same letter, written in September 1814, also contains Jane Austen's well-known comment on Sir Walter Scott. Although Scott's first novel, *Waverley,* was published anonymously, Jane had no difficulty in identifying the author, and wrote: "Walter Scott has no business to write novels, especially good ones.—It is not fair.—He has Fame and Profit enough as a Poet, and should not be taking the bread out of other people's mouths.—I do not like him, & do not mean to like Waverley if I can help it—but I fear I must.—"[48]

Jane Austen's reading was not confined to prose. From childhood she had been a constant reader of English poetry, presumably being introduced to it by her eldest brother, James, himself a versifier. By the time he was fifteen, James had written several technically proficient if somewhat routine sonnets. Between 1782 and 1790, he also composed ten prologues and epilogues for the aforementioned amateur theatricals that were important diversions at Steventon rectory for almost a decade. James Austen's poetic gifts and his mother's knack for improvising occasional verse created a favorable climate for the appreciation of poetry in the Austen household.

The urge to rhyme was mostly derived from the maternal side of Jane's family, for her mother's elder brother, James Leigh-Perrot, was remembered as "a man of considerable natural power" and the writer of "clever epigrams and riddles, some of which, though without his name, found their way into print."[49] Four charades by him that have survived show he had a deft hand with light verse.[50] As for Jane's mother, she was already the author of several "smart pieces" by the time she was six, at which time she was designated as "the poet of the family" by her uncle, Dr. Theophilus Leigh, Master of Balliol College, Oxford, and a celebrated wit.[51] Jane's father is also known to have composed at least one riddle in rhyme, while her sister and her brothers Francis, Henry, and James also composed charades, a favorite family pastime.[52] As for Jane herself, her poetry writing was a lifelong avocation. These ranged from a two-verse jingle written when she was seventeen to accompany a needle case she presented to her friend Mary Lloyd to an elegy in memory of her friend Mrs. Anne Lefroy of Ashe, as well as a lively set of verses on the Winchester Races written three days before her death in 1817. Like most of the Austens, Jane was also a clever charade writer, three being definitely known to have come from her pen.[53]

From the evidence contained in Jane Austen's writings as well as the fortunate survival of several published works by noted eighteenth-century poets known to have belonged to her, it is evident she was well grounded in the British poets from Milton onward. During her Steventon days Jane read Alexander Pope, Matthew Prior, John Gay, Thomas Gray, at least one riddle in rhyme by David Garrick, James Beattie, the Rev. Thomas Moss (whose maudlin "Begger's Petition" she referred to in *Northanger Abbey*), James Thomson (whose complete poems in four elegantly bound volumes were a part of her library), William Hayley, and William Cowper. Besides these, her juvenilia and mature works reveal a long and intimate acquaintance with Shakespeare and Milton.

Of major importance to her poetical development, however, were her browsings in Robert Dodsley's *A Collection of Poems in Six*

Volumes by Several Hands, the foremost British poetical anthology of the eighteenth century. In its pages she encountered not only such well-known poets as Samuel Johnson, Thomas Gray, and William Shenstone but earlier versifiers such as William Whitehead and Isaac Hawkins Brown the Elder, the last two of whom she referred to in *Mansfield Park*. Unfortunately, Jane's set of Dodsley's anthology has been lost, as it was among her books that were sold when she moved from Steventon to Bath in 1801. Writing to her sister in May 1801 Jane commented: "Ten shillings for Dodsley's Poems however please me to the quick, & I do not care how often I sell them for as much."[54] Presumably Jane's Dodsley was bought either by Mrs. Wither Bramston of Oakley Hall near Steventon or by her sister-in-law, Mrs. Augusta Bramston, for Jane added archly: "When Mrs. Bramston has read them through I will sell them again."[55]

There was another contemporary poet whose works Jane Austen admired who has not hitherto been noted. In the second stanza of an unpublished poem dated September 28, 1817, written in memory of his recently deceased aunt by James Edward Austen (later James Edward Austen-Leigh), the line "The Warton whom she loved" occurs in connection with other notable persons beside Jane Austen who are buried in Winchester Cathedral.[56] This "Warton whom she loved" can be none other than Dr. Joseph Warton, headmaster of Winchester College from 1766 to 1793, who not only was buried in Winchester Cathedral but whose grave was marked in 1804 by a celebrated memorial by the sculptor John Flaxman.[57]

Warton, a friend of Samuel Johnson and a member of the Literary Club, was a prominent personage in the Hampshire of Jane Austen's youth. As a clergyman of the same diocese he may well have been an acquaintance of Jane's father. Of more importance here, however, are Warton's poems, particularly his *Odes*, published in 1744 and 1746, in which he not only led the revolt against the straitlaced poetical rules of Alexander Pope but advocated a then unfashionable naturalistic approach to poetry, devoid of the artificial clichés of the Augustans. How Jane Austen first became acquainted with Warton's poems is unknown, but the introduction could have been effected by her brother James, whose poetical output, with the exception of his livelier theatrical pieces, reveals a strong romantic feeling. Even if this did not happen, there was still another and more obvious way in which Jane could have discovered Warton's writings. One of his best known poems, *The Enthusiast: or The Love of Nature,* published in 1744, was included in Dodsley's anthology, which she owned. Therefore, when the family tradition that Jane "loved the country, and her delight in natural scenery was such she would sometimes say it must form one of the delights of heaven"[58] is considered, it is reasonable to assume that Warton's hitherto unrecorded influence might have provided her with the genesis of the dictum in *Sense and Sensibility* concerning the advisability of "admiring Pope no more than is proper."

Besides Dodsley's anthology, Jane Austen would seem to have been familiar with at least two other popular poetry collections. The first was the Fourth Part (1771) of the *New Foundling Hospital for Wit,* a collection in six parts, of various dates, from which she presumably took David Garrick's "Kitty, a fair, but frozen maid"—the only clever riddle in rhyme Mr. Woodhouse in *Emma* could recall.[59] The second was the *Elegant Extracts, or Useful and Entertaining Pieces of Poetry, selected for the improvement of Youth,* compiled by Vicessimus Knox, headmaster of Tonbridge School, where Jane's father had been a pupil. This popular work, which went through numerous editions from 1789 onward and which superseded Dodsley's earlier collection, was mentioned by Jane in *Emma* as the volume from which Robert Martin occasionally read to Harriet Smith and his mother and sisters at Abbey-Mill Farm before they settled for the evening around the card table.

Of major importance in Jane Austen's appreciation of poetry, however, was her admiration of the works of William Cowper, declared by Henry Austen to be her favorite moral writer in verse.[60] Jane could have been acquainted with Cowper's poems during her early years, for the first edition of his collected poems appeared in 1782, when she was six. But the rectory library at Steventon did not contain a copy of Cowper's works until after November 1798, when Jane, then twenty-three, informed her sister that Cowper's poems were to be purchased.[61] Later in December of the same year, she added: "My father reads Cowper to us in the evening, to which I listen when I can."[62] From then on, Jane's letters reveal her intimate acquaintance with Cowper's poetry, while *Sense and Sensibility, Mansfield Park,* and *Emma,* as well as her last unfinished novel, contain quotations or specific mentions of Cowper's works.

There are two possible personal connections between Jane Austen and Cowper that should be mentioned. First, it was Lady Austen, the widow of Sir Robert Austen (d. 1772) of Herendon near Tenterden, Kent, a distant relation of Jane's father, who not only was an intimate friend of Cowper's but also prompted him to write both *The Task* (which Jane quoted in one of her letters) and *The Diverting History of John Gilpin*.[63] Second, Jane Austen was acquainted with Joseph Hill, a lawyer and lifelong friend of the poet, who was also the man of affairs for the branch of the Leigh family to which Jane's mother belonged. Cowper addressed his friend and benefactor in *An Epistle to Joseph Hill* in November 1784, in which he described him as:

> *An honest man, close-buttoned to the chin,*
> *Broadcloth without, and a warm heart within.*

Jane Austen no doubt would have admired this succinct characterization. But the connection here is not only that Hill was a longtime friend, legal advisor, and Berkshire neighbor of Jane's maternal uncle, James Leigh-Perrot, but that Jane and Hill were both guests together at Stoneleigh Abbey in Warwickshire in August 1806.[64] Hill's presence in Warwickshire at that time was primarily connected with the settlement of the Stoneleigh estate, which had only recently come into the possession of Mrs. Austen's cousin, the Rev. Thomas Leigh. It is therefore quite possible that while relaxing from his legal duties Hill discussed his friend the poet (who had died six years previously) with Jane Austen, whose admiration for Cowper's poetry would have stimulated her interest in Hill's recollections of him. That Jane Austen not only continued to admire Cowper's poetry throughout her lifetime but shared her enthusiasm with others is evident from the fact that she presented a copy of his works to her niece Fanny Knight in June 1808, when Jane was a guest of Fanny's parents at Godmersham.[65] Five years later, when Jane was paying her last visit to the same place, she lightheartedly referred thus to Cowper's poem *Verses on Alexander Selkirk*, in a letter to Cassandra: "I am now alone in the Library, Mistress of all I survey—at least I may say so & repeat the whole poem if I like it, without offense to anybody."[66]

Jane Austen's last years at Steventon coincided with the earliest published works of Robert Southey, Thomas Campbell, James

Montgomery, and William Wordsworth, although it is doubtful if she became familiar with any of their poetry until some years later. In any event, she was sufficiently familiar with Campbell, Montgomery, and Wordsworth by 1817 to mention them in *Sanditon.* As for Southey's poetry, she had evidently known it for some time, for in the year of her death she mentioned his latest work in a letter to her lifelong friend Alethea Bigg: "We have been reading the 'Poet's Pilgrimage to Waterloo,' and generally with much approbation. Nothing will please all the world, you know; but parts of it suit me better than much that he has written before."[67]

Again, as in the case of the Joseph Hill-William Cowper connection, Jane's knowledge of Southey the poet was supplemented with personal information concerning Southey the man. This was because Catherine Bigg of Manydown Park, an elder sister of Alethea Bigg's, had become Southey's aunt in 1808 when she married the poet's maternal uncle, the Rev. Herbert Hill, rector of Streatham in Surrey. Since Jane is known to have visited the Hills in May 1811, and probably again in March 1814, she was therefore in a position to learn a good deal concerning the man who became England's poet laureate in 1813. In Southey's "proem" to *The Poet's Pilgrimage to Waterloo* he had lamented the untimely death of his favorite son, Herbert, named for the Rev. Herbert Hill. This caused Jane, in the same letter to Alethea Bigg, to comment: "The opening—the proem I believe he calls it—is very beautiful. Poor man! one cannot but grieve for the loss of the son so fondly described. Has he at all recovered it? What do Mr. and Mrs. Hill know about his present state?"[68]

That Jane Austen's mature poetical reading was not confined exclusively to the Augustans and their late-eighteenth-century successors is reflected in her admiration for Milton, for there are two quotations, one in *Mansfield Park* and the other in *Emma,* that indicate that she was familiar not only with the poet's minor works but with *Paradise Lost* as well. Also, when Jane was staying with her brother Edward at Godmersham in 1813, she described an encounter with Stephen Rumbold Lushington, a member of Parliament, in which a volume of Milton provided a significant detail in her appraisal of that gentleman. Writing to Cassandra in October 1813, she said: "Mr. Lushington goes tomorrow.—Now I must speak of *him*—& I like him very much. I am sure he is clever & a

Man of Taste. He got a vol. of Milton last night & spoke of it with Warmth.—He is quite an M. P.—very smiling, with an exceeding good address, & readiness of Language.—I am rather in love with him.—I daresay he is ambitious & Insincere."[69]

Jane Austen was also sufficiently acquainted with Scott's poetry to use quotations from his works to emphasize salient characteristics of some of her fictional characters. Significantly, Marianne Dashwood in *Sense and Sensibility* was so enamored with Scott's poetry she was accused of wanting to buy up every copy of his works "to prevent them falling into unworthy hands." Jane also used quotations from Scott's *Lay of the Last Minstrel* in describing Fanny Price's reaction to the unromantic family chapel at Sotherton Court in *Mansfield Park*. Anne Elliot in *Persuasion* was quite earnest in her discussions with the poetry-bemused Captain Benwick as to "whether *Marmion* or *The Lady of the Lake* were to be preferred." Later, when Benwick had ceased grieving sufficiently for his lost Fanny Harville to turn his attentions to the flighty Louisa Musgrove, Jane resolved the situation in her best feline fashion by commenting: "He would gain cheerfulness, and she would learn to be an enthusiast for Scott and Lord Byron; nay, that was probably learnt already; of course they had fallen in love over poetry."[70] In *Sanditon* she was even more satirical and used quotations from *Marmion* and *The Lady of the Lake* to emphasize the amorous scheming of Sir Edward Denham, who carried his affected poetical enthusiasms so far as to attribute several "beautiful Lines on the Sea"[71] to Scott that existed only in his hectic fancy, a lapse that Charlotte Heywood, his down-to-earth auditor, pointed out with obvious glee.

Beside the novels, Jane's letters contain references to the writings of the Wizard of the North that reveal her familiarity with his poetry. In June 1808, when she was staying at Godmersham, she expressed her doubts concerning the literary merits of *Marmion* in a letter to her sister, adding that their brother James, who was also a member of the party, was reading the poem aloud to the family in the evenings.[72] A few months later, however, Jane had reversed her unfavorable opinion of *Marmion* and announced her intentions of sending a copy to her brother Charles, then on naval duty on the North American station, to which she added the playful comment: ". . . vry generous in me, I think."[73] On still another occasion when she was visiting her brother James and his family at Steventon rectory, she entertained the company by reading parts of *Marmion* aloud. In recalling the event, the Rev. Fulwar-William Fowle, a nephew of Mrs. James Austen's, wrote to Caroline Austen in 1870 after the publication of the *Memoir:* "Your dear Aunt Jane I can testify to as being the attractive, animated, delightful person her Biographer has represented her. . . . The last time I ever saw her was at Steventon, when she was on a visit to your Mother. . . . She had just finished the first Canto of Marmion. . . . When Mr. W. Digweed was announced it was like the interruption of some pleasing dream."[74]

When *Pride and Prejudice* was published, Jane wrote to her sister and banteringly suggested that the novel was "rather too light, and bright, and sparkling,"[75] adding that "it wants shade, it wants to be stretched out here and there with a long chapter of sense, if it could be had; if not, of solemn specious nonsense, about something unconnected with the story; an essay on writing, a critique on Walter Scott, the history of Buonaparté, or anything that would form a contrast, and bring the reader with increased delight to the playfulness and epigrammatism of the general style."[76] Jane was obviously being facetious, for in an earlier letter, in which she deplored certain technical ambiguities in the same novel, she excused them by ringing the changes on a couplet from *Marmion:*

> *I do not rhyme to that dull elf*
> *Who cannot image to himself . . .*

with a parody of her own on the same couplet:

> *I do not write for such dull elves*
> *As have not a great deal of ingenuity themselves.*[77]

That Jane Austen continued to keep abreast of Scott's poetical works is evident from a letter written to Cassandra in November 1815. Jane had been staying with her brother Henry in London in order to be available for the correction of the proofs of *Emma.* When these were tardy, John Murray, her publisher, lent her two of Scott's latest works, the poem *The Field of Waterloo* and *Paul's Letters to his Kinfolk,* a prose description of post-Napoleonic Paris, to quiet her apprehensions. This caused her to comment: "In short, I am soothed & complimented into tolerable comfort."[78]

According to James Edward Austen-Leigh, Jane was particularly fond of the poetry of George Crabbe, playfully referred to by one of his contemporaries as "Pope in worsted stockings"[79] and characterized by Byron in *English Bards and Scotch Reviewers* as "Nature's sternest painter, yet the best."[80] In commenting on his aunt's fondness for Crabbe's poetry, Jane's nephew wrote: "She thoroughly enjoyed Crabbe; perhaps on account of a certain resemblance to herself in minute and highly finished detail, and would sometimes say, in jest, that if she ever married at all, she could fancy being Mrs. Crabbe; looking on the author quite as an abstract idea, and ignorant and regardless of what manner of man he might be."[81] But Jane's first biographer was not accurate, for although it is obvious Jane was jesting when she declared "she could fancy being Mrs. Crabbe," her nephew did not add that she had a trustworthy source from which she could have learned a good deal concerning Crabbe as a person apart from his reputation as a poet. This source was her maternal aunt, Mrs. Leigh-Perrot, for whom Jane did not much care, but who was a highly intelligent woman with a tenacious memory and a wide knowledge of the society of her time.

Mrs. Leigh-Perrot,[82] born Jane Cholmeley, was a granddaughter of James Cholmeley (d. 1735) of Easton, Lincolnshire, one of whose daughters, Catherine, married William Welby (d. 1792) of Denton House, Lincolnshire.[83] His son and heir, Sir William Welby (d. 1815), also of Denton House, was not only Mrs. Leigh-Perrot's cousin but was for many years an intimate friend of Crabbe's,[84] an acquaintance dating from the 1780s when the poet, who was already the chaplain of the Duke of Rutland at Belvoir Castle in Leicestershire, became the rector of Muston in the same county and also of Allington in Lincolnshire, both parishes being within sight of Belvoir Castle. What is more, Mrs. Leigh-Perrot's favorite niece, Wilhelmina Spry, was the wife of William Earl Welby, the son and heir of Crabbe's good friend. Knowing Jane Austen's interest in the poet, Mrs. Leigh-Perrot could easily have imparted news concerning him to Jane from time to time.

In Jane Austen's novels, Crabbe's poetry is mentioned only once, the reference being to his *Tales in Verse,* which was among the books owned by Fanny Price in *Mansfield Park.* More important, however, is the fact that Jane may have borrowed the name of her heroine in that novel from another Fanny Price, one of the principals in "Marriage," the second part of Crabbe's *The Parish Register*, published in 1807.[85] There is even a superficial resemblance between Crabbe's Fanny Price and Jane's character, for the episode in the poem concerns the unsuccessful efforts of a libertine to seduce the poet's heroine. Unlike Henry Crawford in *Mansfield Park*, however, the would-be Lothario is finally shamed into worthier behavior by his intended victim and ends by becoming a benefactor of her as well as her rustic swain.

Jane's interest in Crabbe as a person is spelled out in several of her letters dating from 1813. In July of that year, Mrs. Crabbe, who had suffered from mental illness for several years, recovered sufficiently to express a desire to visit London. Crabbe granted the wish, and he and his wife and two sons spent nearly two months in a hotel near the Strand.[86] In some way Jane Austen became aware of Crabbe's presence in London, for in a letter written on September 15, 1813, when she was staying with her brother Henry in Henrietta Street, Covent Garden, she told her sister: "I have not yet seen Mr. Crabbe."[87] Later, in the same letter, after she had attended a performance of *The Clandestine Marriage* at Covent Garden Theater, she added: "I was particularly disappointed at seeing nothing of Mr. Crabbe. I felt sure of him when I saw the boxes were fitted up with crimson velvet." Jane's reference was presumably to the line from *The Gentleman Farmer* in Crabbe's *Tales in Verse:*

In full festoons the crimson curtains fell.[88]

Meanwhile, the Crabbes had returned to Muston in Leicestershire, where Mrs. Crabbe died on September 21, 1813. Evidently this information appeared in the newspapers, for Cassandra passed on the news of Mrs. Crabbe's death to Jane. Writing from Godmersham on October 21, 1813, Jane said: "No; I have never seen the death of Mrs. Crabbe," adding, "I have only just been making out from one of his prefaces [presumably the one to *The Borough*] that he probably was married. It is almost ridiculous. Poor woman! I will comfort *him* as well as I can, but I do not undertake to be good to her children. She had better not leave any."[89] Still later, in November 1813, in describing the new governess at Godmersham, Jane wrote: "Miss Lee I found very conversable; she admires Crabbe as she ought.—She is at an age of reason, ten years older than myself at least."[90]

Jane was never serious concerning the desirability of being Crabbe's wife. Even if she had been, she would have been doomed to disappointment. One year after she praised Miss Lee for her admiration of the poet, he fell in love with another woman. While the parson-poet was staying at Sidmouth in South Devon in the autumn of 1814, he met Miss Charlotte Ridout, a lady young enough to be his daughter, who had just rejected a suitor of her own age because he was weak in intellect. An attachment developed between Crabbe and Miss Ridout, and the poet proposed and was accepted, at which time his fiancée presented him with a miniature of herself. Crabbe's love affair with Miss Ridout was unsuccessful, however, for a few months' separation from his inamorata extinguished the flame, and on December 12, 1814, he noted in his diary: "Charlotte's picture was returned."[91] Meanwhile, Jane Austen in some manner had learned of the engagement. That she did not know of its termination, however, is evident from a letter written by Mrs. Austen to her newly wedded granddaughter, Anna Lefroy, on Christmas Day 1814, in which she commented: "Aunt Jane desires me to tell you she has heard some *bad news* lately, namely that Mr. Crabbe is going to be married."[92]

Jane Austen did not confine her interests to the major poets of her time but also enjoyed the lighter works of contemporary versifiers as shown by her admiration of the witty *Rejected Addresses or the new Theatrum Poetarum* by the brothers James and Horatio Smith. This still enjoyable classic of parody aimed at Wordsworth, Southey, Coleridge, Scott, and Byron, among others, purported to be poems unsuccessfully submitted for the prize offered by the proprietors of the newly rebuilt Drury Lane Theater for an address to be recited on the opening night. In commenting on this production by "the two Mr Smiths of the city"[93] in a letter to her sister in January 1813, Jane wrote: "Upon Mrs. Digweed's mentioning that she had sent the Rejected Addresses to Mr Hinton, I began talking to her a little about them, & expressed my hope of their having amused her. Her answer was 'Oh dear yes, very much, very droll indeed—the opening of the House, & the striking up of the Fiddles!' what she meant poor woman, who shall say? I sought no further."[94]

Jane was also familiar with William Combe's popular satire, *The Tour of Dr. Syntax in Search of the Picturesque,* published in 1812 with spirited engravings after drawings by Thomas Rowlandson, who depicted the principal character as a clergyman with an abnormally prominent chin. This gives point to Jane's observation in a letter written from London in March 1814 in which she told Cassandra: "I have seen nobody in London yet with such a long chin as Dr. Syntax."[95] Because of her interest in music, Jane was also acquainted with the sentimental poetical effusions of Thomas Moore, whose verses to "a new set of Irish melodies" were among the music in *Emma* that Frank Churchill chose in London to be sent along with the mysterious gift of the Broadwood square piano to Jane Fairfax in Highbury.

Although the best works of Robert Burns were written when Jane Austen was a child, and even though she was possibly familiar with them while she was still living at Steventon, she did not mention his poetry until she began *Sanditon* in 1817. The passage in the manuscript in which these references appear occurs during a discussion of poetry in general during which Sir Edward Denham, an egotistical seducer, informs Charlotte Heywood, another one of the characters: "Burns is always on Fire.—His soul was the Altar in which Lovely Woman sat enshrined, his Spirit truly breathed the immortal Incense which is her due."[96]

At that point, Charlotte felt it necessary to call on good sense to stem the flow of Sir Edward's bombast and presumably used words similar to those Jane Austen, as a level-headed realist, might have spoken when she commented: "I have read several of Burn's [*sic*] Poems with great delight . . . but I am not poetic enough to separate a Man's Poetry entirely from his Character;—& poor Burns's known Irregularities, greatly interrupt my enjoyment of his Lines.—I have difficulty in depending on the *Truth* of his Feelings as a Lover. I have not faith in the *sincerity* of the affections of a Man of his Description. He felt & he wrote & he forgot."[97]

Finally, what was Jane Austen's opinion of the poetry of Lord Byron? Strangely enough, there is but one reference to his poems in her surviving letters. Writing from London to her sister in March 1814, Jane commented dryly: "I have read the Corsair, mended my petticoat, & have nothing else to do."[98] Even so, Jane mentioned Byron's *The Giaour* and *The Bride of Abydos,* both published in 1813, as being among "the richness of the present age"[99] in the discussion of poetry between Anne Elliot and Captain Benwick in *Persuasion.* Later in the same novel, Benwick quoted Byron's lines from *The*

Corsair beginning "O'er the glad waters of the dark blue sea" to Anne Elliot just before Louisa Musgrove had her memorable fall from the steps of the Cobb at Lyme Regis.[100] This is the sum of Jane Austen's references to the poet who, after the publication of the first two cantos of *Childe Harold's Pilgrimage,* awoke one morning and found himself famous.

But there was a later episode in Byron's turbulent career that would have interested Jane Austen from a personal rather than a poetical standpoint if she had lived to experience it. Byron died at Missolonghi, Greece, on April 19, 1824. His body was brought back to England and lay in state at No. 25 Great George Street, Westminster, on July 9-10 of the same year before being taken to Hucknall Torkard in Nottinghamshire for burial in the family vault. This is a matter of history, but the interesting fact concerning the arrangements as far as Jane Austen is concerned is that the black-draped, candle-lighted front parlor of the house in London where Byron's body lay in state was the town house of her niece Fanny Catherine Knight, who had become the second wife of Sir Edward Knatchbull in 1820.[101]

CHAPTER

8

Jane Austen and Scandal

Even though Jane Austen was a properly reared daughter of a conservative Tory clergyman, she had a lively lifelong interest in scandal as well as other manifestations of human perversity. By the time she had reached early adolescence she was already acquainted with at least two contemporary instances and one earlier case of aberrant human behavior. Later, her surviving letters, ranging from 1796 to 1817, provide ample clues for those interested in the gamier aspects of late Georgian and Regency society to track down the profligate episodes to which she briefly referred.

Jane's introduction to the seamier side of life presumably took place in 1788, when she was twelve. That summer she accompanied her parents and sister, Cassandra, on a visit to her father's kinfolk in Kent and London. While the rectory party was away from Steventon, Thomas Twisleton, thirteenth Baron Saye and Sele, who had married Elizabeth Turner, a second cousin of Jane's mother,[1] committed suicide. He did so in a locked room in his Harley Street town-house in London by cutting his throat with a razor and stabbing himself with his sword.

Whether the Austens learned about this widely publicized scandal from accounts in the London newspapers is not known. Even so, they could hardly have missed the lengthy report of the baron's self destruction that appeared in the *Hampshire Chronicle* on July 18, 1788, since that newspaper had a wide circulation throughout the Steventon area.[2]

Tragic though it was at the time, Lord Saye and Sele's bizarre suicide had an amusing epilogue eighteen years later. In August 1806, Jane Austen and her mother and sister were guests of their cousin, the Rev. Thomas Leigh, at Stoneleigh Abbey in Warwickshire. Another of the house party was the baron's widow, whom the novelist Fanny Burney had described as a compulsive chatterer and celebrity hunter whose "manner spoke a lady all alive."[3] In a letter written by Mrs. Austen while at Stoneleigh to her daughter-in-law Mary Austen at Steventon, she reported: "Our visit has been a most pleasant one, and we all seem in good humour, disposed to be pleas'd, endeavor to be agreeable, and I hope succeed—Poor Lady Saye & Sele, to be sure, is rather tormenting, tho' sometimes amusing, and affords Jane many a good laugh—but she fatigues me sadly on the whole."[4]

Fortunately, an example of Lady Saye and Sele's chatter was subsequently recorded by Jane Austen's niece Anna Lefroy. Many years later Cassandra Austen, remembering her 1806 visit to Stoneleigh with her mother and Jane, recalled that Lady Saye and Sele was asked if she would take "some boiled chicken." To this, her ladyship replied emphatically, "No, I cannot," adding by way of explanation that after her husband had "destroyed himself" she had eaten nothing but boiled chicken for a fortnight in her chamber and "hadn't been able to touch it since."[5]

Lord Saye and Sele's suicide was undoubtedly still being regretted at Steventon rectory when Jane's maternal relations were further embarrassed by another scandal in the Twisleton family. In September 1788, Thomas James Twisleton, the baron's eighteen-year-old stagestruck son, eloped to Scotland with Miss Charlotte Anne Frances Wattell, also a minor, as a result of a liaison begun while they were acting in an amateur production of Jephson's tragedy *Julia* at the Freemason's Hall in London.[6]

Young Twisleton's runaway marriage with Miss Wattell not only caused quite a stir in fashionable society, it also lent support to the long-standing opinion (later capitalized on by Jane Austen in *Mansfield Park*) that private theatricals provided tempting opportunities for nonprofessionals to indulge in dalliance. Even though the surviving Austen archives contain no mention of the Twisleton-Wattell elopement, it is reasonable to surmise that the Steventon household learned of the episode either from newspaper accounts or from letters exchanged between Jane's mother and Lady Saye and Sele's Leigh relations in Gloucestershire.

Twisleton's runaway marriage is highly significant as far as Jane Austen is concerned since it took place only a few months before the last known private theatricals at Steventon rectory. These had begun in December 1782, when Jane was seven, with a performance of Dr. Thomas Francklin's tragedy *Matilda* and ended during the Christmas season of 1788, when *The Sultan, or a Peep into the Seraglio,* a comedy by Isaac Bickerstaffe, and James Townley's farce *High Life Below Stairs* were staged soon after Jane's thirteenth birthday.[7]

The last performances were more or less anticlimactic, however, for the high point of the Steventon theatricals, which paralleled the situation leading up to the Twisleton elopement, had already taken place during the Christmas festivities of 1787. At that time Susannah Centlivre's lively comedy *The Wonder: A Woman Keeps a Secret* was acted with Jane's coquettish cousin Eliza de Feuillide in the leading role.[8]

Eliza, then twenty-six, had descended on Steventon that Christmas like a Parisian bird of paradise, and, according to family tradition, had caused a few heartaches like those later described in *Mansfield Park* by openly flirting with Jane's elder brother James and his younger brother Henry, who later became her second husband.

These intrigues were undoubtedly observed by precocious twelve-year-old Jane, whose recollections of Eliza's dalliance during the highly charged rehearsals and performances of *The Wonder* were apparently drawn on later when she described a similar situation in the *Lovers' Vows* episode of *Mansfield Park*.

Considered separately, there seems to be little relation between the Twisleton-Wattell elopement in September 1788 and the somewhat abrupt termination of the amateur theatricals at Steventon a few months later. Even so, the closeness of time between the two events invites a speculation. Jane's parents, who according to family tradition were already disturbed by Eliza de Feuillide's coquetry during the 1787 production of *The Wonder,* could have felt it was injudicious to encourage further amateur theatricals at the rectory for fear that something similar to young Twisleton's and Miss Wattell's hasty departure for Gretna Green might be duplicated in their own family.

This is merely a surmise, but at least one thing is certain. Jane Austen's later conviction, stressed in *Mansfield Park,* that amateurs are not sufficiently experienced emotionally to cope with the temptations of dilettante performances was apparently not only the result of observations made at the time Steventon rectory was the scene of the provocative performances of *The Wonder,* but was further bolstered by Twisleton's later well-publicized marital difficulties that caused his family and relations additional embarrassment.

Twisleton's subsequent history, with which Jane Austen was well aware, can be briefly told. Eight years after his still stagestruck wife had eloped with him to Scotland, she entered into an adulterous relationship with a lover named John Stein, by whom she had an illegitimate child. After two years of legal wrangling, during which a good deal of dirty linen was washed in public, Twisleton was able to obtain a divorce from his wayward wife.[9] Meanwhile, he had taken Holy Orders and had transferred his histrionic abilities from the amateur stage to the pulpit. After remarrying, Twisleton became secretary and chaplain to the colonial government of Ceylon. Later, he was named the first Archdeacon of Colombo, a post he held until his death in 1824.[10]

Presumably Twisleton had left England under a cloud, for on September 23, 1813, Jane Austen, in discussing the allotment of certain Leigh family clerical livings, passed on the following somewhat acid comment of Mrs. Cassandra Cooke, the wife of her godfather, to her sister Cassandra: "All these and other scrapings from dear Mrs. E. L. [i.e., Elizabeth Leigh] are to accumulate no doubt to help Mr. Twisleton to secure admission again into England."[11]

The next scandal with which Jane Austen was presumably acquainted—the history of a cruel eighteenth-century mother—is important since family tradition maintains it was this woman who was the archetype of the principal character in Jane's early epistolary novel, now known as *Lady Susan.* That this claim is untenable will be obvious when the facts are considered.

The assertion linking Jane's heroine Lady Susan Vernon with a real person was first made by Mary Augusta Austen-Leigh, a great niece of Jane Austen's, in *Personal Aspects of Jane Austen,* in which the presumed original of Jane's scheming adventuress was merely designated as the "cruel Mrs. ———."[12] Research by Austen scholars has identified the person as Mrs. Elizabeth Craven, one of whose daughters, Martha, became the mother of Jane's intimate friends, Martha, Eliza, and Mary Lloyd. Jane undoubtedly learned the ugly facts concerning Mrs. Craven soon after Mrs. Lloyd rented Deane rectory from the Rev. George Austen in the spring of 1789 when Jane was fourteen.

According to Mary Augusta Austen-Leigh, Mrs. Craven was remembered by her descendants for her sadistic meanness. Even so, it should be recalled that Miss Austen-Leigh was writing about a woman who had lived a century and a half earlier, thereby giving ample time for any maternal deficiencies that she might have displayed during her lifetime to be embellished. Moreover, a careful comparison of Miss Austen-Leigh's account with her aunt Caroline Austen's reminiscences plainly shows that the former drew heavily on the latter's recollections to support her shaky hypothesis. Even so, it should also be noted that Caroline Austen, whose family reminiscences can usually be verified by historical facts, made no mention of a Mrs. Craven–Lady Susan Vernon connection in her recollections. Using historical evidence, supplemented with quotations from Caroline Austen's reminiscences, these are the known facts concerning the woman Miss Austen-Leigh claimed was the inspiration for Jane Austen's Lady Susan Vernon.[13]

Mrs. Elizabeth Craven, born Elizabeth Staples in 1698, was the daughter of Colonel John Staples. By her first husband, the Hon. Charles Craven (1682-1754), a brave but light-fingered governor of the province of South Carolina from 1711 to 1717, she was the mother of five daughters and three sons. All of the daughters and one son, who later became the Rev. John Craven of Chilton, Wiltshire, reached maturity, but the other two male children died in infancy. After Charles Craven's death, his widow moved to Sennington (Sevenhampton) in Gloucestershire, and it was there, according to Caroline Austen, that "my grandmother's adventures began." Caroline Austen elaborated on the latter statement thus:

> My grandmother, Martha Craven, and her sisters, had but a rough life of it. Their mother, a most courteous and fascinating woman in society, was of a stern, tyrannical temper, and they were

> brought up in fear, not in love. They were sometimes not allowed proper food, but were required to eat what was loathsome to them, and were often relieved from hunger by the maids privately bringing them up bread and cheese after they were in bed. Perhaps some of the traditions of Mrs. Craven's personal cruelty to her children, as endangering even their lives, went beyond the truth, but there could be no doubt that she was a very unkind and severe mother.

The eldest daughter married "a Squire Cox, of good degree." (Caroline Austen deemed it "a suitable marriage.") This left her four sisters at home with their mother, who was accustomed to taking one of them with her as her personal maid when she made lengthy visits to the country houses of her friends. Finally, matters reached a climax when Mrs. Craven set out for Berkshire with her daughter Jane in attendance as a menial. In her absence, one of her other daughters took matters into her own hands and married a well-to-do yeoman named Hinxman. Her sister Mary, in following her example, however, did not do so well when she hastily married a man named Bishop, whom Caroline Austen described as "a horse dealer . . . with no money and no character." When that happened, Caroline Austen added: "My grandmother Martha, knowing how much Mrs. Craven would resent these misalliances, and foreseeing nothing but increased severity in the house, could not resolve to face her mother's anger, and she also left her home, before Mrs. Craven could return to it, and she never lived under her parent's roof again." Subsequently, after enduring considerable hardship, Martha Craven married the Rev. Nowes Lloyd in 1763 and became the mother of Martha, Eliza, and Mary Lloyd.

Mrs. Craven's later history can be quickly summarized. After marrying her daughter Jane to the Rev. Thomas Fowle, vicar of Kintbury, she took as a second husband Jemmett Raymond of Barton Court, Kintbury. She was also presumably instrumental in arranging the marriage of her son, the Rev. John Craven, to her second husband's much younger, slow-witted half sister, Elizabeth Raymond. Outliving Jemmett Raymond by six years, the former Mrs. Craven died in 1773 at the age of seventy-five. At that time she left a still-existing tangible remembrance for her progeny in the form of a large white marble memorial to her second husband and herself in the Church of St. Mary the Virgin at Kintbury. The tomb is not only decorated with a haughty life-sized bust of herself by Thomas Sheemakers, a fashionable contemporary London sculptor, it also identifies her as "the Widow of the Honbl Charles Craven Esq. Governor of South Carolina In the Reign of Queen Ann [*sic*]."[14]

Jane Austen's frequent visits to Kintbury in her youth would have familiarized her with this memorial. Moreover, as an intimate friend of Mrs. Lloyd and her daughters, she was undoubtedly well acquainted with the factual history of "the cruel Mrs. Craven." But, family tradition to the contrary, there are hardly any parallels between the historical Mrs. Elizabeth Craven-Raymond and Jane's fictitious Lady Susan Vernon with the exception of the latter's shameful bullying of her daughter Frederica.

Scandal more serious than the elopement of an impetuous young distant cousin struck closer to the Austens at Steventon in 1799-1800, when Jane's formidable maternal aunt, Mrs. Leigh-Perrot, was accused by a Bath shopkeeper of stealing a card of white lace, one of many petty crimes punishable at that time by hanging. Mrs. Leigh-Perrot was remanded in custody at Ilchester on August 14, 1799, and was tried and acquitted at Taunton on March 29, 1800, at the Spring Assizes for Somerset.[15] The details of the trial are readily available in any number of biographies of Jane Austen and need not be repeated here. Suffice it to say the acquittal of Jane's aunt on the shoplifting charge should have settled the matter, but there are several tantalizing hints that suggest, despite her protestations of innocence, Mrs. Leigh-Perrot might have been a kleptomaniac.

Seven days before she was declared not guilty of stealing lace, the Rev. William Holland, a Somerset parson, made the following entry in his diary: "At Stowey met Mr. Symes the Lawyer. He told me that Mrs. Parrot [*sic*] had bought off her prosecutor. Alas, alas that money should be able to screen a person from Justice in this Kingdom so remarkable for good laws and uncorrupted Judges. She was accused of stealing lace out of a shop in Bath, is a person of considerable fortune and has a poor Jerry Sneak of a husband who adheres to her through all difficulties."[16]

Even though public opinion had been divided over whether Mrs. Leigh-Perrot was guilty of stealing the card of white lace, and there is ample evidence that most of her friends stood by her during her trouble, there is the strong possibility that she was implicated later in a theft of a different sort.

According to an anonymous manuscript, now in a collection at the University of Florida, the episode is described thus:

> Mrs. Lee [*sic*] Perrot, tried at Ilchester on a charge of stealing lace in a Milliner's shop at Bath, having sometime after been brought before the Magistrates of that City, charged with stealing Plants, the following epigram appeared generally thought to have been written by Dr. Harrington [*sic*].
>
> Sub Judice lis esto
> *To love of plants, which boasts the better claim,*
> *Darwin the Bard, or surreptitious Dame?*
> *Try thou the cause, Judge Botany, we pray*
> *Let him the laurel gain and her the Bay.*[17]

The "Darwin the Bard" referred to was Dr. Erasmus Darwin, the author of several poetical works on botanical subjects and the grandfather of Charles Darwin, the naturalist. "The Bay" and "Judge Botany" alluded to Botany Bay, an all-inclusive term then used for the destination of British criminals sentenced to transportation. Had Mrs. Leigh-Perrot been found guilty of the theft of either the lace or the plant she would have been transported to Australia if the mandatory capital sentence of hanging had been commuted.

The University of Florida manuscript is given added support by two entries in the recently published *A Testimony of her Times: Based on Penelope Hind's Diaries and Correspondence,* edited by Sarah Markham, published in 1990. Mrs. Hind's first reference to the later Leigh-Perrot shoplifting incident, dated November 1804, reads: "On Mrs Leigh Perrott [*sic*] of lace-stealing notoriety, having been detected lately in embezzling some green house plants from a gardener's at Bath, Dr. Harrington [*sic*] of the place wrote the following lines:

> Sub judice lis est
> *To love of plants who has the greater claim,*
> *Darwin the Bard or Perrot's wiley Dame?*
> *Decide the cause Judge Botany, we pray,*
> *Let him the Laurel take and her the Bay.*[18]

The author of the two almost identical epigrams was Dr. Henry Harington (1727-1816), a magistrate and mayor of Bath.

Shortly after recording Dr. Harington's *jeu d'esprit,* Penelope Hind, the wife of the Rev. John Hind, vicar of Finden in Sussex, received further information concerning Mrs. Leigh-Perrot's plant stealing from a friend, Miss Matilda Rich of Sonning, who was well informed concerning what was going on in Bath. Mrs. Hind's later information, dated June 5, 1805, reads:

> Miss Rich says that since Mrs. Perrott's [*sic*] stealing the plants everybody has dropped her acquaintance, and she is universally shunned. It seems she was cheapening plants at a gardener's and wanting to buy a small one then growing which he refused to sell at the price she proposed; on his back being turned a young lady in the garden saw her stooping down to the border and appearing very busy with her hands which was to loosen it from the ground, for on rising she dropped her pocket handkerchief on the spot, and then stooped to pick up that and the plant together, and put both in her pocket. The young lady told the gardener, who taxed her with it. She positively denied the charge, but he insisted on searching her pockets where it was found; she then burst into tears, and intreated that it might not be put into the papers. The man resolved on prosecuting her, but this was put a stop to from the father of the young lady precipitately taking her from Bath to prevent her appearing in a court of justice as a witness against this infatuated woman.[19]

In commenting on this incriminating information, Sarah Markham wrote in an excellent survey of the episode titled "A gardener's question for Mrs. Leigh-Perrot," published in the 1981 annual report of the Jane Austen Society:

> Although it was certainly an exaggeration to say that Mrs. Leigh-Perrot was universally shunned, there are still questions to be asked. Who could have released the information but the gardener or the father of the young lady so hurriedly removed? No onlooker could have known that the gardener was later prevented from prosecuting by the girl's absence. As for Mrs. Leigh-Perrot—did she enter the garden with a large pocket-handkerchief for the express purpose of lifting a plant or was it done on a sudden impulse? Could her partial deafness have been the cause of some misunderstanding? She is known to have been careful with money, but it does seem unlikely that after her previous dreadful experiences she should have risked another prosecution for the sake of such a small reward. All that can safely be said is that a

> number of people in and around Bath did not give her the benefit of the doubt.[20]

The last-known reference to Mrs. Leigh-Perrot's alleged kleptomania is to be found written in a copy of *Northanger Abbey* and *Persuasion,* now in the collection of the Victoria and Albert Museum in London. This volume once belonged to the Shakesperian scholar Alexander Dyce, an Oxford contemporary of the Rev. James Edward Austen-Leigh, Jane's first biographer. In it Dyce made a notation in 1844 that his friend had inherited Mrs. Leigh-Perrot's money. He then added: "The lady mentioned . . . had an invincible propensity to stealing, and was tried at Bath [*sic*] for stealing lace; the printed account of her trial still exists. The family were dreadfully shocked at the disgrace which she brought upon them. For many years she lived in seclusion at Scarlets (a handsome place) where she died."[21]

This poses an interesting question. Could Jane Austen have known of or suspected her aunt's kleptomania, and although deploring the frailty, been angered at the selfish weakness that would have constantly threatened the family as well as herself with disaster or disgrace? We probably shall never know the answer, for all contemporary evidence pointing to Mrs. Leigh-Perrot's guilt with the exception of the items mentioned has apparently disappeared. But the fact that Alexander Dyce was told, presumably by James Edward Austen-Leigh, that "the family were dreadfully shocked at the disgrace which she brought upon them" indicates that the verdict of not guilty handed down at Taunton in 1800 and the later plant-stealing episode could have been regarded by Jane Austen as a lucky escape for her aunt, whose light-fingered propensities were either known or at least suspected by her family.

The next mention of scandal in Jane Austen's correspondence invites an intriguing speculation. Writing to her sister on January 8, 1801, Jane said that their friend Eliza Fowle had seen her cousin, Lord Craven, whom she expected to visit her shortly, adding: "She found his manners very pleasing indeed.—The little flaw of having a Mistress now living with him at Ashdown Park, seems to be the only unpleasing circumstance about him."[22] Later, on January 21, 1801, Jane wrote: "Lord Craven was prevented by Company at home, from paying his visit at Kintbury, but as I told you before, Eliza is greatly pleased with him, and & they seem likely to be on the most friendly terms."[23] Although no name is mentioned it could be possible that the woman referred to in Jane's letter was none other than the notorious courtesan Harriette Wilson, later the celebrated queen of "The Fashionable Impures," whose witty memoirs, published in 1825, present a vivid picture of the racier side of Regency society.

The "Lord Craven" mentioned by Jane was William, seventh Baron Craven of Ashdown Park and Hamstead Marshall, Berkshire, and an aide-de-camp to George III. As a great favorite of Queen Charlotte, he was also "caressed by the ladies of the court, who were eager to match him with their daughters."[24] Lord Craven also commanded The Buffs military unit (or 3rd of Foot), and it was with him that his cousin, the Rev. Thomas Fowle, who had become engaged to Cassandra Austen, went on a military expedition to the West Indies, where he died of yellow fever in 1797.

More relevant here, however, is the fact that Lord Craven was also a well-known rake. In 1801, the year of Jane Austen's letter just quoted, he had taken the fifteen-year-old Harriette Dubochet, later known as Harriette Wilson, as his mistress. Although there is no mention in Harriette's memoirs of any visit to Berkshire before she and Lord Craven took up residence in Brighton while his regiment was stationed at nearby Lewes, he might have brought her to Ashdown Park before moving on to Brighton. In that case, his cousin Eliza Fowle would have been in the position to pass on the information concerning the "little Flaw of having a Mistress now living with him at Ashdown Park" to Jane.

Harriette states in her memoirs that she found Lord Craven insufferably dull because he insisted on drawing pictures of coconut trees and mapping out his former West Indian campaign "on the best vellum paper" instead of making love to her. She finally left him because of his addiction to drawing coconut trees instead of adoring her.[25]

The woman Craven subsequently married was also connected peripherally with Jane Austen. In 1807 he wed Louisa Brunton, a provincial actress, whose father, once a greengrocer in Drury Lane, London, had been the manager of the Norwich Theater, where his daughter appeared with considerable success. In 1815, when *Emma* was published and Jane Austen was collecting her readers' opinions, she noted the following: "Countess Craven—admired it very much, but did not think it equal to P&P [i.e., *Pride and Prejudice*], which she ranked as the very first of its sort."[26]

In February 1801, when Jane Austen was visiting her friends the Bigg sisters at Manydown Park, she referred to another scandal—an irregular affair in the royal family—in a letter to her sister. Jane had just received a communication from her youngest brother, Charles John Austen, then serving as a lieutenant in the *Endymion* under the command of Sir Thomas Williams. Jane wrote: "Charles spent three pleasant days in Lisbon.—They were very well satisfied with their Royal Passenger, whom they found fat, jolly & affable, who talks of Ly [i.e., Lady] Augusta as his wife & seems much attached to her."[27]

The "Royal Passenger" referred to by Jane was Prince Augustus Frederick, later Duke of Sussex, the sixth son of George III. Prince Augustus, one of the more respectable of the royal dukes, a generally dissolute lot, was a discerning bibliophile and a great lover of music. He was inordinately vain of his three-octave tenor voice, but was nonetheless plagued by serious bouts of asthma. It was this complaint that had obliged him to sail on the *Endymion* to Portugal early in 1801 in order to escape the fog-cursed British winter. However, the scandal, or rather the irregularity concerning him, obliquely referred to by Jane Austen, dated from a few years earlier.[28]

In 1792, when he was in Rome, the prince encountered Lady Augusta Murray and her mother, the Countess of Dunmore, while visiting the church of San Giacomo. Noticing that the string of one of Lady Augusta's shoes was untied, the nineteen-year-old prince knelt down and tied it. From then on he began a regular courtship of Lady Augusta, a lady six years older than himself.

On one occasion he arrived with a copy of *The Tempest,* which he insisted that Lady Augusta read. When she complied, she discovered the prince had heavily underlined the lines:

> *O if a virgin, and your affections not gone forth,*
> *I'll make you the Queen of Naples.*

This declaration was followed by an avalanche of love letters in which the prince referred to Lady Augusta either as "my amiable Goosy" or "my Gussy." But Lady Augusta was wary and refused to wed the prince until he signed a statement agreeing to honor their marriage despite any objections that might be advanced later by his father. Only when this document, properly drawn up and signed by the prince, was produced did Lady Augusta consent to marry Prince Augustus. The ceremony was performed in April 1793 by the Rev. William Gunn, an Anglican clergyman acting as a Protestant chaplain in Rome. Later, when the prince and Lady Augusta had returned to London, they were again married in December 1793, in St. George's Church, Hanover Square, under the assumed names of Mr. Augustus Frederick and Miss Augusta Murray. They did so to forestall any question of the validity of their Roman marriage.

When this became known to George III, however, he declared the marriage invalid, since it violated the Royal Marriage Act of 1772, which made it illegal for any member of the royal family to marry before the age of twenty-five without the king's permission. A decree annulling the marriage in St. George's was pronounced by the Dean of Arches in the summer of 1794; the previous marriage in Rome being dismissed as "a show and effigy of a marriage." Even so, Prince Augustus held out and continued to live with his "Goosy," by whom he had a son and a daughter, until after his return from Lisbon in the summer of 1801. Later he is said to have preferred the solid worth of a dukedom and twelve thousand pounds a year to the charms of a forty-year-old wife.

Jane Austen's Twisleton cousins seemed to have a propensity for getting into scandalous scrapes. It will be remembered that while still a minor, Thomas James Twisleton eloped to Scotland with Miss Charlotte Anne Frances Wattell, with whom he had formed a liaison while they were performing in amateur theatricals in London. Ten years after Twisleton's youthful fall from grace, his youngest sister, Mary-Cassandra Twisleton, whose older sister, Julia-Judith Twisleton, had married Jane's cousin, James Henry Leigh of Adlestrop, in 1786, was featured in another family scandal that was mentioned by Jane Austen in two of her letters. As the details of the affair were probably already too well known to the Austens from family correspondence and the newspapers, Jane merely referred to it obliquely on November 20, 1800, at which time she told Cassandra that their erring cousin and her mother, Lady Saye and Sele, were about to move to Bath.[29] Later, on May 12, 1801, after Jane herself had moved from Steventon to Bath, she attended a ball in the Upper Rooms where she met the guilty party face to face.

In describing the encounter to Cassandra, Jane wrote: "By nine o'clock my Uncle, Aunt & I entered the rooms & linked Miss Winstone on to us. . . . I then got Mr. Evelyn to talk to, and Miss Twisleton to look at; and I am proud to say I have a very good eye at an Adultress [*sic*], for tho' repeatedly assured that another in the same party was the *She,* I fixed upon the right one from the first—A resemblance to Mrs. Leigh was my guide. She is not so pretty as I expected; her face has the same defect of baldness as her sister's, & her features not so handsome;—she was highly rouged, & looked rather quietly and contentedly silly than anything else."[30]

Since there have been any number of erroneous speculations concerning the identity of Mary-Cassandra Twisleton's lover, it might be well to provide the exact information from the journals of the House of Lords, from which her husband finally secured a civil divorce.

Born in 1774, and while still a minor, Mary-Cassandra Twisleton married Edward Jervis Ricketts on January 29, 1790, in the Church of Saint Mary-le-Bone in London. The marriage broke up in October 1797 when Ricketts discovered incriminating letters between his wife and her lover, Charles William Taylor of Margaret Street, off Cavendish Square, London. Shortly thereafter, Mary-Cassandra returned to her mother's home.

On June 30, 1798, the Bishop of London granted Ricketts an Episcopal divorce from Mary-Cassandra. Ricketts then set in motion a civil divorce action, which came before the House of Lords on December 10, 1798. At the hearing, several witnesses swore they had seen Mary-Cassandra visit her lover's house surreptitiously, while others commented on her disheveled state when she left. The most damaging evidence was provided by a maid who testified that Mary-Cassandra had bragged in graphic detail concerning Taylor's prowess as a lover compared to Ricketts's performance as a husband. The action ended in Ricketts's being granted a civil divorce on January 3, 1799, two years before Jane Austen stigmatized her cousin as an "Adultress."[31] Seven years later, Mary-Cassandra married Charles Head-Graves, the son of a Suffolk parson, whom she survived, dying at the age of sixty-nine in 1843.[32]

The next mention of scandal in Jane Austen's correspondence is particularly important inasmuch as the affair referred to could have served as the catalyst for the climax of *Mansfield Park,* which was begun about February 1811. The incident took place in June 1808, when Jane was staying with her brother Edward at Godmersham in Kent. In commenting on the affair, which involved two of her Southampton acquaintances, Jane wrote on June 20, 1808, to Cassandra: "This is a sad story about Mrs. Powlett. I should not have suspected her of such a thing.—She staid the Sacrament I remember, the last time that you & I did.—A hint of it, with Initials, was in yesterday's Courier; and Mr. Moore guessed it to be Ld [Lord] Sackville, beleiving [*sic*] there was no other Viscount S. in the peerage, & so it proved—Ld Viscount Seymour not being there."[33] There does not seem to be any reference in the London *Courier,* but the *Morning Post* for June 18, 1808, printed the following notice: "Another elopement has taken place in high life. A Noble Viscount, Lord S., has gone off with a Mrs. P., the wife of a relative of a Noble Marquis."[34] Later, on June 21, 1808, the same paper published this further detail: "Mrs. P's faux pas with Lord S— — —e took place at an inn near Winchester."[35] Like many journalistic tidbits of that time as well as today, the statement was not accurate. As the scandal referred to, combined with the Twisleton-Wattell affair of 1788, could have provided Jane Austen with the inspiration for the Rushworth-Crawford elopement in *Mansfield Park,* it deserves to be recounted in detail.[36]

The principals in the affair were Charles Sackville Germain, second Viscount Sackville, later fifth Duke of Dorset, and the wife of Colonel Thomas Norton Powlett, a member of an old Hampshire family well known to the Austens. In 1798, Powlett, then thirty-one, married Miss Letitia Mary Percival, who was ten years his junior. Shortly thereafter, while the Powletts were living in London, they became acquainted with Lord Sackville, after which he and Mrs. Powlett, according to later testimony in court, arranged to meet at her home on any number of occasions when her husband was "in the Country." The affair continued after the Powletts moved to Southampton but did not come to the attention of the gossip columnists of the London newspapers until after June 10, 1808, when Mrs. Powlett and Lord Sackville were discovered in a compromising situation in a Winchester inn. This resulted in an action for ten thousand pounds in damages by Colonel Powlett against Lord Sackville on the grounds of adultery with Mrs. Powlett.

According to an account of the trial in the *Hampshire Chronicle* for August 1, 1808, Lord Sackville met Colonel Powlett and his wife at the Stockbridge race course on June 9, 1808, at which time Sackville heard Powlett make plans to accompany a friend on an all-day yachting party the following day. Apparently some secret communication between Sackville and Mrs. Powlett took place, for the next morning, after the colonel had set out for Southampton Quay, Mrs. Powlett sent for post horses for her carriage and ordered the postilion to drive her to the White Hart Inn in Winchester. When she arrived, the innkeeper, named Bell, accommodated her with a room up one flight of stairs. Shortly afterward Lord Sackville arrived and was shown into a room on the ground floor where he ate a light breakfast, after which he lounged at the open door of his room and talked with the landlord. Meanwhile, Mrs. Powlett came downstairs and walked about near the two men, but spoke to neither of them. She then returned upstairs and was followed shortly by Lord Sackville. They went into her room and closed the door.

Suspecting "they were going to act improperly," Bell asked his wife to investigate but she did not go immediately. When she finally knocked on Mrs. Powlett's door she was told not to come in. Mrs. Bell then went into an adjoining room with a connecting door and finding that it had been locked on the other side, demanded that it be opened. When this was done, after some delay, she noticed that the shutters were "put to" and the curtains had been drawn, while Lord Sackville was stooping down on the other side of the bed. Mrs. Powlett then confronted the landlady and demanded an explanation for the intrusion. At first Mrs. Bell refused to answer, but after the question was repeated she accused Mrs. Powlett of impropriety. At that point, Lord Sackville came forward and he and Mrs. Powlett demanded that Mrs. Bell say nothing of the assignation. She replied that it would be useless for her to try to hush up the matter as one of her chambermaids knew about it. That caused Mrs. Powlett to weep; Lord Sackville made matters worse by warning Mrs. Bell "not to hurt Mrs. Powlett." He then left the room, ordered his carriage, and drove away. Mrs. Powlett was driven back to Southampton, hoping that her rendezvous with Lord Sackville would be forgotten.

At the trial, which took place after Jane Austen had returned from Godmersham to Southampton, the jury awarded Colonel

Powlett three thousand pounds in damages. In commenting on the case the *Hampshire Chronicle* said: "No private subject has so much occupied the attention of the neighborhood, as this affair. We have been cautious of retailing the numberless stories of which the circumstance has given birth, having waited till a Court of Law should sanction the detail." But apparently that was not the end of the story for Jane Austen. When she came to write *Mansfield Park,* the Sackville-Powlett scandal and the Twisleton-Wattell elopement presumably provided her with hints for the denouement of the Maria Rushworth–Henry Crawford affair. Under her pen the coy factual entries in the *Morning Post* were transformed into a similar fictional scandal that climaxed with: ". . . it was with infinite concern the newspaper had to announce to the world, a matrimonial fracas in the family of Mr. R. of Wimpole Street. . . . "[37]

In 1811, when Jane Austen was visiting her brother Henry in London, she was the guest of a French count and his wife whose murders a year later caused a sensational scandal. Writing to Cassandra from London on April 18, 1811, Jane said that Henry's wife, Eliza, the former Madame de Feuillide, had made a particular point of inviting three French acquaintances, Louis Emmanuel Henri Alexandre de Launai, Comte d'Antraigues, and his wife and son, Comte Julien d'Antraigues, to a grand musical evening party. The d'Antraigues declined the invitation because they were already engaged but responded by inviting the Henry Austens and Jane to visit them on an earlier evening before the party. This caused Jane to remark: "It will be amusing to see the ways of a French circle."[38]

The Comte d'Antraigues, a well-known continental diplomat who had incurred the implacable hatred of Napoleon and who was then living in retirement in England, was the husband of Madame Saint-Huberti, the celebrated French dramatic soprano. Her triumphs at the Theatre Français before the French Revolution, particularly in the operas of Gluck and Piccinni, were familiar to Eliza Austen, Jane's sister-in-law, when she lived in Paris with her first husband, Jean-François Capot de Feuillide. Jane enjoyed her visit to the d'Antraigues' (she spelled the name "d'Entraigues" in her letter) and described the evening thus:

> Eliza enjoyed her eveng [*sic*] very much & means to cultivate the acquaintance—& I see nothing to dislike in them, but their taking quantities of snuff.—Monsieur the old Count, is a very fine looking

> man, with quiet manners, good enough for an Englishman—& I believe is a Man of great Information & Taste. He has some fine Paintings, which delighted Henry as much as his Son's music gratified Eliza—& among them, a Miniature of Philip 5. of Spain, Louis 14.s Grandson, which exactly suited My capacity.—Count Julien's performancc is very wonderful. We met only Mrs Latouche & Miss East—& we are just now engaged to spend next Sunday Eveng [*sic*] at Mrs L.s—& to meet the D'Entraigues;—but M. le Comte must do without Henry. If he wd but speak english, *I* would take to him.[39]

Although she did not realize it, Jane was mixing in dangerous company that evening, for although the Comte d'Antraigues was then past sixty, he was still secretly engaged in intrigue against Napoleon for the Russian and British governments. Threatened by the French with instant execution if captured, he had arrived in England in 1806 from the continent, bearing a letter of introduction from the emperor of Russia.[40]

He had also acted for years, sometimes simultaneously, as a secret agent for Royalist France, Russia, and Prussia, as well as operated as a successful expert forger of supposedly rediscovered ancient Roman historical writings. His intrigues made it dangerous for him to remain in Dresden, where he spied for Russia. He therefore fled with his wife and son to England, settling in a house on Barnes-terrace at Barnes, in Surrey. Fate caught up with him there a little more than a year after Jane Austen visited him. He and his wife were stabbed to death by an Italian servant named Lorenzo, who then took his own life. The motive for the murder was never satisfactorily explained. As the British government seized the Comte's private papers immediately after the murder and discovered secrets of the highest importance among them, the crime was presumed to have been a case of political vengeance.[41]

Later in the same year Jane Austen referred to another scandal in a letter written to her sister from Chawton on May 29, 1811: "You certainly must have heard before I can tell you that Col. Orde has married our cousin, Margt. Beckford, the Marchess. of Douglas's sister. The papers say that her father disinherits her, but I think too well of an Orde to suppose that she has not a handsome independence of her own."[42]

This introduces the question of how "our cousin Margt. Beckford," who was the elder daughter of the celebrated William Beckford of

Fonthill Abbey, could have been related to Jane Austen. The puzzle can be answered conjecturally either one of two ways. Lady Albinia Bertie, a daughter of Peregrine Bertie, the second duke of Ancaster, married Francis Beckford of Basing, Hampshire, who was an uncle of William Beckford of Fonthill Abbey.[43] One of her sisters, Lady Jane, was the wife of General Edward Mathew and the mother of Anne Mathew, the first wife of Jane Austen's elder brother, James. Lady Albinia was therefore the great-aunt of William Beckford's two daughters, both of whom are mentioned in the excerpt from Jane Austen's letter just quoted, as well as the great-aunt of Jane Austen's niece Jane Anna Elizabeth Lefroy, James Austen's only child by his first wife.

It may be that Mary Austen, James Austen's second wife, was in the habit of speaking of the wealthy Beckford sisters as "our cousins," and that Jane was quoting Mary. But there is another possible explanation. After Lady Albinia's death, Francis Beckford married again, his second wife being Susanna Love of Basing. By her he had four children, three of whom are significant in this context: Charlotte Beckford (d.1803), who married John Charles Middleton, the tenant of Chawton Manor, the property of Jane's brother Edward, from 1808 to 1813; Maria Beckford, who lived with her brother-in-law at Chawton Manor and is frequently mentioned as "Miss Beckford" in Jane Austen's letters; and Francis Beckford, who married Johanna Leigh, a descendant of the Leighs of Cheshire from whom Jane Austen's mother was also descended.[44] This connection may account for Jane Austen's usage of the phrase "our cousin" in connection with William Beckford's daughter Margaret, which brings us to the scandal that Jane mentioned in her letter to Cassandra.

Having successfully married his second daughter, Susannah Euphemia Beckford, to the Marquis of Douglas in 1810, William Beckford endeavored to marry off his elder daughter equally well. But Margaret Beckford preferred Colonel James Orde, a relatively poor relation of the Duke of Bolton, to any of the titled and wealthy suitors that her father proposed. When she could bear her father's importunities no longer she decided to take matters into her own hands. In May 1811, shortly before Jane wrote her letter to Cassandra, a hastily scribbled note from Lady Ann Hamilton, under whose protection Margaret Beckford had been living in

London, was delivered to William Beckford enclosing a note from his daughter. Lady Hamilton's note read: "Margaret went out this morning to take her usual walk in the Park and I thought with Mlle, and she has just sent me the enclosed instead of returning. I dread to think—She must have gone off with Orde." Margaret Beckford's note confirmed Lady Hamilton's suspicions. It read: "No longer able to bear the very unpleasant situation in which I am placed I have *at length* resolved upon a step which I feel assured will ensure my Happiness and have now adopted this mode of communication in preference to speaking to you on the subject and when you receive this I shall *no longer* have the name of Beckford."[45]

Margaret Beckford, as Jane Austen reported in her letter, was disinherited by her father, who not only furiously scrawled "Off! Off! Off!" on the blank side of his daughter's note but referred to her as "Mrs. Ordure" from that time on. The breach was not resolved until nine years later when she died at the age of thirty-nine, at which time Beckford sent a note of condolence to Colonel Orde.[46] Margaret Beckford's father had himself been involved in a well-publicized homosexual scandal with the seventeen-year-old William ("Kitty") Courtenay at Poderham Castle in 1784. This prompted the *Morning Herald* to print a highly suggestive paragraph beginning: "The rumour concerning a Grammatical mistake of *Mr. B* and the *Hon Mr. C,* in regard to the genders, we hope for the honour of Nature originates in Calumny! etc.," which caused Beckford to leave England temporarily.[47]

Jane Austen also makes casual reference to the tarnished reputation of the woman who was then Lord Byron's mistress in a letter to her friend Martha Lloyd in February 1813. There is no evidence that Jane was aware of Byron's current connection with the person mentioned in her letter, but the woman's previous love affairs had been so public that they were common gossip of Regency society. In commenting on the matrimonial troubles of the Prince Regent and his wife, Jane added: ". . . & the intimacy said to subsist between her [i.e., the princess] and Lady Oxford is bad."[48]

The lady mentioned so disparagingly by Jane Austen was Jane Elizabeth Scott, born in 1773, a daughter of a Hampshire rector, the Rev. James Scott. Unlike Jane Austen's father, who was a conservative Tory, the Rev. Mr. Scott was a liberal thinker, and his daughter was reared in the ardor of French Revolutionary thought.

In 1794, when she was twenty-two, she married Edward Harley, fifth Earl of Oxford and Mortimer, who was so good-natured he merely winked at the extramarital amours of his beautiful wife. With her liberal views in politics and love, Lady Oxford was therefore given free rein to pursue her fondness for good-looking young men who espoused the reform movement, her first lover having been Sir Francis Burdett, the Whig politician and an acquaintance of Jane Austen's brother Henry.[49]

After her affair with Burdett, Lady Oxford's lovers became so numerous that she soon acquired a large family of children of such uncertain parentage that the wits referred to them as the "Harleian Miscellany." This situation was given an ironic twist by her indulgent husband, who was so amiable and complacent that no divorce was ever contemplated. Lady Oxford was forty when twenty-four-year-old Byron met her in 1812, on the rebound from his tempestuous affair with Lady Caroline Lamb. Byron told Lady Blessington that Lady Oxford's "autumnal charms" suited him exactly, and for a time he reveled in her company "in the bowers of Armida" at Eyewood, the Oxfords' country house. It is also a matter of record that Lady Oxford encouraged Byron in his "Senatorial duties," and persuaded him to join the party of her friend, the Princess of Wales, which confirms Jane Austen's derogatory reference to her intimacy with the princess.[50]

The Byron–Lady Oxford affair ended in June 1813 when Lady Oxford sailed for the Mediterranean with her husband and the "Harleian Miscellany," presumably to escape Byron's Wertherism, the continual jealousy of his former mistress, Lady Caroline Lamb, and the fear of being dragged "into some scene, and put in peril by the scissors and bodkin of the enemy."[51]

Even as late as four months before her death, Jane Austen was able to comment, albeit wearily, on scandal in high society. In a letter dated March 13, 1817, she told Fanny Knight: "If I were the Duchess of Richmond, I should be very miserable about my son's choice. What can be expected from a Paget, born & brought up in the centre of conjugal Infidelity & Divorces?—I will Not be interested about Lady Caroline. I abhor all the race of Pagets.—"[52]

Jane's vehement statement was in reference to the forthcoming marriage of Lady Caroline Paget, the daughter of Henry William Paget, later Marquis of Anglesey,[53] to Charles, fifth Duke of

Richmond. The bride's father, known at that time as Lord Paget, was subsequently referred to as "One Leg" because he lost his right leg at the Battle of Waterloo. The man that Lady Caroline Paget married was the son of the Duchess of Richmond who gave the celebrated ball on the eve of the same battle.

Jane's phrase "conjugal Infidelity & Divorces" in regard to the Pagets needs further clarification, for with the facts in mind, and they were widely publicized, it is a good indication of how assiduously she followed the happenings of her time—scandalous and otherwise.

On July 25, 1795, Lord Paget married Lady Caroline Elizabeth Villiers, the third daughter of the fourth Earl of Jersey and his wife, the notorious Lady Frances Jersey, an early mistress of Jane's *bête noire,* the Prince Regent. At the time that Lord Paget entered into an adulterous relationship with Lady Charlotte Wellesley (née Cadogan), the wife of Henry Wellesley, a younger brother of the man who later became the Duke of Wellington, he and his wife were the parents of three sons and a daughter. When Lady Charlotte's husband learned of his wife's infidelity, he brought an action against Lord Paget and was awarded twenty thousand pounds in damages. After that, Wellesley divorced his wife.[54]

Meanwhile efforts were made by his family and friends to induce Lord Paget to reconcile with his wife, but these were futile, and he slipped off with the newly divorced Lady Charlotte for a tour of the Highlands. At that point, Lady Caroline Paget sued her unfaithful husband for infidelity and was granted a divorce in 1810. After that, Lord Paget and the former Lady Caroline Wellesley were married and became the parents of three sons and three daughters.[55]

Lord Paget, who was created Marquis of Anglesey in 1815, was a great favorite of the Prince Regent and was entertaining the latter at a partridge shoot at Beaudesert, his country home in Staffordshire, when the Rev. James Stanier Clarke, the Regent's librarian, was showing Jane Austen around Carlton House just before the publication of *Emma.*[56]

Concerning Jane Austen's connection with the marriage she condemned so roundly, there is evidence that she had a closer acquaintance with Lord Anglesey's family than asserted by R. W. Chapman, the editor of *Jane Austen's Letters.* In his note to the letter from Jane to Fanny Knight, Chapman merely mentioned that Sir Arthur Paget, a younger brother of Lord Paget, had married Lady

Augusta Fane, the divorced wife of Lord Boringdon, later the Earl of Morley, whose second wife, Frances, Countess of Morley, not only received a presentation copy of *Emma,* but praised it in her letter of thanks to Jane Austen.[57]

But Chapman missed another and more important connection that placed Jane Austen in a better position to know more about the Pagets. Jane's main source of information regarding the family of which she spoke so slightingly was probably her younger brother, Charles John Austen, who served for a year and a half as the first lieutenant in the frigate *Endymion* under the command of Captain Charles Paget, later Vice Admiral Sir Charles Paget, another brother of Henry William Paget, later first Marquis of Anglesey. During his time of service in the *Endymion* under Captain Paget, Charles Austen was active in cruising in the Channel and the Bay of Biscay and on the coasts of Spain and Portugal. On the recommendation of Captain Paget, Charles Austen was subsequently promoted to the command of the *Indian,* attached to the North American station.[58]

It is therefore reasonable to surmise that Charles Austen was in the position to pass on information concerning the Pagets to his sister at Chawton, the nature of which we now have no way of knowing. But as Jane Austen was a fair-minded woman, she no doubt had a good reason for asserting "I abhor all the race of Pagets," even though some might regard the vehemence of her statement as uncharitable.

CHAPTER

Jane Austen's Journeyings

Jane Austen's frequent journeys away from Steventon, Bath, Southampton, and Chawton, the four places where she lived more or less permanently, qualified her as a well-traveled woman for her time. Unlike many contemporaries of her class, Jane never left her native land during her forty-one years, but she is known to have traveled extensively in the south and west of England, as far north as Staffordshire, and also into Wales. She also lived for varying lengths of time in Oxford, Reading, and London. All these places provided her with carefully observed background material, not only for some of her juvenilia and the six novels of her maturity, but also for her last, unfinished novel, now known as *Sanditon.*

As far as is known, Jane Austen's first journey away from home took place in 1783, when she was seven. In spring of that year she and her sister, Cassandra, were enrolled in a boarding school at Oxford run by Mrs. Ann Cawley, a sister of their uncle, Dr. Edward Cooper.[1] Later in the same year, Mrs. Cawley moved her school to Southampton, taking Jane and Cassandra and their cousin Jane Cooper[2] with her. Because of the prevailing stench of "stinking fish" at Southampton, which Jane recalled amusingly in *Love and Freindship* (*sic*), written when she was fourteen, she presumably was unfavorably impressed with the town.[3] Jane had not been there long, however, when she was stricken with "putrid fever," now believed to have been typhus fever. According to tradition, Mrs. Cawley failed to realize the gravity of the situation and refused to notify the Austen girls' parents. But the quick-thinking Jane Cooper felt otherwise and sent an urgent appeal to her mother and Mrs. Austen to come to Southampton immediately. When they arrived, Jane and Cassandra were taken back to Steventon, where Jane came very close to dying. Mrs. Cooper was not so fortunate. Before removing her daughter from Mrs. Cawley's indifferent care she, too, contracted the fever and died in October 1783, shortly after her arrival home, and was buried at Whaddon near Bath.

Two years later, Jane and her sister became pupils at the Abbey School in Reading, where the enrollment was mainly made up of girls from the families of the landed gentry, professional classes, and clergy. The school, located in the former gate-house of Reading Abbey, was run by Mrs. Sarah La Tournelle, a stout, motherly woman with a cork leg, and a Miss Pitts, an excellent needlewoman who played and sang well, spoke French fluently, and "danced remarkably well, but with too much of the Scotch style, which was then in fashion."[4] Earlier biographers of Jane Austen have maintained that her regular schooling ended in 1784, when she was nine, but later research indicates the sisters presumably remained at the Abbey School until 1786.[5]

In the summer of 1788, Jane Austen, then twelve, traveled in the company of her parents and sister to West Kent, where they visited her ninety-year-old great-uncle, Francis Austin, a wealthy solicitor, who lived at the Red House in Sevenoaks.[6] While in Kent, they also visited William Hampson Walter (a half brother of Jane's father) and his family at nearby Seal, and possibly also Tonbridge, where Jane's father was born and attended Tonbridge School. It may have been on that trip that Jane and her sister acquired the "2 Tunbridge ware work boxes of oval shape, fitted up with ivory bands containing reels for silk—yard measures, &c." that Jane's niece Anna Lefroy recalled seeing later in her aunt's "Dressing Room" at Steventon.[7] This trip into Kent also included what was possibly Jane's first visit to London, since her cousin Eliza de Feuillide, who was then living in Orchard Street, London, mentioned in a letter that Jane, her parents, and her sister had "dined with us on their way back to Hampshire."[8]

Whether Jane Austen's 1788 London visit included any sightseeing is not known, but her juvenilia contain several references indicating she was familiar with some parts of the city either from her 1788 visit or other unrecorded ones a short time afterward. In *Frederic & Elfrida,* written between 1787 and 1790, one of the characters drowns herself in "a deep stream which ran thro' her Aunt's pleasure Grounds in Portland Place"[9] in the Marylebone district of London. Also, in *The Beautifull* (*sic*) *Cassandra,* dating from the same period, Jane described the adventures of "the only Daughter of a celebrated Milliner in Bond Street" in the Mayfair, Bloomsbury, and Hampstead areas of London.[10] Later in *Love and Freindship* (*sic*), finished in 1790, Jane mentioned the Holborn area of London as well as Newgate Prison.[11] The most interesting London reference in Jane Austen's juvenilia, however, occurs in *Lesley Castle,* dating from 1792, when she was sixteen. In it one of the characters longs "to go to Vaux-hall, to see whether the cold Beef there is cut so thin as it is reported."[12] Jane was in error as far as her choice of meat was concerned, for it was ham rather than beef that was then reputedly cut with astonishing thinness at the fashionable London pleasure garden. Even so, Jane's mistake did not detract from the point she was trying to make, for the myth survived until the time of Charles Dickens. In "Vauxhall Gardens by Day" in *Sketches by Boz,* Dickens observed: "It was rumoured too . . . that there, carvers were exercised in the mystic art of cutting a moderate sized ham into slices thin enough to pave the whole of the grounds."[13]

Travel in Jane Austen's day would have been difficult without horses, and her juvenilia also furnish proof she was well acquainted (in name at least) with the wide variety of vehicles then used by people who traveled either for business or pleasure. In *The Memoirs of Mr Clifford,* written between 1787 and 1790, she began her story:

> Mr Clifford lived at Bath; & having never seen London, set off one monday [*sic*] morning determined to feast his eyes with a sight of that great Metropolis. He travelled in his Coach & Four, for he was a very rich young Man & kept a great many Carriages of which I do not recollect half. I can only remember that he had

> a Coach, a Chariot, a Chaise, a Landeau, a Landeaulet, a Phaeton, a Gig, a Whiskey, an italian [*sic*] Chair, a Buggy, a Curricle & a wheelbarrow. He had likewise an amazing fine stud of Horses. To my knowledge he had six Greys, 4 Bays, eight Blacks & a poney.[14]

In the same story Jane used the slang phrase "pretty tight work,"[15] then a common expression employed by travelers to describe the slow progress on country roads that were usually in deplorable condition, particularly during the winter months. Throughout the last quarter of the eighteenth century, however, the main highways in England were gradually improved, and this encouraged people to travel for pleasure.

At that period the writings of the Rev. William Gilpin, rector of Boldre in Hampshire, did a great deal toward interesting the English in their own country and its natural beauties. Among his enthusiastic readers was the young Jane Austen, for according to her brother Henry: "At a very early age she was enamoured of Gilpin on the Picturesque. . . ."[16] Gilpin's *Observations, relative chiefly to Picturesque Beauty, made in the year 1776 in Several Parts of Great Britain, particularly the Highlands,* was published when Jane was thirteen, and she referred to it as "Gilpin's Tour to the Highlands"[17] in *Love and Freindship* (*sic*). Although Jane never visited Scotland, her interest in reading of far-off places, beginning with Gilpin's works, never palled, for books about travel were among her favorite reading matter.

Jane Austen's love of beautiful scenery and romantic ruins remained constant, but she never carried it to excess, and her *History of England,* finished in 1791 when she was fifteen, contains a fling at the affectation for dilapidated fanes that had become something of a cult during her childhood. In describing Henry VIII, Jane observed: ". . . nothing can be said in his vindication, but that his abolishing Religious Houses & leaving them to the ruinous depredations of time has been of infinite use to the landscape of England in general, which probably was a principal motive for his doing it. . . . "[18]

Jane's first recorded visit to Bath was in 1797, when she visited her maternal uncle and aunt, Mr. and Mrs. Leigh-Perrot, in the company of her mother and sister. The possibility that Jane visited Bath earlier, however, is suggested by a reference in her brief juvenile novel *Evelyn,* dating from around her sixteenth year. It includes a letter dated from a place called Westgate Buildings, the same address Jane used later for Mrs. Smith in *Persuasion.*[19] How Jane knew about Westgate Buildings when *Evelyn* was written is not known, but a glance at the history of her Cooper relations possibly contains the clue. Dr. Edward Cooper, who married Mrs. Austen's sister, Jane, was appointed Holcomb Prebendary of Wells Cathedral in 1770. Wells, then as now, was a part of the diocese of Bath and Wells. In November 1772, Jane's mother, in referring to the Coopers, wrote: ". . . they are quite settled in Bath."[20] As Cooper was a wealthy and cultivated man, it is possible he chose to reside in sophisticated Bath rather than in the then provincial backwater of nearby Wells. It is therefore possible Jane Austen visited him there as a child in the company of her parents, at which time she could have become acquainted with Westgate Buildings, then a much more fashionable address than it was when *Persuasion* was written.

An event that took place in December 1791 opened up an entirely new world to Jane Austen. Two days after Christmas of that year her brother Edward married Elizabeth Bridges, a daughter of Sir Brook Bridges of Goodnestone Park, Kent. The marriage was to prove of major importance to Jane, both in a social as well as a literary sense, for it gave her the entrée into the world of the wealthy landowners of East Kent, a society entirely different from the quiet country life of Steventon. Edward Austen and his wife resided first at Rowling, a Georgian house near Goodnestone Park, but later moved to Godmersham, where they lived in elegance and comfort. Elizabeth Austen's family was well connected, including close ties with the royal court and the higher ranks of the clergy. As her relations stayed frequently at Rowling or Godmersham, Jane, during several long visits to her brother's homes, was provided with suggestions and raw material for her mature fiction.

In the latter part of 1793, Jane and Cassandra attended a ball in Southampton while visiting their cousins, the Butler-Harrisons. The visit was apparently planned to coincide with the return of their brother Francis from the East Indies, in which case the home station vessel to which he had been assigned could have been anchored in nearby waters. Fifteen years later Jane attended a ball in the same place and wrote her sister: "It was the same room in which we danced 15 years ago! I thought it all over—& in spite of the shame of being so much older, felt with thankfulness that I was quite as happy now as then."[21]

In the autumn of 1794, Jane and Cassandra paid their first recorded visit to Edward at Rowling, passing through London on the way. No details of this Kentish visit are known other than the fact that Jane referred to it later in a letter as "our hot journey into Kent fourteen years ago."[22] Jane's visit to Rowling in 1796 is well documented, however, for five letters written to Cassandra at Steventon from London and Kent in August and September of that year have survived. Jane, then twenty, set out for Kent in the company of her brother Edward and others, with an overnight stop in London where they stayed at a hotel on Cork Street. In announcing her arrival there, Jane informed Cassandra gaily: "Here I am once more in this scene of dissipation and vice, and I begin already to find my morals corrupted."[23] Then, after recounting the details of her journey, she added: "We are to be at Astley's tonight, which I am glad of."[24] Jane was referring to the circus and equestrian exhibition known as Astley's Ampitheater of the Arts, then one of London's most popular places of entertainment. Opened in 1780 by Philip Astley, a spectacular equestrian performer and theatrical impresario, the theater had already burned down twice before the erection of the third one on the same site. By then Astley's was under the patronage of the Duke of York, and was a roofed-over structure consisting of a huge ampitheater, the largest stage in London, elaborate boxes for the more affluent, and a pit for the populace.[25]

Jane's visit coincided with the first performance in England of Signor Lionardi and his celebrated "Cabinet of Monkies,"[26] which had just arrived from Hamburg, where they had "for a long time been the admiration of the curious on the Continent." The entertainment was supplemented on that occasion with exhibitions on the slack rope, tightrope dancing, elaborate equestrian displays, a minuet danced by two horses, fireworks, and a comic pantomime called *Harlequin's Fancy,* a rewarding experience for the four shillings Jane's brother had paid for the box from which he and the rest of his party enjoyed the performance. As far as is known, Jane's 1796 visit to Astley's was the only one she ever made, but it left such an impression in her memory she used it later as the setting for one of the pivotal actions in *Emma.*

In the four letters Jane Austen wrote to her sister from Rowling in 1796, she unwittingly revealed the primary source for the country house comedy she later developed so brilliantly in her six completed novels—the leisurely but intellectually monotonous existence of the greater majority of the landed gentry, the wining and dining, balls, parties, and field sports, and even the concern of a poor but proud young woman like herself who was often hard pressed to meet the demands of servants accustomed by years of precedent to expect gratuities, or "vails" as they were then called, for services rendered to house guests.[27]

Notable, as far as *Pride and Prejudice* is concerned, was Jane's mention of having danced the "Boulangeries" at a ball she attended at that time.[28] Presumably she and her sister had learned this new French dance from their cousin Eliza during the Christmas festivities at Steventon in 1787, after Eliza had danced it for the first time that autumn at Tunbridge Wells.[29] By the time Jane was at Rowling in 1796, however, it was apparently so popular she may well have mentioned it in *First Impressions,* the earlier version of *Pride and Prejudice,* which she began that year after returning to Steventon. It is also worth noting that Rowling was only a few miles from Canterbury, where, according to a suggestion in one of Jane's 1796 letters, the presence of a "a new set of Officers" was then causing a flutter among the Lydia Bennets of East Kent.[30]

Since Jane had traveled from Hampshire in a family party, she experienced no difficulties in getting to Rowling. When the time came for her to leave, however, she ran into trouble. Her brother Henry, who had been there briefly, left for Yarmouth to consult his regimental physician, while her brother Francis, who was also of the party, had to depart abruptly when he received a summons to a new naval posting. Although Henry promised to return in time to escort Jane back to Steventon, he proved so dilatory she told Cassandra despairingly that depending on him was the equivalent of "waiting for Dead-men's Shoes."[31] But Henry came up with a scheme he felt would spare Jane the risk of depending on a stagecoach as a means of transportation, a mode of travel then frowned on for unaccompanied single women of her class. Henry was then courting a young woman named Mary Pearson, whose father was one of the officers of Greenwich Hospital. His suggestion was that Jane should meet Mary Pearson at Greenwich, after which the two young women would be escorted back to Steventon by Jane's father, who would come to London for that purpose.

The plan evidently appealed to Jane, who was anxious to return home, for she told Cassandra: "My father will be so good as to fetch home his prodigal Daughter from Town, I hope, unless he wishes me to walk the Hospitals, Enter at the Temple, or mount Guard at St. James [*sic*]."[32] Later, when it became evident it might not be convenient for Mary Pearson to meet her at Greenwich, Jane commented: ". . . for if the Pearsons were not at home, I should inevitably fall a Sacrifice to the arts of some fat Woman who would make me drunk with Small Beer."[33] This was apparently a wry reference either to the fate of Moll Hackabout as shown in the first plate of Hogarth's *The Harlot's Progress* or to the misfortune of countless other unaccompanied country girls who arrived in London only to be snared by procuresses. It is not known how Jane Austen got back to Steventon from Rowling, for the next thing definitely known concerning her appears in Cassandra Austen's memorandum on the dating of her sister's novels. In this Cassandra recorded: "First Impressions begun in Oct 1796 Finished in Augt 1797. Published afterwards, with alterations & contractions under the Title of Pride & Prejudice."[34]

About the time Jane began transforming *Elinor and Marianne* into *Sense and Sensibility* (1797), she and her sister accompanied their mother, who was not well, to Bath in November of that year on a visit to Mr. and Mrs. Leigh-Perrot, with whom they remained until just before Christmas. Little is known concerning what happened while Jane was in Bath. As *Susan*, her novel that later was published as *Northanger Abbey*, was written between 1798 and 1799, it is reasonable to assume that many of the Bath details in it were observed during Jane's visit there late in 1797. It is also possible the surviving set of David Hume's *The History of England*, bearing the inscription "Jane Austen/1797" in the first volume, was presented to her by her uncle during her visit to Bath in that year.[35] Other elegantly bound books from her library containing James Leigh-Perrot's armorial bookplate still survive, and although the Hume volumes do not contain his bookplates, the superior quality of the bindings agrees with that of other volumes her uncle presented to her. In any event, Jane apparently lost no time dipping into Hume's history, for in *Susan* (*Northanger Abbey*), which she began after her return to Steventon from Bath, she has Eleanor Tilney admit to having read "the productions of Mr. Hume" with pleasure.[36]

Late in 1797 another family event took place that exerted a far-reaching personal as well as literary influence on Jane Austen. Mrs. Thomas Knight, the adoptive mother of Jane's brother Edward, handed over her extensive Kentish and Hampshire properties to him and retired on an annual income of two thousand pounds to a house in Canterbury known as The White Friars. One of the first things Edward did after moving from Rowling to Godmersham was to invite his parents and sisters to spend a long summer holiday with him in his handsome Palladian house beside the river Stour. The party set out for Godmersham in August 1798 and remained there for two months. As far as is known, this was Jane Austen's first visit to Godmersham, one of the stateliest country houses in East Kent, begun in 1732 by Thomas Knight I, the father of the man who adopted Edward Austen.[37] Including this 1798 visit and the last one that she paid to Godmersham in 1813, Jane was the guest of her brother at least eight times. Although, according to her niece Anna Lefroy, she was not as popular with her Kentish relations as her sister Cassandra,[38] Jane enjoyed the good living and diversified company she encountered there.

Jane Austen's next known visit to Bath was probably more pleasant than the one she had made two years earlier. In 1799, Jane's wealthy brother Edward began to suffer from nervous complaints. His doctors at first recommended sea bathing for his troubles, and for a time it appeared he would go to some nearby seaside resort other than Brighton. Unlike her fictional Lydia Bennet, for whom "a visit to Brighton comprised every possibility of earthly happiness," Jane Austen, who had been asked to join the party, heartily disapproved of the scheme. Apparently Cassandra had also been included in the invitation, for Jane wrote: "I assure you that I dread the idea of going to [name unclear] as much as you do, but I am not without hopes that something may happen to prevent it."[39] Jane was not alone in her dislike of fashionable seaside pleasure grounds, for a contemporary, the Rev. John Styles, taking "the sea is His and He made it" as his text, had recently preached a well-publicized sermon on the moral traps of the seaside in general, and of Brighton in particular. In this he thundered: "Many young persons, now lost to society, have to attribute their ruin to a career of novel reading begun at a watering-place."[40] Jane, as an avid novel reader, would hardly have agreed with these sentiments, but she was obviously relieved when Edward's doctors later substituted Bath for the seaside place that was first considered.

Leaving the three youngest children at home, Edward and his wife and their two older children, Fanny and Edward, drove to Steventon in style in the family coach, picked up Mrs. Austen and Jane, and proceeded to Bath in a leisurely manner. After staying overnight at an inn at Devizes, where they dined on lobster and asparagus, with cheesecakes for the children,[41] they set out again the next morning for Bath, where Edward had taken comfortable lodgings at No. 13 Queen Square kept by "a fat woman in mourning" whose little black kitten delighted Jane by running about the staircase.[42] On the way they encountered three friends who provided Jane with a satirical touch for her first letter from Bath: "In Paragon we met Mrs. Foley and Mrs. Dowdeswell with her yellow shawl airing out, and at the bottom of Kingsdown Hill we met a gentleman in a buggy, who on minute examination, turned out to be Dr. Hall—and Dr. Hall in such very deep mourning that either his mother, his wife, or himself must be dead."[43]

Although the mineral waters of Bath did little to alleviate Edward's troubles, he nevertheless gained some compensation for the long journey from Kent by buying a handsome matched pair of black coach horses for sixty guineas each on the recommendations of an old friend, Mr. Evelyn. This gave Jane an opportunity to remind Cassandra that she had not forgotten *Gulliver's Travels* by commenting: ". . . & if the judgement of a Yahoo can ever be depended on, I suppose it may now, for I believe Mr. Evelyn has all his life thought more of Horses than of anything else."[44] Meanwhile, the Austen party reveled in the delights of Bath, attended a gala outdoor concert at Sydney Gardens in honor of the king's birthday, saw Kotzebue's drama *The Birth-Day* and the "pleasing spectacle of Blue Beard" at the theater,[45] and made purchases at the well-stocked shops. In the meantime, Jane's friend Martha Lloyd had expressed a desire to reread *First Impressions,* a request Cassandra conveyed to Jane, who replied: "I would not let Martha read 'First Impressions' again upon any account, and am very glad that I did not leave it in your power. She is very cunning, but I saw through her design; she means to publish it from memory, and one more perusal must enable her to do it."[46] The phrase "I did not leave it in your power" poses an interesting speculation. Could Jane have taken the manuscript of *First Impressions* with her to Bath for further emendations in spare moments?

A few days after this was written the Austen party prepared to leave Bath. Before doing so, however, Jane called at No. 1 Paragon Buildings, where her uncle, James Leigh-Perrot, made her a present of another set of elegantly bound books: Oliver Goldsmith's *A History of the Earth, and Animated Nature,* in the first volume of which she wrote "Jane Austen/1799."[47] Less than two months after her arrival home, Jane Austen's family was horrified to learn that Mrs. Leigh-Perrot had been arrested on a charge of stealing a card of white lace of the value of twenty shillings from a Bath haberdashery shop. The details of Mrs. Leigh-Perrot's trial and acquittal at Taunton in March 1800 need not be repeated here. But it should be mentioned to her credit that even though Jane Austen did not like her aunt, the latter considerately saved Jane from what undoubtedly would have been a very painful experience when she refused to permit Mrs. Austen to send her daughters to Ilchester while their aunt was remanded in custody awaiting trial.[48]

Jane Austen's visit to her friend Martha Lloyd, at Ibthorpe, a few miles west of Steventon, in November 1800, was ended by one of the most traumatic experiences of her life. On her return home Jane learned that her parents had decided to leave Steventon, where she had spent her first twenty-five years, and move to Bath, a decision that caused her great unhappiness. From then until early in May 1801, when she and her mother left Steventon for Bath, with a stop at Ibthorpe on the way, Jane remained at home to help with the preparations for the move. By prearrangement, Jane and her mother stayed with the Leigh-Perrots in Paragon at Bath while awaiting the arrival of her father and Cassandra.[49] Meanwhile, as a "desperate walker," Jane explored the lovely open countryside surrounding Bath to escape from the boredom of the Leigh-Perrots' staid household.

In recording the details of one of these excursions, she wrote:

> The friendship between Mrs. Chamberlayne & me which you predicted has already taken place, for we shake hands whenever we meet. Our grand walk to Weston was again fixed for Yesterday,

> & was accomplished in a very striking manner; Every one of the party declined it under some pretense or other except our two selves, (&) we had therefore a tete a tete: but *that* we should equally have had after the first two yards, had half the Inhabitants of Bath set off with us.—It would have amused you to see our progress;—we went by Sion Hill, & returned across the fields;—in climbing a hill Mrs. Chamberlayne is very capital; I could with difficulty keep pace with her—yet would not flinch for the world.—On plain ground I was quite her equal—and so we posted away under a fine hot sun, She without any parasol or any shade to her hat, stopping for nothing, & crossing the Church Yard at Weston with as much expedition as if we were afraid of being buried alive.—[50]

After Jane's father and sister arrived in Bath in early June, the combined family party set out for Sidmouth, an ancient fishing village on the south coast that had become increasingly popular as a seaside resort since George III had stayed there briefly in 1781.[51] As Sidmouth is in Devon, Jane's holiday there may have provided her later with background material for the final revision of *Sense and Sensibility*.[52] The town is backed by the rolling hills of the Sid valley, then topped with open commons, which Jane perhaps transformed into the breezy downs where Marianne Dashwood and Willoughby met for the first time. Also, as a "desperate walker," Jane conceivably could have discovered the Georgian cottage near Sidmouth now called Rose Hill that some believe to have been the original of Barton Cottage in the novel. Still another excursion from Sidmouth toward Honiton (mentioned in *Sense and Sensibility*) would have brought her to Sand Barton, the late Tudor mansion of the Huish family, which could either have suggested the name for her fictional Barton Park or have served as an inspiration for Allenham Court. The important point about Sidmouth, however, is that it was either there or at some other seaside resort that she visited between 1801 and 1804 that Jane Austen met and presumably fell in love with an unidentified suitor, the only man her sister ever considered worthy of her.

By October 1801 the Austens had returned to Bath. Early the next summer they were again in Devon when they visited Dawlish and probably Teignmouth, which would have provided Jane with further topographical observations for the final revision of *Sense and Sensibility*. Meanwhile, the Peace of Amiens, which became effective in March 1802, had brought many British naval officers home from active service at sea. One of these was Jane's brother Charles, who took his parents, and possibly his sisters, on a tour of Wales from which they returned in mid-August.[53] The possibility that Jane and her sister accompanied Charles and their parents to Wales at that time is supported by Jane's niece Caroline Austen. Writing of that period of her aunt's life Caroline Austen said: "They were in Devonshire, and in Wales."[54] Further evidence is also furnished in a letter written by Anna Lefroy in 1862: "She [i.e., Jane] was once I think at Tenby—and once they went as far north as Barmouth."[55]

According to Sir Egerton Brydges, Jane Austen was at Ramsgate in the summer of 1803, presumably visiting her brother Francis, then in charge of the North Foreland unit of the Sea Fencibles, a home guard raised to repel any attempted invasion by Napoleon's Grand Army, then encamped across the English Channel at Boulogne. Later in November of the same year Jane and Cassandra were at Lyme Regis. Writing to Cassandra later, Jane compared a recent fire in Southampton with one that had taken place in Lyme Regis on November 3, 1803, which both had presumably witnessed.[56] It will be remembered it was at that time of the year she later sent the party from Uppercross to the same place in *Persuasion,* thereby enabling her to describe off-season Lyme Regis with authority.

In the summer of 1804, Jane and Cassandra Austen and their parents joined Henry and his wife for "rambles" throughout southwestern England, ending at Lyme Regis in early September. During that summer one of the two authentic contemporary likenesses of Jane Austen was painted by her sister.[57] The first, bearing no date or signature, is the well-known bust portrait now in the National Portrait Gallery in London. The second and lesser known watercolor is signed "C.E.A. 1804." This drawing shows a back view of Jane, dressed in blue, wearing a blue bonnet and seated on a grassy knoll. Unfortunately the bonnet hides Jane's face, but Sir Egerton Brydges's assertion that Jane's cheeks were "a little too full"[58] is borne out by the generous curve of her left cheek that Cassandra included in her sketch. This drawing is the one referred to by Anna Lefroy in a letter written in August 1862: "I would give a good deal, that is as much as I could afford, for a sketch which Aunt Cassandra made of her on one of their expeditions—sitting down out of doors on a hot day with her bonnet strings untied."[59]

The drawing was eventually acquired by Anna Lefroy and was inserted by her in the existing volume of family history now known as the Lefroy Manuscript.

It was fortunate that Jane Austen and her parents declined to accompany Cassandra and the Henry Austens when they left Lyme Regis for Weymouth, for the decision was responsible for one of Jane's best letters, written on September 14, 1804, in which she told her sister, among other things, it had "been all the fashion this week in Lyme"[60] to have a fever, Jane being one of the sufferers. But that did not prevent her from enjoying the sea bathing, although she felt unreasonably tired afterward. In the meantime, she assured Cassandra she was doing her best to fill her sister's accustomed role as the family housekeeper by attending to "the general dirtiness of the house & furniture & all its inhabitants."[61] Becoming more specific, Jane added: "I endeavour as far as I can to supply your place & be useful, & keep things in order. I detect dirt in the water-decanter as fast as I can & give the Cook physic which she throws off her stomach."[62] Later, Jane praised the Austens' manservant, James, calling him "quite an Uncle Toby's annuity to us,"[63] thereby revealing her familiarity with Sterne's *Tristram Shandy.*

Jane, then twenty-eight, and therefore beyond that period of her development when her desire for dancing "was not suffering under the insatiable appetite of fifteen,"[64] was also singled out as a prospective partner one evening when she visited the Assembly Rooms by a presumptuous visitor whom she described as "a new odd-looking man who had been eyeing me for some time, and at last, without any introduction, asked me if I meant to dance again." To this she added: "I think he must be Irish by his ease, and because I imagine him to belong to the honbl [*sic*] Barnwalls, who are the son, and the son's wife of an Irish viscount, bold queer-looking people, just fit to be quality at Lyme."[65]

A few months after the Austens returned to Bath, Jane's father died, leaving Mrs. Austen and her two daughters temporarily in straitened circumstances. Family loyalty came to the rescue, and Mrs. Austen's annual income was fixed at £460 by yearly contributions from four of her sons.[66] This assurance enabled Jane and her mother and sister to continue to travel on a modest scale. Even so, money was never in great supply, for during the summer after her father's death, when Jane was staying at Godmersham, she complained in a letter to Cassandra, then staying at nearby Goodnestone Farm: "As I find by looking into my affairs, that instead of being very rich I am likely to be very poor, I cannot afford more than ten shillings for Sackree [the Godmersham nursemaid]; but as we are to meet in Canterbury I need not have mentioned this. It is well however, to prepare you for the sight of a Sister sunk in poverty, that it may not overcome your Spirits."[67] This was badinage, of course, for other letters written by Jane at the same time reveal she and her sister stayed at Worthing, a seaside resort on the Sussex coast twelve miles west of Brighton with their mother and Martha Lloyd on their way back to Bath.[68] Worthing's popularity had begun in 1798 when the Princess Amelia, the youngest and favorite daughter of George III, had been sent there for the benefit of her health. Unlike its bawdy neighbor, Brighton, Worthing made a point of discouraging the rakish and rowdy crowds that flocked to the latter place. If a print called "The Sands at Worthing," from a painting by John Nison, issued in 1808, is accurate, the place was notable only for a few bathing machines and a cluster of boarding houses—the equivalent of seaside Sanditon, described in Jane's last, unfinished novel.[69]

Following the death of her husband in early 1805, Mrs. Austen and her daughters moved from one set of furnished lodgings to another in Bath before finally leaving the city on July 2, 1806, going first to Clifton, a small spa near Bristol. From there they proceeded to Adlestrop in Gloucestershire for a visit that was to bear fruit when Jane wrote *Mansfield Park*.

In June 1799, before Jane Austen moved from Steventon to Bath in 1801, she and her sister had visited their mother's first cousin, the Rev. Thomas Leigh, at Adlestrop. The trip was recalled in a letter, written to her sister in May 1801, in which Jane commented on the renewal of her acquaintance with a Mrs. Chamberlayne who "remembers us in Gloucestershire when we were very charming young women."[70] Mrs. Chamberlayne was the wife of Edmund Chamberlayne of Maugersbury, Gloucestershire, a cousin of the Rev. Thomas Leigh.[71]

At the time of Jane's two earlier known visits to Gloucestershire in 1794 and 1799, the old formal gardens at Adlestrop House still included "clipped yew walks, a summer house on a mound to the south, an orangery and a bowling green, said to be one of the best in England," which had been laid out by William Leigh, one of her maternal ancestors during the seventeenth century. By the time of Jane's 1806 visit, however, all traces of these old-fashioned gardens had been swept away by Humphry Repton, the fashionable landscape gardener. Repton, under the guidance of the Rev. Thomas Leigh, who prided himself on being a great "improver," had transformed the grounds and garden at Adlestrop House into a fastidiously landscaped prospect. While this work was in progress, Jane's clerical cousin had also remodeled the Adlestrop rectory garden into a semblance of the plan later suggested by Henry Crawford for the fictional Thornton Lacey in *Mansfield Park,* a change Jane would have observed during her 1806 visit to Adlestrop. Since all of these changes at Adlestrop were spelled out in Repton's *Observations on the Theory and Practice of Landscape Gardening* (1803), it is possible Jane Austen became acquainted with this work in the library of the Rev. Thomas Leigh while she was his guest.[72]

Meanwhile, while she and her mother and sister were guests at Adlestrop rectory in 1806, the Rev. Thomas Leigh was notified of the death of his (and Mrs. Austen's) distant cousin, the Hon. Mary Leigh, whose brother, Edward, the fifth and last Lord Leigh of the first creation, had provided in his will that his handsome estate, Stoneleigh Abbey in Warwickshire, should pass to "the first and nearest of his male kindred of his blood" who was alive at the time of his sister's death. As the Rev. Thomas Leigh, who eventually became master of the princely estate, was one of the three claimants, he set out immediately for Stoneleigh, accompanied by Jane and her mother and sister. By Jane's time, the older parts of Stoneleigh Abbey, which had been in her mother's family since 1561, had been dwarfed by the erection during the early eighteenth century of a magnificent three-story classical mansion filled with family memorabilia and many paintings and works of art brought back by earlier Leighs from the Grand Tour.[73]

This has led to the supposition that Jane later used some of the details of Stoneleigh as archetypes of Mr. Rusworth's Sotherton in *Mansfield Park.* Certain features of Stoneleigh, particularly the position of the village church and the Leigh almshouses in relation to the mansion itself, and the mahogany-pewed, rococo plaster-decorated family chapel, are certainly too close to the fictional Sotherton to be ignored. What is more, much of the formal garden, the wilderness, and the bowling greens that are known to have been at Stoneleigh during Jane's 1806 visit, but were later swept away by Humphry Repton, could have provided her with further topographical details for her novel.[74] Repton's work at Adlestrop was already familiar to Jane from her visit there before she visited Stoneleigh. As the new owner had immediately enlisted Repton's advice for a fee of five guineas a day on how to improve his princely inheritance, conversations with her clerical cousin concerning his "improvements" and the cost involved could also have given Jane useful facts for *Mansfield Park*, begun in February 1811.

For some years Jane Austen's cousin, the Rev. Edward Cooper, had tried to induce her and her mother and sister to visit him at Hamstall-Ridware in Staffordshire, where he was rector, and in 1806, she and her mother and sister decided to accept the invitation.[75] After remaining for more than a week at Stoneleigh Abbey, from which they took excursions to Warwick Castle and the ruins of Kenilworth Castle,[76] they set out for Staffordshire on August 14, 1806,[77] remaining there for about five weeks. Jane was already well acquainted with the route by hearsay as her brother Edward had taken it in 1791 when he and his adoptive parents, the Knights of Godmersham, and a party of friends had made a tour of the Lake District.[78] The route was also the one that Jane's fictional Elizabeth Bennet and the Gardiners later took in *Pride and Prejudice,* all of which serves to introduce an interesting digression.

In 1958, Elizabeth Jenkins, one of Jane Austen's more distinguished biographers, saw a notice outside a first-floor room of the Rutland Arms in Bakewell in Derbyshire, three miles from Chatsworth, the home of the Dukes of Devonshire. The notice claimed Jane Austen had stayed at the inn in 1811 when she was revising *Pride and Prejudice* and had made that particular room the scene of two episodes in her novel. Miss Jenkins was surprised at the announcement and telegraphed R. W. Chapman, the Jane Austen scholar, asking if it were true. Chapman replied: "No evidence that she was ever north of the Trent." This statement is in error, for Hamstall-Ridware is definitely north of the Trent. Despite Chapman's assertion, however, Miss Jenkins did an excellent job of demolishing the Rutland Arms story, for after Jane Austen's 1806 trip to Hamstall-Ridware, her travels never again took her north of the Trent. Miss Jenkins then ended her otherwise well-reasoned article, "Birth of a

Legend," in the Jane Austen Society Report for 1965 with the statement: ". . . that the Committee of the Jane Austen Society regard the notice, long, confident and circumstantial as it is, as entirely without foundation."[79]

Even so, as the Austens were at Hamstall-Ridware for almost two months, it is reasonable to surmise they were not confined to the rectory grounds for the duration of their stay. It is therefore possible that their host would have arranged several excursions in his carriage to enable them to visit the more celebrated scenic and architectural attractions of the area. Since Chatsworth has always been the most splendid attraction in the neighborhood they could have been taken there to admire its well-known magnificence, even though it is more than forty miles from Hamstall-Ridware. With this theory in mind, Donald Greene of the University of Southern California has spent considerable time in an on-the-spot investigation of the possibility that Jane Austen might have visited Chatsworth during the late summer of 1806, at which time she presumably garnered sufficient information concerning the lay of the land to use later in describing Pemberley, the fictitious home of Fitzwilliam Darcy, the hero of *Pride and Prejudice.*

Many of the topographical details described in Jane's novel, as Greene has shown in his *The Original of Pemberley* (1980), tally with the layout of the grounds and park at Chatsworth, not only then but now.[80] This is not meant to suggest that Jane Austen used Chatsworth as the exact model for Darcy's home, however, for even before it was greatly enlarged during the nineteenth century, Chatsworth was a palace, whereas Pemberley was merely a handsome and elegantly appointed country gentleman's seat. Even so, if Jane Austen did visit Chatsworth in 1806, she could have later utilized selective details of the great house, and the surrounding landscape she observed at that time, in describing fictitious Pemberley without straining the credulity of her readers, as far as Darcy's wealth and position were concerned. In the absence of any written record or oral tradition in either the Austen or the Cooper families to prove that the Chatsworth expedition took place, Greene's theory can be entertained only as a plausible suggestion. Nevertheless, as Jane Austen, despite Chapman's categorical denial, had definitely traveled north of the Trent, and as Hamstall-Ridware was within driving distance from Chatsworth, it is reasonable to assume that

Edward Cooper might have included it among the places to which he took his aunt and cousins while they were his guests in 1806, a theory that can easily be postulated without recourse to the highly questionable Rutland Arms tourist tale.

While Mrs. Austen and her daughters lived in Southampton (1806-09), Jane's travels seem to have been limited to Hampshire visits, a stay in London with the Henry Austens at Brompton, and a visit in the company of her brother James and family to Godmersham in 1808. While she was in London staying with the Henry Austens, Jane "saw the ladies go to Court"[81] for the celebration of George III's seventieth birthday. The event was described in the *Annual Register* thus: "Their majesties received the junior part of the royal family at Buckingham-house in the morning, where they breakfasted, and congratulated their royal parents on the return of the day. Soon after one o'clock, the queen and the princesses prepared to leave Buckingham-house, and they arrived at St. James's at quarter past two, escorted by a party of life guards."[82]

As for Jane's 1808 visit to Godmersham, her surviving letters reveal that the time was spent in a constant round of visits to and from the local gentry, excursions to Canterbury, and hospitality at home. Mrs. Knight, Edward Austen's adoptive mother, who was still living at The White Friars in Canterbury, invited Jane to visit her while she was in Kent, including "the usual Fee, & all the usual Kindness"[83] in her letter in order that Jane might have sufficient pocket money while she was her guest. Jane Austen undoubtedly appreciated Mrs. Knight's generosity, but it still hurt her pride to have to accept gratuities from anyone, causing her to comment later in a letter on a similar occasion: ". . . but till I have a travelling purse of my own, I must submit to such things."[84] Even so, Jane accepted Mrs. Knight's well-intentioned "fee," telling Cassandra: "I sent my answer by them [i.e., Jane's brothers James and Edward] to Mrs. Knight, my double acceptance of her note & her invitation, which I wrote without much effort, for I was rich—& the rich are always respectable, whatever be their stile [*sic*] of writing."[85]

In 1809, Mrs. Austen decided to move from Southampton to Chawton in Hampshire where her son Edward had provided a permanent home for her daughters and herself. Before taking up their residence there, however, the Austen party set out for a summer vacation at Godmersham, presumably with a brief stop along the way at Great Bookham in Surrey, where Jane's godfather, the Rev. Samuel Cooke, was vicar and where the Austens had made an earlier visit in 1799. Cooke had married Cassandra Leigh, a first cousin of Jane Austen's mother, and he and his wife were great friends of Fanny Burney, (Madame d'Arblay), one of Jane Austen's favorite novelists, who had lived at nearby Camilla Cottage from 1793 to 1797.[86]

Since the d'Arblays moved away from Great Bookham before Jane's first visit in 1799, it is impossible to say if she ever met her godfather's celebrated literary neighbor. But as *Emma,* written between January 1814 and March 1815, is set in Surrey, and more particularly in that area of the county where the Cookes lived, and as Jane Austen is definitely known to have been their guest in 1814, it is reasonable to surmise that much of the local color for *Emma,* including the setting for the crucial scene at Box Hill, was noted by Jane while she was a guest at Great Bookham vicarage.[87]

During the eight years that Jane Austen lived at Chawton she was actively engaged in writing. Her travels therefore were more or less limited to visits to London to consult with her brother Henry, who handled the business transactions relative to the publication of *Sense and Sensibility, Pride and Prejudice, Mansfield Park,* and *Emma,* and to her last visit to Godmersham during the latter part of 1813. On that journey Jane accompanied her brother Edward and his family from Chawton to Kent, and sent an amusing account of the large party's progress to her brother Francis, then at sea: "We left Chawton on ye 14th,—spent two entire days in Town and arrived here on ye 17th.—My Br [Brother], Fanny, Lizzy, Marianne & I composed this division of the Family, & filled his Carriage, inside & out.—Two post chaises under the escort of George conveyed eight more across the Country, the Chair brought two, two others came on horseback & the rest by the Coach—and so by one means or another we all are removed.—It puts me in mind of the account of St. Paul's shipwreck, when all are said by different means to reach the shore in safety."[88]

Earlier in the same year when Jane traveled up to London with her brother Henry, she was particularly struck by the beauty of the magnificent garden created by William Kent at Esher Place in Surrey, which Horace Walpole had earlier called "Parnassus, as Watteau would have painted it."[89] Jane's description was less flamboyant but equally enthusiastic. She wrote to Cassandra: "I was very much pleased with the country in general. Between Guildford and Ripley I thought it particularly pretty, also about Painshill & everywhere else; and from a Mr. Spicer's grounds at Esher, which we walked into before our dinner, the views were beautiful. I cannot say what we did *not* see, but I should think there could not be a wood, or meadow, or palace, or a remarkable spot in England that was not spread out before us on one side or the other."[90]

Jane Austen's visits to London between 1809 and 1815 were responsible for many *douceurs* (as she liked to refer to them) in the way of sophisticated pleasures, but there was one experience she was invited to share that she politely declined—a meeting with Madame de Staël. The events leading up to the publication of *Mansfield Park* were responsible for the invitation to meet the formidable Frenchwoman. It could not have been "after the publication" of the novel, however, as reported later by Henry Austen, for it is a matter of record that Madame de Staël left London for Paris on March 8, 1814, the day before *Mansfield Park* was published.[91] Nevertheless, the anecdote is worth noting, not only to correct a mistake that has appeared in earlier biographies of Jane Austen, but also to indicate she was by then not quite so unknown an author as has previously been suggested.

As far as can be ascertained, at some time between the completion of *Mansfield Park* soon after June 1813 and its publication on May 9, 1814, Jane Austen was invited to meet Madame de Staël, who had arrived in London in the summer of 1813, accompanied by her son and daughter and the handsome young husband whose hand, but not his name, she had accepted. She was immediately taken up by society and was such a sensation that Lady Holland, the great Whig hostess, told Thomas Creevey, the political diarist: "The great wonder of the time is Madame de Staël. She is surrounded by all the curious, and every sentence she utters is caught up and repeated with various commentaries."[92]

Shortly after Madame de Staël's arrival in England, Sir James Mackintosh, the Scottish philosopher and historian, who was a great admirer of Jane Austen's novels, recommended that the distinguished visitor read *Pride and Prejudice,* which had been published in January 1813. After reading the novel, Madame de Staël called it "*vulgaire,*" a criticism that disturbed Mackintosh, who later wrote:

". . . there is no book which that word would suit so little. . . . Every village could furnish matter for a novel to Jane Austen. She did not need the common materials for a novel—strong passion, or strong incident."[93]

Jane Austen's knowledge of Madame de Staël was not confined to the latter's 1813-14 visit to England, however, for the formidable Frenchwoman had earlier been a near neighbor of Jane's godfather, the Rev. Samuel Cooke, when she lived with a group of aristocratic French emigrés at Juniper Hill near Great Bookham, Surrey, at the time Louis XVI and Marie Antoinette were guillotined in Paris.[94] It is therefore likely that Jane had heard a good deal about the French writer from the Cooke family. Jane is also known to have been familiar with at least one of Madame de Staël's novels, for in 1808, while living at Southampton, she had recommended that a friend read *Corinne, or Italy* (1807), which had recently been published in two English translations.[95]

Although Henry Austen's account of his sister's refusal to meet the woman whom Byron characterized as one who "writes octavos and *talks* folios"[96] is somewhat pompous, it is nevertheless the only surviving account of the incident:

> When Miss Austen was on a visit to London soon after the publication of Mansfield Park, a nobleman, personally unknown to her, but who had good reason for considering her to be the authoress of that work, was desirous of her joining a literary circle at his home. He communicated his wish in the politest manner, through a mutual friend, adding, what his Lordship thought would be an irresistible enducement, that the celebrated Madam de Staël would be of the party. Miss Austen immediately declined the invitation. To her truly delicate mind such a display would have given her pain instead of pleasure.[97]

By the time Henry wrote this, sixteen years after Jane's death, he had become a deadly serious Evangelical clergyman, so we may regard the last two sentences with some reservations. Although Jane Austen undoubtedly had her own reasons for not wanting to encounter the redoubtable French writer, it is probable they were not as censorious as Henry Austen's account would indicate.

After 1815, during which Jane Austen spent a good deal of time in London prior to the publication of *Emma,* her traveling days were numbered. In 1816 she became seriously ill, and Cassandra accompanied her to Cheltenham in hopes of a cure from its spa waters. In commenting on this last journey of Jane Austen, her niece Caroline wrote: "In May, 1816, my two Aunts went for a few weeks to Cheltenham—I am able to ascertain the date of this and some similar occurrences by a reference to old pocket books [i.e., diaries] in my possession—It was a journey in those days, to go from Hampshire into Gloucestershire and their first stage was to Steventon."[98] In speaking of her aunt's return journey to Chawton, Caroline continued: "They made also a short stay at Mr. Fowle's at Kintbury, I believe *that* was, as they returned—Mrs. Dexter, then Mary Jane Fowle, told me afterwards that Aunt Jane went over the old places, and recalled old recollections associated with them, in a very particular manner—looked at them, my cousin thought, as if she never expected to see them again."[99]

Even so, after completing *Persuasion* in July 1816, Jane Austen made an effort to begin a new novel, which her family believed she meant to call *The Brothers,* but which is now known as *Sanditon.*[100] Putting aside the sustained romantic tone of *Persuasion,* Jane reverted to the satirical vein of her earliest writings in her last composition, which, apart from any love element that it might have contained, appears to have been intended as a satire on hypochondria and the seaside towns that claimed to be health resorts. Jane was thereby agreeing with her favorite moral poet, William Cowper, when she chose the shore as the setting for her proposed novel:

Your prudent grandmammas, ye modern belles,
Content with Bristol, Bath and Tunbridge Wells,
When health required it would consent to roam
Else more attached to pleasures found at home.
But now alike, gay widow, virgin, wife
Ingenious to diversify dull life,
In coaches, chaises, caravans, and hoys,
Fly to the coast for daily, nightly joys,
And all, impatient of dry land agree
With one consent to rush into the sea.[101]

Apparently Jane Austen was prepared to augment Cowper's satire with her own seaside observations made earlier at Sidmouth, Dawlish, Teignmouth, Lyme Regis, and Worthing. But her last novel had to be abandoned early in 1817 shortly before she took her last journey in May 1817, when she went to Winchester in the company of her sister in search of better medical attention. She died there on July 18, 1817, and was buried in Winchester Cathedral, where her grave is now visited annually by admirers who travel there from all over the world to pay her homage.

CHAPTER

10

Jane Austen and Religion

Jane Austen wrote three prayers for the use of her family's evening devotions. The manuscript, inscribed in Cassandra's handwriting "Prayers composed by my ever dear sister Jane," contains the following: "Above all other blessings oh! God, for ourselves and our fellow-creatures, we implore thee to quicken our sense of thy mercy in the redemption of the world, of the value of that holy religion in which we have been brought up, that we may not, by our own neglect, throw away the salvation thou hast given us, nor be Christians only in name."[1] This petition, characteristic of others uttered throughout the three prayers in question, is in direct contrast to statements made by insensitive critics who have accused Jane of being indifferent in religious matters, of giving merely a formal allegiance to Christianity, or of being "a profoundly irreligious woman."[2]

Nothing could be further from the truth. From her childhood until her death, Jane Austen's life and religious beliefs were governed by the rites and teachings of the Anglican Church. The basic tenets of Christianity, with a firm but quiet insistence on the superiority of the seven Christian virtues over the seven deadly sins are amply reflected in her novels as well as in her surviving letters. As Jane herself once expressed it: "Wisdom is better than Wit, & in the long run will certainly have the laugh on her side."[3]

Unfortunately for Jane Austen's religious reputation, her brother Henry, "an earnest preacher of the evangelical school," included this ponderous evaluation of her spiritual life in the biographical sketch he wrote immediately after his sister's death: "She was thoroughly religious and devout; fearful of giving offense to God, and incapable of feeling it toward any fellow creature."[4] This pietistic appraisal, admittedly written when Henry was grieving over Jane's untimely death, continued to be believed by many of her admirers until the publication of Jane Austen's letters revealed her as a more fallible human being.

As a daughter and a granddaughter of conservative Anglican clergymen, Jane Austen belonged to a High Church Tory family that believed in rendering unto Caesar the things that are Caesar's, and unto God the things that are God's, the commonly accepted approach to religion at that time. Although Methodism had gained a considerable foothold among the lower classes, as well as influenced a few of the theatrically pious in high places, its zeal during Jane's girlhood had not made much of an impression on such contented members of the Established Church as the Austens. Nor had it caused them to question their enjoyment of the good things of this world while hopefully preparing for those of the next. That Jane Austen was well instructed in orthodox Christianity and firmly believed its tenets is apparent from a more plausible statement from Henry Austen's biographical sketch: "On serious subjects she was well instructed, both by reading and meditation, and her opinions accorded strictly with those of our Established Church."[5] That Jane's religious thinking became more serious as she grew older is also apparent from the letters of her maturity.

Jane Austen's religious reticence was succinctly summed up by Richard Whately, Archbishop of Dublin, in a review of *Northanger Abbey* and *Persuasion* in the *Quarterly Review* for January 1821: "Miss Austen has the merit (in our judgment most essential) of being evidently a Christian writer: a merit which is much enhanced, both on the score of good taste, and of practical utility, by her religion being not at all obtrusive."[6] Whately's perceptive observation was later emphasized by Jane Austen's nephew in the *Memoir:* "They [the novels] certainly were not written to support any theory or inculcate any particular moral, except indeed the great moral which is to be equally gathered from an observation of the course of actual life—namely, the superiority of high over low principles, and of greatness over littleness of mind."[7]

Jane Austen's youth coincided with that period of Anglican history during which a great deal of laxity existed. Many of the clergy paid curates pittances to take their services in country parishes while they (i.e., the actual incumbents) lived in comfort elsewhere. Many clergymen were also pluralists (i.e., holders of several livings at the same time), a category that included Jane Austen's father, who was simultaneously rector of the adjoining parishes of Steventon and Deane. In the Rev. George Austen's case, however, there seems to have been no unseemly irregularities. He lived among his parishioners and set them a good example by his kindness and upright behavior in the manner Sir Thomas Bertram in *Mansfield Park* believed a conscientious rector should do.

In the second number of *The Loiterer* (February 7, 1789), Jane's eldest brother, James, himself a keen rider to hounds and soon to take Holy Orders, published this fictitious advertisement: "Wanted—a Curacy in a good sporting country, near a good pack of fox-hounds, and in a sociable neighborhood; it must have a good house and stables, and a few acres of meadow ground would be very agreeable—To prevent trouble, the stipend must not be less than 80 pounds. The Advertiser has no objection to undertaking three, four, or five Churches of a Sunday, but will not engage where there is any weekly duty. Whoever has such a one to dispose of, may suit themselves by sending a line, directed to A. B. to be left at the *Turf Coffee House,* or the gentleman may be spoken with, any tuesday [*sic*] morning at Tattersall's Betting Room."[8]

Granted, this was a satire, but there were rectors within Jane Austen's circle of acquaintance who saw nothing wrong with combining their clerical duties with more worldly matters. Notable among these was the Rev. Charles Powlett, a sporting parson who had sown a good deal of wild oats while at Cambridge, after which he became a member of the fast set surrounding the Prince of Wales.[9] On a more dignified but still worldly level, was the social-minded Rev. Isaac Peter George Lefroy of Ashe, in whose hospitable home Jane Austen was a frequent visitor from earliest childhood.[10] There was also the clerical Fowle family of Kintbury, one of whose members, the Rev. Fulwar-Craven Fowle, a former pupil of Jane Austen's father, was praised by George III for being the best preacher, rider to hounds, and cavalry officer in Berkshire.[11] These, and many other clerical connections of the Austens' during Jane's early womanhood, were sociable men of varying spiritual orientation who saw no inconsistency in combining riding to hounds and attending dancing assemblies or convivial dinner parties with their more serious duties on Sunday.

Like all other professional classes, the clergy of Jane Austen's day included the dedicated as well as those who were little credit to their calling, and these nuances were not lost on Jane Austen during her formative years. It was therefore from personal observation, rather than imagination, that she was later enabled to create a representative fictitious portrait gallery of the Anglican clergy in her novels, ranging from the exemplary Edmund Bertram (one of her favorite characters) and the gluttonous Dr. Grant in *Mansfield Park,* to the conscientious Dr. Shirley in *Persuasion,* the witty Henry Tilney in *Northanger Abbey,* the obsequious Mr. Collins in *Pride and Prejudice,* and the odious Mr. Elton in *Emma.*

Apart from her private baptism at home on December 17, 1775, and her public christening in Steventon Church on April 5, 1776,[12] nothing is known concerning Jane Austen's religious activities during her childhood. As a rector's daughter she would have been expected to attend the Sunday services of Morning and Evening Prayer in his church as well as participate in evening devotions at home. That Jane and all of the Austen children were carefully trained to behave reverently in church can be presumed from the fact that in an age when most worshippers stood during the reading of the prayers in church, her brother Francis was later singled out for comment as "*the* officer who knelt in church."[13] This precision as far as ecclesiastical formality is concerned no doubt stemmed from the fact that Jane's mother came from a family that stressed the niceties of ritual over the less ceremonious practices then in vogue. Mrs. Austen's uncle, Dr. Theophilus Leigh, Master of Balliol College, Oxford, was considered singular because he "not only bowed to the Altar on entering and leaving the college chapel, but at his country living of Huntspill . . . he always wore *a distinctive vestment*"—presumably a cope—practices that were then considered extreme manifestations of High Church Anglicanism.[14]

As a born humorist, Jane Austen did not neglect the opportunity to notice any aberrant behavior on the part of worshippers in her father's church, however, for later, in looking back on those times, she recalled one parishioner thus:

> *Happy the lab'rer in his Sunday clothes!*
> *In light-drab coat, smart waistcoat, well-darned hose,*
> *And hat upon his head, to church he goes;*
> *As oft, with conscious pride, he downward throws*
> *A glance upon the ample cabbage rose*
> *That, stuck in button-hole, regales his nose,*
> *He envies not the gayest London beaux.*
> *In church he takes his seat among the rows,*
> *Pays to the place the reverence he owes,*
> *Likes best the prayers whose meaning least he knows,*
> *Lists to the sermon in a softening doze,*
> *And rouses joyous at the welcome close.*[15]

The first mention of religion in Jane Austen's writings occurs in *The History of England,* dating from 1791, when she was fifteen. Like most of her Leigh ancestors, Jane was an ardent admirer of the Stuarts, a devotion that apparently had been enhanced in her case by a recent reading of *Mary Queen of Scots Vindicated* (1787), by John Whitaker, an author mentioned by name in her burlesque history. Jane was then enamored of the more romantic aspects of Catholicism, but she did not let her enthusiasm run away with her. In writing of James I, she said: "As I am myself partial to the roman catholic religion, it is with infinite regret that I am obliged to blame the Behaviour of any Member of it; yet Truth being I think very excusable in an Historian, I am necessitated to say that in this reign the roman Catholics of England did not behave like Gentlemen to the protestants."[16] One year later and probably just prior to her confirmation, Jane was deep in the study of Archbishop Thomas Secker's *Lectures on the Catechism of the Church of England,* for she mentioned the book in *Catharine or The Bower,* the last of her juvenilia, dating from 1792.[17]

Jane Austen's confirmation presumably took place in 1794. A still extant prayer book titled *A Companion to the altar shewing the nature & necessity of a Sacramental preparation in order to our Worthy receiving the Holy Communion to which are added prayers and meditations*

(London, ca. 1790), has this inscription on its flyleaf: "Jane Austen, April 24, 1794."[18] Jane was eighteen at that time, the exact age George III had specified for the confirmation of the Princess Charlotte, the only child of the Prince of Wales. Another point in favor of Jane's having been confirmed at that time is that the minimum age of sixteen had been a requirement in Anglican practice for the rite since the beginning of the eighteenth century.[19] The exact place of Jane Austen's confirmation is not known, but it could have been in Winchester Cathedral or in Basingstoke's largest parish church, the latter being the preferred place for confirmations in North Hampshire at that time.

The only direct reference to religion in Jane Austen's Steventon letters occurs in one written in April 1798 to her cousin Philadelphia Walter, whose father had just died. As Cassandra Austen was not at home, Jane undertook writing a letter of condolence to the Walter family on behalf of her parents and herself. Although it is couched in the formal language of the period, it contains one sentence that is indicative of Jane's own Christian convictions: "But the very circumstance which at present enhances your loss, must gradually reconcile you to it the better;—the Goodness which made him valuable on Earth, will make him blessed in Heaven."[20] Although Jane was unquestionably sincere in the sentiments just quoted, she was still a carefree young woman and could refer to penance in a lighthearted manner. Her cousin Edward Cooper, rector of Hamstall-Ridware in Staffordshire, had joined the ranks of the Evangelicals, the contemporary equivalent of today's Christian fundamentalists. In 1800 Jane told Cassandra that Cooper's letters were surprisingly "chearful [*sic*] & amusing," adding: "He dares not write otherwise to *me*—but perhaps he might be obliged to purge himself from the guilt of writing Nonsense by filling his shoes with whole pease for a week afterwards."[21]

Meanwhile, Jane Austen had written *Susan* (*Northanger Abbey*) in 1798-99, in which she created Henry Tilney, one of her most delightful young parsons. The novel also contains a clue to her serious reading then or earlier. In the scene in which Tilney, his sister, and Catherine Morland walk to the top of Beechen Cliff in Bath, there is a reference to the works of Hugh Blair, a fashionable minister of the Church of Scotland. His *Lectures on Rhetoric and Belles Lettres* had been published a few years before Jane Austen began her novel, while the first volume of his sermons had appeared in 1777. Jane was indeed already familiar with Blair's sermons before *Susan* (*Northanger Abbey*) was written, for she mentioned them as early as 1792 in *Catharine or The Bower.*[22]

That Jane Austen disapproved of William Godwin, the dissenting minister and advocate of free love who had become an atheist but was later converted by Coleridge to theism, is also evident from a tart remark she included in a letter to Cassandra in May 1801: "The Pickfords are in Bath & have called here. . . . He is as raffish in his appearance as I would wish every Disciple of Godwin to be."[23] There is no record that Jane Austen ever read the *Vindication of the Rights of Women* by Godwin's wife, the former Mary Wollstonecraft. As an omnivorous novel reader, however, she presumably had read Godwin's *The Adventures of Caleb Williams* and *St. Leon,* both of which were published before she moved to Bath.

Only nine of Jane's letters survive from the period she lived in Bath, 1801 to 1806. This makes it difficult to chart her regular activities, much less her spiritual life, during that time. But it is known that it was not a happy period of her life. Her uprooting from Steventon had been traumatic and was followed by what is believed to have been her only serious love affair, which presumably took place between 1801 and 1804 and ended with the death of her suitor. These were trials enough to have tested even the strongest faith, but worse was to come. On December 16, 1804, Jane's twenty-ninth birthday, her lifelong friend, Mrs. Anne Lefroy of Ashe, died as the result of a fall from her horse. Nothing survives concerning Jane's reaction at the time to this tragedy, but four years later she commemorated the event by writing her only known serious poem, in which she described Mrs. Lefroy as the "friend and ornament of human kind."[24] Jane's poem, which is too long to quote here, also included the fervent hope she would one day be reunited in another and better world with the woman who had encouraged her from her earliest childhood.

Jane Austen's sorrow over the death of Mrs. Lefroy was further compounded a little over a month later by an even greater loss: the death of her father in January 1805. At that time she wrote two letters to her brother Francis, then at sea. In breaking the news in her first letter, she said: "Our dear Father has closed his virtuous & happy life, in a death almost as free from suffering as his Children could have wished. . . . Next to that of the consciousness of his worth & constant preparation for another World, is the remembrance of his having suffered, comparatively speaking, nothing."[25] Jane's second letter was more personal: "It has been very sudden! . . . We had however some hours of preparation, & when we understood his recovery to be hopeless, most fervently did we pray for the speedy release which ensued. To have seen him languishing long, struggling for Hours, would have been dreadful! & thank God! we were all spared from it."[26] In concluding Jane observed: "The Serenity of the Corpse is most delightful! — It preserves the sweet, benevolent smile which always distinguished him. — "[27]

Later in 1805, when Jane was staying in Kent, she included a reference in one of her letters to her sister that indicates the seriousness of her reading after the death of her father: "I am glad you recommended 'Gisborne,' for having begun, I am pleased with it, and I had quite determined not to read it."[28] Jane was referring to *An Enquiry into the Duties of the Female Sex* (1797) by the Rev. Thomas Gisborne, a Staffordshire neighbor of her pious cousin, the Rev. Edward Cooper. Gisborne, an ardent Evangelical, was a close friend of William Wilberforce, Hannah More, and other contemporary reformers (known as the Clapham Sect) who were then endeavoring to curb the more liberal social mores of the Georgian world. Jane's approbation of Gisborne's book is therefore significant, for although she never adopted the puritanical excesses advocated by the more violent Evangelicals, it has been suggested there are parallels between some of Gisborne's pronouncements and certain passages in the novels of Jane's maturity, particularly *Mansfield Park*.[29]

Jane Austen's religious feelings were again revealed in the comments she made following the death of her brother Edward's wife at Godmersham, Kent, in 1808. Soon after giving birth to her eleventh child, Elizabeth Austen died suddenly. Cassandra had gone to Godmersham earlier to assist at the confinement, and was therefore present at Elizabeth's death. In speaking of her brother in her letter of consolation to Cassandra, Jane said: "God be praised! that you can say what you do of him — that he has a religious Mind to bear him up, & a Disposition that will gradually lead him to comfort . . . May the Almighty sustain you all — & keep you my dearest Cassandra well. . . ."[30] Concerning Elizabeth Austen, she continued: "We need not enter into a Panegyric on the Departed — but it is sweet to think of her great worth—of her solid principles, her true devotion, her excellence in every relation of Life. It is also consolatory to reflect on the shortness of the sufferings which led her from this World to a better.—"[31] Even so, Jane felt it was no time for heavy-handed piety, for she added: "I have written to Edward Cooper [i.e., her Evangelical cousin] and hope he will not send one of his letters of cruel comfort to my poor brother. . . ."[32]

As a good aunt, Jane tried to comfort Edward Austen's two oldest boys, Edward and George, who came from Winchester College to stay temporarily with their grandmother and aunt at Southampton. In describing her efforts, Jane wrote to Cassandra: "We do not want amusement: bilbocatch, at which George is indefatigable, spillikins, paper ships, riddles, conundrums, and cards, with watching the flow and ebb of the river, and now and then a stroll out, keep us employed. . . ."[33] Jane also took her nephews to church, at which time she was pleased that young Edward "was much affected by the sermon,"[34] the text of which was taken from the words of the Litany: "All that are in danger, necessity, or tribulation."[35] As was the custom in the Austen family, a part of Sunday evening was devoted to reading the Psalms and Lessons for the Day, followed by a sermon read aloud from a book of devotions, to which Jane reported her nephews were very attentive. But the boys switched to conundrums as soon as the devotions were over, on which Jane commented amusingly: "George is most industriously making and naming paper ships, at which he afterwards shoots with horse-chestnuts, brought from Steventon on purpose; and Edward equally intent over the 'Lake of Killarney,' twisting himself about in one of our great chairs."[36]

Jane Austen minced no words concerning her distaste for the earnest evangelical sermons preached and published by her cousin Edward Cooper, as well as her disapproval of the unnatural piety in which his eldest son, Edward, had been reared. In January 1809 she wrote to Cassandra: "A great event happens this week at Hamstall, in young Edward's removal to school; he is going to Rugby & is very happy in the idea of it;—I wish his happiness may last, but it will be a great change, to become a raw school boy from being a pompous Sermon-Writer, & a domineering Brother—It will do him good I dare say."[37] In an earlier letter written the same year, Jane also included this slyly disapproving comment on a volume of sermons that had just been published by the boy's father: "Miss M conveys to us a third volume of sermons from Hamstall, just published; and which we are to like better than the two others;—they are professedly *practical*, and for the use of country Congregations.—"[38] Six years later, after moving to Chawton, Jane continued to register her dislike of the type of Evangelical piety that the rector of Hamstall-Ridware preached. In September 1816, a little less than a year before her death, she wrote to Cassandra: "We do not much like Mr. Cooper's new Sermons;—they are fuller of Regeneration & Conversion than ever—with the addition of his zeal in the cause of the Bible Society.—"[39]

In 1809, in a letter to her sister, Cassandra Austen mentioned reading Hannah More's *Coelebs in Search of a Wife*, an Evangelical tale published the same year. It went into eleven editions in nine months, indicating, as the Rev. Sydney Smith wittily remarked, the "advantage from a worldly point of view of writing orthodox, didactic works."[40] Cassandra had evidently urged Jane to read the work, which contained a manifesto against the theater, poetry, and novels as vehicles of "unparalleled vice and infidelity," for Jane replied with some asperity: "You have by no means raised my curiosity after Caleb [*sic*];—My disinclination for it before was affected, but now it is real; I do not like the Evangelicals.—"[41] Then, realizing she had been unkind as far as Cassandra's choice of reading matter was concerned, she added wryly: "Of course I shall be delighted, when I read it, like other people, but till I do I dislike it."[42] Jane's emphatic remark: "I do not like the Evangelicals," indicates she was repelled by the restrictive moral straitjacket the sect was then attempting to impose on the more liberal and compassionate clergy and public.

Like many other thoughtful people of her class and time, however, it is evident that she gradually modified her feelings concerning religious and social changes. Five years after expressing her dislike of the Evangelicals as a sect, she used the same word, but perhaps in a different sense, when she wrote to Fanny Knight: "I am by no means convinced that we ought not all to be Evangelicals, & am at least persuaded that they who are from Reason and Feeling, must be happiest & safest.—"[43] This might seem a sudden change of thinking, except for the fact that an excerpt from a later letter to Fanny Knight clearly revealed exactly what Jane meant the word "Evangelical" to convey. Strangely enough, even though the passage from the earlier letter has been frequently quoted to support the theory that Jane underwent a radical change of religious thinking during the last years of her life, the statement in the later letter has heretofore been neglected. It reads: "I cannot suppose we differ in our ideas of the Christian Religion. You have given an excellent description of it. We only affix a different meaning to the word *Evangelical.*"[44] Jane's emphasis of the word is significant, for it indicates she used the word "Evangelical" in its original meaning—of or pertaining to the Gospel narrative or to the basic teachings embodied in the four Gospels.[45]

Jane Austen could never have been an Evangelical in the narrowest sense, for she never at any time in her life relinquished her pleasure in the theater, novel reading, dancing, music, nature, or the fine arts, all of which were considered instruments of the Devil by the Clapham Sect. Jane could even joke about Satan (she called him the Black Gentleman in *Emma*). In a letter from London to her sister at Chawton at the time she was writing the last chapters of *Mansfield Park,* she said: "Before I say anything else, I claim a paper full of halfpence on the drawing-room mantlepiece; I put them there myself, and forgot to bring them with me. I cannot say that I have yet been in any distress for money, but I chuse to have my due, as well as the Devil."[46]

Earlier, Jane also indulged in a sly private joke involving the rector of All Saints' Church, Southampton, something no strait-laced Evangelical would ever have done. For some time she and Cassandra had playfully teased their friend Martha Lloyd for her innocent admiration of Dr. Richard Mant, a dignified clergyman with a wife and ten children. Evidently Martha joined in the fun, for Jane took the opportunity of Cassandra's being at Godmersham in January 1809 to add another imaginary episode to the saga of the supposed flirtation: "Martha and Dr. Mant are as bad as ever; he runs after her in the street to apologize for having spoken to a Gentleman while *she* was near him the day before. Poor Mrs. Mant can stand it no longer; she is retired to one of her married Daughters."[47] This was followed a few days later with: "Martha pleases herself in believing that if *I* had kept her counsel, you wd never have heard of Dr M.'s late behaviour. . . . I am willing to overlook a venial fault; and as Dr. M. is a Clergyman their attachment, however immoral, has a decorous air."[48]

The strongest argument in favor of Jane's never having been unduly influenced by the Evangelicals is the fact that of all the thirteen characters in the six novels of her maturity who were either already clergymen or candidates for ordination, none of them betray the slightest affinity with the more restrictive brand of Christianity that was then being militantly promulgated by the Clapham Sect. Edward Ferrars in *Sense and Sensibility* frankly acknowledged that he had temporarily abandoned his desire to become a clergyman because his family did not consider the profession to be smart enough, a revelation of a lack of willpower not indicative of religious zeal. As for Dr. Davis in the same novel, little is known of him except that pink was his favorite color and that he drove up to London in his own carriage for the annual social season, indicating he preferred the fleshpots of the metropolis to the duties of his parish during that time of the year when the theater, opera, and evening parties were more readily available in London than in the country. As for the Rev. William Collins in *Pride and Prejudice,* he was so busy toadying to Lady Catherine de Bourgh he had only leftover time for the formalities of his ecclesiastical duties. In George Wickham's case, although he was never able to join the ranks of the clergy because of the estimable efforts of Fitzwilliam Darcy, Jane Austen left no doubts in the minds of her readers he would have been a disgrace to the Church.

As the original versions of *Sense and Sensibility* and *Pride and Prejudice* dated from Jane Austen's Steventon period, the clergymen or would-be clergymen depicted in them were presumably indicative of some of the flesh-and-blood parsons she had observed at that time. With *Mansfield Park,* however, the characterization became more complex. But even though Edmund Bertram and his friend, the shadowy Mr. Owen, were more earnest than the clergymen Jane had depicted in her earlier novels, their orthodoxy, at least as far as Edmund was concerned, reflected the opinions common to serious-minded Tory Church of England clergymen devoid of the priggish zealotry that characterized Evangelical teachings. Dr. Grant in the same novel was typical of the earlier sybaritic eighteenth-century clergy such as the real-life Rev. James Woodforde, whose delightful diary gives ample evidence that he had no scruples against mixing his clerical duties with the abundant pleasures of the table. As for the Rev. Mr. Norris in *Mansfield*

Park, little is known concerning him except that he was sickly and had too much of a cross to bear with a dictatorial wife to trouble himself with Evangelical hair-splitting.

In *Emma,* Jane Austen reverted to the toadying type of parson she had depicted in Mr. Collins in *Pride and Prejudice.* But Mr. Elton, the vicar who plays such an important role in Emma Woodhouse's scheming and in the affairs of Highbury in general, is only a more physically attractive Mr. Collins with the added vices of spitefulness and meanness of spirit. In *Northanger Abbey,* written at Steventon but published after Jane Austen's death, she was content to depict a charming, well-bred clergyman in Henry Tilney, a witty younger son who had no scruples against combining the not too arduous duties of his parish with the pleasures of the secular world. As for the Rev. Richard Morland in the same novel, we are told only that he "was a clergyman, without being neglected, or poor, and a very respectable man." In the case of his son James Morland, who was to have been his father's successor, he would automatically have been condemned in strict Evangelical circles for wasting his time on so frivolous a young woman as Isabella Thorpe. In *Persuasion,* Jane Austen merely sketched in young Charles Hayter, who was only too anxious to exchange a presumably poorly paid curacy for the comfortable rectorship of Uppercross, where Dr. Shirley, a conscientious old-fashioned rector like Jane Austen's father, had zealously discharged all of the duties of his office for more than forty years.

Jane Austen maintained her artistic integrity in depicting the clergymen in her novels as flesh-and-blood human beings rather than paragons of impossible holiness. In doing so, however, she did not escape criticism, for after *Emma* was published one reader, a Mrs. Wroughton, complained she "Thought the Authoress wrong, in such times as these to draw such Clergymen as Mr Collins & Mr Elton."[49] The same criticism was leveled at Jane twenty years after her death by Cardinal Newman. Writing to a sister in January 1837, he stigmatized Jane's clergymen thus: "What vile creatures her parsons are! she has not a dream of the high Catholic ethos."[50] Even so, a more objective critic came to Jane's rescue at about the same time. Although he grew up under the influence of the Clapham Sect, Thomas Babington Macaulay had only the highest praise for Jane Austen's clergymen, particularly Edward Ferrars, Henry Tilney,

Edmund Bertram, and Mr. Elton. Macaulay's praise is too lengthy to quote here, but it included: "Who would not have expected them to be insipid likenesses of each other? . . . No such thing. . . . And almost all this is done by touches so delicate, that they elude analysis, that they defy the powers of description, and that we know them to exist by the general effect to which they have contributed."[51]

Jane Austen did not lose the opportunity of quietly infusing her novels with solid principles having their roots in her basic Christian beliefs. Nor did she hesitate to use the name of God if the action or situation being described required it to emphasize emotion. Since she had been taught not to take the name of God in vain, however, she was extremely careful in her usage of the name of the deity unless it rose spontaneously to the lips of those characters who used it in a crisis. In *Sense and Sensibility,* Marianne Dashwood, on being rebuffed by Willoughby at the evening musical party, blurted out: "Good God! Willoughby, what is the meaning of this?" In *Pride and Prejudice,* the formerly haughty Fitzwilliam Darcy betrays his changed attitude toward Elizabeth Bennet as well as his Christian solicitude when Elizabeth is prostrated at the news of Lydia's elopement by exclaiming: "Good God! What is the matter!" In *Mansfield Park,* the name of the deity is used sparingly even though the theme of the novel is the eventual triumph of Christian principles over worldly ones. When it does occur, however, it emphasizes the emotional point forcibly. When Fanny Price contemplates the horrible possibility that her beloved Edmund Bertram might be snared by the charming, but morally flawed, Mary Crawford, she steels herself by imploring: "God grant that her influence do not make him cease to be respectable." In *Emma,* the heroine uses the name of the deity six times in the last chapters of the novel without any sacrilegious intent, finally exclaiming: "Oh God! that I had never seen her!" in referring to Harriet Smith when she fears the latter has supplanted her in Mr. Knightley's affections. In *Northanger Abbey,* it is not the heroine who uses the name of the Almighty in a time of stress but her brother, James Morland, who expresses his obvious relief in losing the fickle Isabella Thorpe by writing: "Thank God I am undeceived in time." As for *Persuasion,* Jane puts the name of the deity in the mouth of the one person in the novel least likely to use it, the disciplined and self-contained Captain Frederick Wentworth. On the occasion of

Louisa Musgrove's fall from the Cobb at Lyme Regis, he loses control momentarily, staggering against a wall for support, "exclaiming in the bitterest agony: Oh God! her father and mother!"

The letters of Jane Austen's maturity contain so many allusions to her unostentatious but enduring faith that only a few can be mentioned here. In July 1813 in a letter to her brother Francis, then on naval duty in the Baltic, she betrayed an anti-Catholic attitude when she wrote: "I have great respect for former Sweden. So zealous as it was for Protestan[t]ism!"[52] Later in the same year when she was staying at Godmersham, she commented on the Rev. Joseph Godfrey Sherer, the rector of the parish: "I heard him for the first time last Sunday, & he gave us an excellent Sermon—a little too eager sometimes in his delivery, but that is to me a better extreme than the want of animation, especially when it evidently comes from the heart as in him."[53]

Jane also mentions the works of two well-known contemporary serious authors in one of her letters written to her sister in 1813. These were Thomas Clarkson, the abolitionist and author of *A History of the Abolition of the Slave Trade* (1808) and the *Memoir of William Penn* (1813), and Claudius Buchanan, a clergyman who had been active in the establishment of the Anglican Church in India, whose *Eight Sermons* was published in 1811, followed by his *An Apology for Promoting Christianity in India* (1813).[54] It is also known that she was particularly fond of the sermons of the great eighteenth-century divine, the Rev. Thomas Sherlock, for in September 1814, she told her niece Anna [Mrs. Benjamin Lefroy]: "I am very fond of Sherlock's Sermons, prefer them to almost any.—"[55] That Jane Austen was not averse to the mention of religion in a work of fiction is also evident from another letter written to the same niece later that year. In commenting on a recently published novel by Letitia Matilda Hawkins, Jane said: "We have got 'Rosanne' in our Society, and find it much as you describe it; very good and clever, but tedious. Mrs. Hawkins' great excellence is on serious subjects. There are some very delightful conversations and reflections on religion; but on lighter topics I think she falls into many absurdities."[56]

Further evidence of Jane Austen's religious views during the same period are included in a letter she wrote to her friend Martha Lloyd in September 1814. In commenting on the unsatisfactory progress of the War of 1812 between Great Britain and the United

States, in which the British had suffered several naval defeats, Jane said: "If we are to be ruined, it cannot be helped—but I place my hope of better things on a claim to the protection of Heaven, as a Religious Nation, a Nation in spite of much Evil improving in Religion, which I cannot believe the Americans to possess."[57] Jane's letter was written from London, where her brother Henry had taken her to see Benjamin West's enormous painting, "Christ Rejected by the Elders," now in the Pennsylvania Academy of Fine Arts. Jane's enthusiasm over the painting was evident for she wrote: "I have seen West's famous Painting, and prefer it to anything of the kind I ever saw before. I do not know that it is reckoned superior to his 'Healing in the Temple,' but it gratified me much more, and indeed is the first representation of our Saviour which ever at all contented me. 'His Rejection by the Elders,' is the subject.—I want to have You and Cassandra see it.—"[58]

Jane Austen's faith did not falter when she was stricken with what is believed to have been Addison's disease in 1816. When the disease was in remission, she still had hopes of recovering, but even then she had steeled herself to accept the possibility of death with stoical Christian fortitude. In a letter she wrote to her friend Anne Sharpe, a former governess at Godmersham, she said:

> How to do justice to the kindness of all my family during this illness, is quite beyond me!—Every dear Brother so affectionate & so anxious!—and as for my Sister!—Words must fail me in any attempt to describe what a Nurse she has been to me. Thank God! she does not seem to be worse for it *yet*, & as there was never any sitting-up necessary, I am willing to hope she has no after-fatigue to suffer from. I have so many alleviations & comforts to bless the Almighty for! . . . But the Providence of God has restored me—& may I be more fit to appear before him when I *am* summoned, than I shd have been now![59]

Later, in writing of her steady decline she said: "But I am getting too near complaint. It has been the appointment of God, however secondary causes may have operated."[60]

Jane Austen's hopes of recovery did not materialize, and according to Henry Austen's biographical sketch: "She made a point of receiving the sacrament [i.e., Holy Communion] before excessive bodily weakness might have rendered her perception unequal to her wishes."[61]

In describing Jane's last hours in a letter to her niece Fanny Knight, Cassandra wrote:

> I thank God that I was enabled to attend to her to the last & amongst my many causes of self-reproach I have not to add any wilfull [*sic*] neglect of her comfort. She felt herself to be dying about half an hour before she became tranquil and apparently unconscious. During that half an hour was her struggle, poor soul! she said she could not tell us what she suffered, tho she complained of little fixed pain. When I asked her if there was any thing she wanted, her answer was she wanted nothing but death and some of her words were "God grant me patience, Pray for me oh Pray for me!"

Later in the same letter, Cassandra added: "The last sad ceremony is to take place on Thursday morning, her dear remains are to be deposited in the cathedral—it is a satisfaction to me to think they are to lie in a Building she admired so much—her precious soul I presume to hope reposes in a far superior Mansion."[62]

ABBREVIATIONS TO THE NOTES

AP	R. A. Austen-Leigh, *Austen Papers, 1704-1856* (London, 1942).
AR	*Annual Reports of the Jane Austen Society,* 1966-1991. Separate issues with individual pagination for each year.
Aunt	Caroline Mary Craven Austen, *My Aunt Jane Austen.* (Winchester, 1952).
Biographical Notice	Henry Thomas Austen, "Biographical Notice of the Author," pre fixed to the first edition of *Northanger Abbey* and *Persuasion* (1817). Reprinted in *The Novels of Jane Austen,* ed. R. W. Chapman, vol. 5 (Oxford, 1923).
Brabourne	*Letters of Jane Austen,* ed. with an introduction and critical remarks by Edward, Lord Brabourne, 2 vols. (London, 1884).
Chawton MSS	Manuscript album of James Austen's miscellaneous works owned by the Jane Austen Memorial Trust, Chawton.
CR	*Collected Reports of the Jane Austen Society 1949-1965,* with an introduction by Elizabeth Jenkins (London, 1967).
DNB	*The Dictionary of National Biography,* ed. Sir Leslie Stephen and Sir Sidney Lee, 63 vols. (London, 1885-1900; 1921-22).
Emma	*The Novels of Jane Austen (Emma),* ed. by R. W. Chapman, vol. IV (Oxford, new ed., 1971).
FP	R. W. Chapman, *Jane Austen: Facts and Problems* (Oxford, 1948 [1970]).
FR	William and Richard Austen-Leigh, revised and enlarged by Deirdre Le Faye. *Jane Austen: A Family Record* (London, 1989).
GH	George Holbert Tucker, *A Goodly Heritage: A History of Jane Austen's Family* (Manchester, 1983).
Gilson	David John Gilson, *A Bibliography of Jane Austen* (Oxford, 1982).
Hill	Constance Hill, *Jane Austen: Her Homes and Her Friends* (London, new ed. 1904 [1923]).
Honan	Park Honan, *Jane Austen: Her Life* (New York, 1987).
LCR	C. H. Collins Baker, "Lady Chandos' Register," *Genealogists' Magazine* 10 (1947-50), 255-64, 299-309, 339-52.

Letters	*Jane Austen's Letters to Her Sister Cassandra and Others,* collected and ed. R. W. Chapman (Oxford, 1969; reprint of the 1952 second ed.).
Life and Letters	William and Richard Arthur Austen-Leigh, *Jane Austen, Her Life and Letters: A Family Record,* first ed. (London, 1913 [1965]).
Marshall	*Jane Austen's Sanditon: A Continuation, with "Reminiscences of Aunt Jane" by Anna Austen Lefroy,* ed. Mary Gaither Marshall (Chicago, 1983).
Memoir	James Edward Austen-Leigh, *A Memoir of Jane Austen* (Oxford, 1926 [1967]).
Memoir of Miss Austen	Henry Thomas Austen, "Memoir of Miss Austen," prefixed to the edition of Jane Austen's novels published by Richard Bentley (London, 1833).
MP	*The Novels of Jane Austen (Mansfield Park),* ed. R. W. Chapman, vol. III (Oxford, new ed., 1973).
MW	*The Novels of Jane Austen (Minor Works),* ed. R. W. Chapman with revisions of B. C. Southam, vol. VI (Oxford, new ed., 1972).
NA/P	*The Novels of Jane Austen (Northanger Abbey and Persuasion),* ed. by R. W. Chapman, vol. V (Oxford, new ed., 1972).
OFH	Agnes Leigh, "An Old Family History," *National Review,* no. 49 (1907).
PA	Mary Augusta Austen-Leigh, *Personal Aspects of Jane Austen* (London, 1920).
Piggott	Patrick Piggott, *The Innocent Diversion: Music in the Life and Writings of Jane Austen* (London, 1979).
PP	*The Novels of Jane Austen (Pride and Prejudice),* ed. R. W. Chapman, vol. II (Oxford, new ed., 1973).
RCA	Caroline Mary Craven Austen, *Reminiscences of Caroline Austen* (Winchester, 1986).
Sailor Brothers	J. H. and E. C. Hubback, *Jane Austen's Sailor Brothers* (London, 1906).
Southam	*Jane Austen: The Critical Heritage,* vol. I (1811-70), ed. B. C. Southam (London, 1968).
SS	*The Novels of Jane Austen (Sense and Sensibility),* ed. R. W. Chapman, vol. I (Oxford, new ed., 1974).

Chapter 1 — Presenting Miss Jane Austen

1. *Letters* (120) 443.
2. Ibid. (142) 486-87.
3. *Biographical Notice*, 6.
4. *Memoir of Miss Austen*, xiv.
5. *Aunt*, 10.
6. Brabourne, I, ix-xv.
7. *GH*, 15-36.
8. Ibid., 53-81.
9. Steventon Baptismal Register.
10. Brabourne, II, 3; also D. G. Le Faye, "Anna Lefroy's Original Memories of Jane Austen," *Review of English Studies*, August 1988, 418.
11. Steventon Baptismal Register.
12. *Letters* (81) 314.
13. *GH*, 99-114.
14. Ibid., 115-17.
15. Ibid., 118-32.
16. Ibid., 133-48.
17. Ibid., 149-64.
18. Ibid., 165-90.
19. *Memoir*, 176.
20. *AP*, 32.
21. Ibid., 131.
22. Ibid., 142.
23. Ibid., 144.
24. Ibid., 148.
25. Marshall, 155-65.
26. *Letters* (13) 35.
27. *Biographical Notice*, 5.
28. Henry Fielding, *Tom Jones*, Book IV, Chapter II.
29. *Biographical Notice*, 5.
30. Marshall, 157.
31. *Memoir*, 87.

32. *Aunt*, 5.
33. Ibid., 7.
34. Sir Egerton Brydges, *The Autobiography, Times, Opinions and Contemporaries of Sir Egerton Brydges* (London, 1834), II, 41.
35. "Jane Austen," *Times Literary Supplement*, September 17, 1954.
36. D. G. Le Faye, "Recollections of Chawton," *Times Literary Supplement*, May 3, 1985.
37. *Letters* (4) 8.
38. Lady Knatchbull, "Aunt Jane," *The Cornhill Magazine*, 1947, 72-73.
39. Ibid.
40. *MW*, 403.
41. *Memoir*, 210-11.
42. Rev. A. G. K. L'Estrange, *The Life of Mary Russell Mitford* (New York, 1870), I, 235.
43. Vera Watson, *Mary Russell Mitford* (London, 1949), 1-12; 119-20.
44. Ibid., 2.
45. *Letters* (Other Persons Index).
46. *CR* (1965), 294-95.
47. *Aunt*, 5.
48. Alexander Pope, "An Essay on Man," line 13.
49. *Letters* (15) 43.
50. L'Estrange, *The Life of Mary Russell Mitford*, I, 235.
51. M. W. DeWolfe Howe, "A Jane Austen Letter," *The Yale Review*, vol. 15, October 1926-July 1926, 321-22.
52. *Letters* (17) 49; (18) 53.
53. Ibid. (28) 98.
54. Hill, 91.
55. *Letters* (120) 443.
56. *Biographical Notice*, 3.
57. Ibid., 7.
58. *Aunt*, 9.
59. *Memoir*, 102-3.
60. *AR* (1972), 21.
61. *Letters* (76) 297.
62. Ibid. (90) 367.
63. Sir Zachary Cope, "Jane Austen's Last Illness," *British Medical Journal*, July 18, 1964, 140, 182-83.
64. *Letters*, 515.
65. Gilson, 470-71.
66. *Memoir*, 176.
67. *GH*, 112-14.
68. Gilson, 471.
69. *Memoir*, 176.

Chapter 2 — Homes, Environments, and Friends

1. *Letters* (126) 452.
2. Keith Irons, *Steventon and the Austens* (Steventon, 1975), 10.
3. Arthur Willis, "Last Days of a Great House," *Hampshire Chronicle,* May 30, 1970, 5, columns 1 and 2.
4. Irons, *Steventon and the Austens,* 10-11; also Maggie Lane, *Jane Austen's Family, Through Five Generations* (London, 1984), 197.
5. *Memoir,* 21.
6. *Sailor Brothers,* 9-10.
7. *Letters* (29) 101.
8. *FR,* 69, 83.
9. *AR* (1975), illustration; also Gilson, 440-41.
10. *Memoir,* 11.
11. *Letters* (Authors, Books, and Plays Index).
12. *OFH,* 277-86.
13. Ibid., 286.
14. A. Walton Litz, "The Loiterer: A Reflection of Jane Austen's Early Environment," *Review of English Studies,* August 1961, 251-61.
15. Sir Zachary Cope, "Who Was Sophia Sentiment? Was She Jane Austen?" *The Book Collector,* 1966, 143-51.
16. *PA,* 147-8.
17. *MW,* 44, 74, 138, 192.
18. *Memoir,* 10-11.
19. *AP,* 21, 29-30.
20. Lady Knatchbull, "Aunt Jane," *The Cornhill Magazine,* 1947, 72-73.
21. National Trust, *The Vyne* (London, 1973).
22. G. F. Prosser, *Select Illustrations of Hampshire* (London, 1883), article on Laverstoke House.
23. James Edward Austen-Leigh, *Recollections of the Early Days of the Vine Hunt* (London, 1865), 69-80.
24. Prosser, *Select Illustrations of Hampshire,* article on Laverstoke House.
25. Sir Egerton Brydges, *The Autobiography, Times, Opinions and Contemporaries of Sir Egerton Brydges* (London, 1834), I, 5, 137.
26. *Memoir,* 57.
27. Brydges, *Autobiography,* I, 5, 137.
28. *Letters* (9) 21.
29. Ibid. (Other Persons Index).
30. *MW,* 433.
31. A. M. W. Stirling, ed., *The Diaries of Dummer* (London, 1934).
32. James Edward Austen-Leigh, *Recollections of the Early Days of the Vine Hunt,* 66.

33. *Letters* (32) 117.
34. *Life and Letters*, 69.
35. *MW*, 3.
36. Rev. R. F. Bigg-Wither, *Materials for a History of the Wither Family* (Winchester, 1907), 52-53.
37. *Letters* (145) 495.
38. Ibid. (29) 99.
39. Ibid. (35) 123.
40. Jean Freeman, *Jane Austen in Bath* (Winchester, 1969), 23-24.
41. *Letters* (32) 115.
42. Ibid. (39) 141.
43. Ibid.
44. Ibid. (29) 100.
45. *AP*, 237.
46. *Letters* (54) 208.
47. Ibid. (43) 148.
48. Richard Arthur Austen-Leigh, *Jane Austen and Southampton* (London, 1949), vi.
49. Ibid., 15-19.
50. *Letters* (49) 178; also William Cowper, "The Task," vi, 150.
51. Joan Grigsby, "The House in Castle Square," *AR* (1978), 20-25.
52. *Memoir*, 82.
53. Patrick Piggott, "Jane Austen's Southampton Piano," *AR* (1980), 6-9.
54. Burial records of St. Nicholas Church, Chawton.
55. Brabourne, II, 120.
56. *Letters* (59) 226.
57. Ibid. (66) 262.
58. Ibid. (62) 243.
59. Ibid., 243-44.
60. Ibid. (68) See Chapman's note to this letter.
61. *Oxford Dictionary of Quotations* (1979), 512.
62. *GH*, 174-75.
63. *Letters* (68) 266.
64. T. Edward Carpenter, *The Story of Jane Austen's Home* (Jane Austen Memorial Trust, 1954), 1-8.
65. *Aunt*, 3-4.
66. Ibid., 4.
67. Ibid., 7-8.

Chapter 3 — Beaux and a Blighted Romance

1. *FR*, xvii.
2. *Memoir*, 16.
3. Ibid.
4. *Letters* (141) 483.
5. Ibid. (13) 35.
6. Ibid. (34) 121.
7. Ibid. (55) 210.
8. Ibid. (140) 480; see also entry under William Deeds (1761-1834) in Other Persons Index.
9. Ibid. (142) 468.
10. *NA/P* (*Northanger Abbey*), 110-11.
11. For information concerning Edward Taylor of Bifrons and his family, see John Bernard Burke's *A Genealogical and Heraldic History of the Commoners of Great Britain and Ireland*, III (London, 1823-1838), 107-109; Joseph Foster's *Alumni Oxonienses 1715-1886* (London, 1887); Nigel Nicolson's *The World of Jane Austen* (London, 1991), 61, 75; and Sir David Waldron Smithers's *Jane Austen in Kent* (Westerham, Kent, 1981), 62, 107.
12. *Letters* (6) 14.
13. Ibid. (25) 87.
14. For information concerning Edward Bridges, see J. A. Venn's *Alumni Cantabrigienses* (Cambridge, 1922); and *FR*, 134, 150.
15. *Letters* (5) 11.
16. Ibid. (15) 45.
17. Ibid. (46) 165.
18. Ibid. (54) 205.
19. Ibid. (56) 217.
20. Ibid. (85) 339.
21. Ibid. (89) 362.
22. Ibid. (Other Persons Index); Also *FR*, 46, 156.
23. Ibid. (9) 21.
24. Honan, 156
25. *Letters* (75) 293; (76) 298.
26. For information on Charles Fowle and his family see *AR* (1982), 20-26; also *FR*, 39, 53, 85, 147.
27. Letters (1) 3; (2) 4.
28. Ibid. (2) 6.
29. For information on John Willing Warren, see Joseph Foster's *Alumni Oxonienses;* George Richard and Charles Shadwell's *The Provosts and Fellows of Oriel College*, 152; C. S. Emden's "Oriel Friends of Jane

Austen," II, *Oriel Record,* 1950; and R. W. Chapman's "Jane Austen's 'Warren,'" *Times Literary Supplement,* May 14, 1931.

30. For information on the Rev. Charles Powlett and his family, see Arthur Collins's *The Peerage of England* (Brydges edition, London, 1812) under the heading "Powlett, Marquis of Winchester," II, 384-86, with particular attention to the footnote on p. 386; Thomas Crawford's "Boswell's Temple and the Jane Austen World," *Scottish Literary Journal,* vol. 10, no. 2, December 1983, 53-57; Joseph Foster's *Alumni Oxonienses;* and *FR,* 80, 85, 87, 114. For Powlett's obituary see the *Gentleman's Magazine,* vol. 100, 1830, part 2, 471-72.
31. *Letters* (27) 91.
32. Ibid. (2) 6.
33. Ibid. (92) 378.
34. Ibid. (2) 6.
35. Ibid. (14) 39.
36. Ibid. (30) 105.
37. For information on Thomas Langlois Lefroy and his family see: J. A. P Lefroy's "Jane Austen's Irish Friend: Rt. Hon. Thomas Langlois Lefroy, 1776-1869," *Proceedings of the Huguenot Society in London* (London, 1979), 148-55; J. A. P. Lefroy's "A Walloon Family, Loffroy of Cambray," *Proceedings of the Huguenot Society in London* (London, 1966), 604-25; Helen Lefroy's "Strangers," *AR* (1982), 6-11; and *FR,* 85-87, 251-52.
38. Thomas Langlois Lefroy, "The Late Chief Justice LeFroy," *Dublin University Magazine,* vol. 79, January 1872, 65.
39. *Letters* (1) 1-2.
40. Ibid., 3.
41. Henry Fielding, *Tom Jones,* Book VII, Chapter XIV.
42. Information Furnished by J. G. Lefroy of Carrigglas Manor, Longford, Ireland, March 2, 1978.
43. *Letters* (2) 5.
44. Ibid., 6.
45. Ibid.
46. Ibid.
47. Ibid. (11) 27.
48. *FP,* 57-58.
49. Ibid., 58.
50. For information on Samuel Blackall and his family, see Venn's *Alumni Cantabrigienses; DNB,* II, 579-81; Frank Stubbings, "Samuel Blackall and Jane Austen," *Emmanuel College Magazine,* Oxford, 1984, 40-45; and *FR,* 96-97, 182, 241. Blackall's obituary appeared in the *Gentleman's Magazine,* N.S., vol. 17, 1844, 2.

51. Jane Townley Pryme and Alicia Bayne, *Memorials of the Thackeray Family* (London, 1883), 163.
52. *Letters* (11) 27-28.
53. Ibid. (81) 316-17.
54. Ibid. (17) 51.
55. Ibid. (29) 103.
56. *FP,* 64.
57. *Letters* (8 through 22) 19-73.
58. *FP,* 67-68.
59. Ibid., 67.
60. Ibid., 66.
61. *Memoir,* 28-29.
62. *FP,* 65.
63. Constance Pilgrim, *Dear Jane: A Biographical Study of Jane Austen* (London, 1971).
64. Mary Moorman, *William Wordsworth: A Biography. The Early Years 1770-1803* (Oxford, 1957), 4-5, 472-73; also Mary Moorman, *William Wordsworth: A Biography. The Later Years 1803-1850* (Oxford, 1965), 32-46.
65. *AP,* 159.
66. Moorman, *William Wordsworth: The Early Years,* 64, 472.
67. *Life and Letters,* 91.
68. For information on Harris Bigg-Wither and his family see the Rev. R. F. Bigg-Wither's *Materials for a History of the Wither Family* (Winchester, 1907), 52-59; Park Honan's "Jane Austen and Marriage," *Contemporary Review,* November 1984, 253-59; and *FR,* 121-22, 250.
69. *Letters* (17) 50-51.
70. Ibid. (18) 56.
71. Honan, "Jane Austen and Marriage," 256.
72. *Letters* (23) 75; (25) 85.
73. *FP,* 177-78.
74. Ibid., 67.
75. *Life and Letters,* 93.
76. Honan, "Jane Austen and Marriage," 258.
77. *Letters* (61) 236; also Venn's *Alumni Cantabrigienses;* and *AR* (1987), 11-15.
78. *Letters* (75) 293.
79. *FP,* 67.

CHAPTER 4 — JANE AUSTEN AND THE EVENTS OF HER TIME

1. *Letters* (126) 452.
2. Original letter dated November 10, 1913, now the property of Dorset County Museums. Quoted by permission of Roger Peers, R.N.R., Curator.
3. Laura M. Ragg, "Jane Austen and the War of Her Time," *Contemporary Review*, 1940, 547-48.
4. *AP*, 30.
5. Frances Bertram Pinion, *A Jane Austen Companion: A Critical Survey and Reference Book* (London, 1973), 193-94.
6. Information furnished by Sir Robin Macworth Young, KCVO, H. M. Librarian, Windsor Castle.
7. *MW*, 72, 194-95.
8. H. W. Earney, "The Man Who Caused the American Revolution," *Hampshire Magazine*, October 1982, 41-42.
9. *The Loiterer*, I, No. II, February 7, 1789, 5.
10. *Letters* (Other Persons Index); also *DNB*, III, 1002-4.
11. *Letters* (Other Persons Index); also *GH*, 105.
12. *AP*, 86-97; 99-119.
13. William Austen-Leigh and Montague George Knight, *Chawton Manor and Its Owners* (London, 1911), 157-58.
14. *AP*, 177.
15. Ibid.
16. William R. O'Byrne, *A Naval Biographical Dictionary* (London, 1861), I, 29.
17. William R. O'Byrne, *Naval Biographical Dictionary* (London, 1849), 26-27.
18. *Aunt*, 9.
19. *Letters* (see entry under Henry Thomas Austen in section devoted to *Jane Austen's Family*; also *GH*, 136-140.
20. *The Loiterer*, I, February 28, 1789, 13-14.
21. *AP*, 321-23.
22. *Letters* (133) 465; also *Life and Letters*, 45.
23. Lord James Dumfermline, *Lieutenant General Ralph Abercromby, K.B., 1793-1801: A Memoir by His Son* (Edinburgh, 1864), 54-60.
24. *Letters* (18) 54, 57.
25. O'Byrne, *Naval Biographical Dictionary* (1849), 26-27; also *Letters* (38) 137.
26. O'Byrne, *Naval Biographical Dictionary* (1861), I, 29; also *Sailor Brothers*, 60-64.
27. *Letters* (18) 57-58.
28. *Memoir*, 26.
29. *Sailor Brothers*, 114.

30. Sir Egerton Brydges, *The Autobiography, Times, Opinions and Contemporaries of Sir Egerton Brydges* (London, 1834), II, 41.
31. *Sailor Brothers*, 122.
32. Ibid., 15-56.
33. Ibid., 176.
34. *AP*, 237.
35. *Sailor Brothers*, 196.
36. Arthur Bryant, *The Years of Victory, 1802-1812* (London, 1945), 249-50.
37. *MW*, 446.
38. *Letters* (63) 246.
39. Ibid.
40. Ragg, "Jane Austen and the War of Her Time," 546.
41. *Letters* (66) 261-62.
42. Ibid. (Note in Letters 66).
43. Ibid. (70) 276.
44. *MP*, 119.
45. *Letters* (73) 317.
46. Ibid. (81) 317.
47. Ibid., 314.
48. Ibid.
49. Ibid. (87) 354.
50. Ibid. (91) 372.
51. Ibid.
52. J. R. Priestley, *The Prince of Pleasure and His Regency 1811-20* (London, 1969 [1971]), 116.
53. Ibid., 113-137.
54. *Letters* (96) 389.
55. Ibid.
56. Ibid. (97) 390.
57. John Timbs, *Clubs and Club Life in London* (London, 1967), 103.
58. *Letters* (97) 390.
59. Ibid. (99.1) 508.
60. *FP*, 181; also *GH*, 177.
61. *GH*, 186-87.

Chapter 5 — The Elegant Amenities

1. *Biographical Notice*, 5.
2. Evelyn Howe, "Amateur Theatre in Georgian England," *History Today*, October 1970, 695-703.
3. Ibid., 695.

4. Ibid., 696.
5. *Life and Letters*, 63-64.
6. *AP*, 126.
7. Ellen Jordan, "Mansfield Park," *Times Literary Supplement*, June 23, 1972, 719.
8. *DNB*, VII, 622-24.
9. *Chawton MSS*, poems 1 and 2; also *GH*, 100-1.
10. Rev F. Thoyts, *A History of Esse or Ashe, Hampshire* (London, 1888), 58.
11. Ibid., 79.
12. *AP*, 67, 115.
13. Ibid., 124.
14. Ibid., 126.
15. *Chawton MSS*, poems 5 and 6.
16. Ibid., poem 6.
17. *The Poetical Register and Repository of Fugitive Poetry*, vol. 2, 1802 (London, 1803), 58-59.
18. Mary Katherine Woodworth, *The Literary Career of Sir Samuel Egerton Brydges* (Oxford, 1935), 7-8.
19. *Chawton MSS*, poem 7.
20. Ibid., poem 8.
21. Ibid., poem 9.
22. *AP*, 138; also *Life and Letters*, 66.
23. *Chawton MSS*, poem 10.
24. *AP*, 138.
25. J. H. Hubback, "Pen Portraits in Jane Austen's Novels," *The Cornhill Magazine*, July 1928, 24-33.
26. *MW*, 49.
27. *Webster's Biographical Dictionary* (Springfield, MA, 1971), 1355.
28. *MW*, 109.
29. *DNB*, XI, 1079-81; also XVI, 543-46.
30. *MW*, 65.
31. *Letters* (134) 469.
32. *MW*, 173.
33. B. C. Southam, ed., *Jane Austen's "Sir Charles Grandison"* (Oxford, 1980), 5.
34. Ibid., 10-11.
35. *MP*, 124.
36. Barbara Carpenter Turner, *Winchester* (Southampton, 1930), 145-46.
37. *Letters* (22) 71.
38. *Bath Herald and Register*, Saturday, June 29, 1799, 3.
39. Samuel Taylor Coleridge, *Biographica Literaria* (1907), II, 159.
40. William Reitzel, "Mansfield Park and Lovers' Vows," *Review of English Studies*, 1933, 454.

41. *Letters* (30) 107.
42. Ibid. (33) 118.
43. *AP*, 238.
44. *AR* (1980), 7.
45. Richard Arthur Austen-Leigh, *Jane Austen and Southampton* (London, 1949), 46.
46. *Letters* (62) 242.
47. Ibid. (61) 235-36.
48. Ibid. (60) 233.
49. Richard Arthur Austen-Leigh, *Jane Austen and Southampton*, 31.
50. *SS*, 330.
51. *PP*, 319.
52. *Letters* (70) 275.
53. Ibid.
54. Ibid. (82) 321.
55. Ibid., 319.
56. Ibid., 323.
57. Ibid.
58. Ibid.
59. Ibid. (85) 338.
60. Ibid. (82) 323.
61. Ibid. (93) 380.
62. Ibid., 381.
63. Ibid., 380.
64. Ibid., 384.
65. Ibid.
66. Piggott, 25, 150.
67. *Letters* (94) 385.
68. Ibid.
69. Paul Henry Lang, *George Frederick Handel* (New York, 1977), 194.
70. Ackerman's *Repository of Arts* (London, 1813), 230-31; also *The Times* (London), March 1814.
71. *Letters* (105) 415.
72. Ibid. (106) 419.
73. *NA/P* (*Northanger Abbey*), 14
74. Ibid., 16.
75. Piggott, 131-64.
76. *AR* (1975), 12.
77. Piggott, 5, 6, 8, 9 (illustration), 54, 160, 167.
78. B. Matthew, *The Music of Winchester Cathedral*, 21.
79. Percy A. Scholes, *The Oxford Companion to Music* (Oxford, 1970), 559.
80. Piggott, 145.

81. Ibid., 17-18.
82. *Letters* (20) 65.
83. Piggott, 19-20, 41.
84. *NA/P (Persuasion)*, 193.
85. *Letters* (44) 154.
86. *Aunt*, 6-7.
87. *Letters* (70) 274.
88. Piggott, 8, 14 (illustration).
89. Ibid., 21.
90. *Letters* (91) 370-71.
91. Ibid. (117) 437.
92. Ibid. (116) 435.
93. Ibid. (118) 440.
94. *Biographical Notice*, 5.
95. *FR*, 47.
96. *Letters* (20) 63 (illustration); also *CR* (1949-1965) 49 (illustration).
97. *Letters* (11) 30.
98. Ibid. (69) 267.
99. Richard D. Altic, *The Shows of London* (London, 1978), 235.
100. *Letters* (69) 267.
101. Ibid. (80) 309-10.
102. Ibid., 312.
103. Sir Joshua Reynolds, *Catalog of Pictures by the Late Sir Joshua Reynolds Exhibited by the Permission of the Proprietors in Honour of That Distinguished Artist and for the Improvement of British Art* (London, 1813), 15, 19, 20.
104. *Letters* (90) 368.
105. *Biographical Notice*, 5.
106. *Letters* (15) 44.
107. Ibid. (17) 51-52.
108. Ibid. (27) 90.
109. Ibid. (91) 370.

CHAPTER 6 — JANE AUSTEN AND THE PRINCE REGENT

1. *Memoir*, 157.
2. *Letters* (78.1) 504.
3. Shane Leslie, *George the Fourth* (Boston, 1926), 22.
4. Ibid., 22-23.
5. Ibid.
6. G. F. Prosser, *Select Illustrations of Hampshire* (London, 1883), article on Kempshott Park.

7. *Chawton MSS*, poem 14.
8. A. M. W. Stirling, ed. *The Diaries of Dummer* (London, 1934), 78.
9. Ibid.
10. Ibid., 74-75.
11. Ibid., 75.
12. Ibid., 79.
13. Ibid.
14. Ibid.
15. Jane Austen, *Volume the Third*, ed. R. W. Chapman (Oxford, 1951), 69.
16. Alan Lloyd, *The King Who Lost America* (New York, 1971), 317.
17. Stirling, ed., *The Diaries of Dummer*, 77-78.
18. Ibid., 79-80.
19. William R. O'Byrne, *A Naval Biographical Dictionary* (London, 1861), I, 29.
20. Sidney Dark, *Twelve Royal Ladies* (New York, 1929), 322.
21. James Edward Austen-Leigh, *Recollections of the Early Days of the Vine Hunt* (London, 1865), 37.
22. Herbert Cole, *Beau Brummell* (New York, 1977), 41.
23. Lewis Melville, *The First Gentleman of Europe* (London, 1906), 30.
24. Stirling, ed., *The Diaries of Dummer*, 80.
25. Ibid.
26. *CR* (1964) "Extracts from the Morning Chronicle," 262-64.
27. *FR*, 102.
28. *Letters* (78.1) 504.
29. Melville, *The First Gentleman of Europe*, 107-30.
30. *Letters* (78.1) 504.
31. Ibid.
32. J. B. Priestley, *The Prince of Pleasure and His Regency, 1811-20* (London, 1969 [1971]), 33; also J. H. Plumb, *The First Four Georges* (New York, 1937), 147.
33. Percy B. Shelley, *Sonnet: England in 1819*.
34. Priestley, *The Prince of Pleasure*, 47.
35. *Letters* (96) 389.
36. Ibid. (97) 391.
37. Ibid. (Other Persons Index).
38. Winifred Watson, "Two Chelsea Doctors," *The Lady*, vol. 27, October 1960, 533-34; also Sir Zachary Cope, "Dr. Charles Haden (1786-1824), a Friend of Jane Austen," *British Medical Journal*, April 16, 1966, 974.
39. *Aunt*, 12.
40. *Memoir*, 118.
41. "Jane Austen," *St. Paul's Magazine*, March 1870, 634.
42. Brabourne, II, 245-47.

43. *DNB,* IV, 429-30; *Gentleman's Magazine* (1835), 328; and J. A. Venn's *Alumni Cantabrigienses* (Cambridge, 1922).
44. Information furnished by Gilbert P. Hoole, retired librarian and member of the teaching staff of Tonbridge School, Kent.
45. Joanna Richardson, *George the Magnificent: A Portrait of King George IV* (New York, 1966), 98.
46. Priestley, *The Prince of Pleasure,* 36.
47. W. H. Pyne, *The History of the Royal Residences* (London, 1819), II, 1-92.
48. Ibid.
49. Ibid.
50. *London Times,* Friday, November 17, 1815, 3, column 1.
51. *Aunt,* 12.
52. Ibid.
53. *Letters* (113) 429.
54. Ibid. (113a) 429-30.
55. Ibid. (120) 442-43.
56. Ibid., 443.
57. Ibid. (1202) 444.
58. Ibid., 444-45.
59. Ibid., 445.
60. Ibid.
61. Ibid.
62. Ibid. (1262) 451.
63. Ibid. (49) 181.
64. Ibid. (126) 452.
65. Ibid., 452-53.
66. Ibid. (117) 436.
67. Ibid. (121) 446.
68. *Emma* (dedication page).
69. *Letters* (122) 447.
70. Ibid. (118) 441.
71. Gilson, 74; also Roger Fulford, "Address Given by Mr. Roger Fulford at the Annual General Meeting 1957," *AR* (1957), 120.

CHAPTER 7 — JANE AUSTEN'S READING

1. Robert Halsband, "The Female Pen," *History Today,* October 1974, 709.
2. *DNB,* XIII, 689.
3. *Letters* (120) 443.
4. *Biographical Notice,* 7.
5. Gilson, 442.

6. *MW,* 65, 93, 139, 141, 144, 199, 232.
7. Gilson, 438-39.
8. *Letters* (25) 82.
9. *Emma,* 461.
10. *Letters* (48) 173.
11. Ibid.
12. Gilson, 441.
13. *PA,* 27; also Gilson, 441-42.
14. *Letters* (56) 218-19; also Sir Zachary Cope, "Dr. Thomas Percival and Jane Austen," *British Medical Journal,* 1969, 55-56.
15. Gilson, 431-446.
16. Ibid., 436, 438, 440, 442, 445.
17. *Letters* (26) 89.
18. Ibid. (14) 38-39.
19. Gilson, 444-45.
20. Ibid., 89.
21. Ibid., 439-40.
22. *NA/P* (*Northanger Abbey*), 306-12.
23. Gilson, 434.
24. *Letters* (9) 21.
25. Michael Sadlier, *The Northanger Novels: A Footnote to Jane Austen,* English Association Pamphlet No. 68, Oxford, 1927; also Michael Sadlier, *Things Past* (London, 1944), 167-200.
26. *Letters* (31) 111.
27. Gilson, 432-46.
28. *Letters* (63) 248.
29. Ibid. (64) 251.
30. Ibid. (65) 256.
31. Ibid. (62) 242.
32. Charles Dudley Warner, ed., *Library of the World's Best Literature Ancient and Modern* (New York), vol. 23, 13, 830.
33. *Letters* (55) 212.
34. Ibid. (75) 292, 294.
35. Ibid., 292.
36. Ibid.
37. Ibid.
38. Ibid. (101) 406.
39. Ibid. (Index to !! Addenda).
40. Ibid. (78) 304.
41. Ibid. (91) 371; also *Letters* (Authors, Books, and Plays Index).
42. Ibid. (98) 393.
43. *NA/P* (*Persuasion*) 317, 320.

44. Marshall, 160.
45. *Letters* (109) 423.
46. Ibid. (92) 377.
47. Ibid. (101) 405.
48. Ibid. (100) 404.
49. *Memoir,* 71.
50. *PA,* 160-62.
51. *GH,* 66-67.
52. *PA,* 162-69.
53. *MW,* 440-52.
54. *Letters* (37) 133.
55. Ibid.
56. Original poem (unpublished) inscribed "Edward Austen on the death of his aunt Miss Austen the author," dated "Sunday September 28th 1817." Owned by David J. Gilson of Oxford, England, and quoted with his permission.
57. J. M. G. Blakiston, "Flaxman's Monument to Joseph Warton: Its Genesis and Evolution," *Winchester Cathedral Record,* no. 42, 1973, 22-38.
58. Hill, 91-92.
59. *Emma,* 78.
60. *Biographical Notice,* 7.
61. *Letters* (12) 33.
62. Ibid. (14) 39.
63. David Cecil, *The Stricken Deer or the Life of Cowper* (Indianapolis, 1930), 209-29.
64. *Life and Letters,* 194-197; also *AP,* 247.
65. Gilson, 434.
66. *Letters* (84) 335.
67. Ibid. (139) 476.
68. Ibid., 476-77.
69. Ibid. (87) 353.
70. *NA/P* (*Persuasion*), 167.
71. *MW,* 396.
72. *Letters* (52) 197.
73. Ibid. (63) 248.
74. *FP,* 97-98.
75. *Letters* (76) 299.
76. Ibid., 299-300.
77. Ibid., 298.
78. Ibid. (116) 433.
79. Stanley Kunitz and Howard Haycraft, *British Authors of the Nineteenth Century* (New York, 1936), 154.

80. Ibid.
81. *Memoir,* 89-90.
82. *AP* (Cholmeley Pedigree), 342; also *AP,* 180-81.
83. John Bernard Burke, *Peerage and Baronetage* (London, 1970), 2778-79.
84. Rene Huchon, *George Crabbe and His Times* (London, 1907), 373, 377.
85. Sharon Footerman, "The First Fanny Price," *Notes and Queries,* June 1978, 217-219.
86. Huchon, *George Crabbe and His Times,* 375.
87. *Letters* (82) 319.
88. Ibid., 323; also Chapman's note to this letter.
89. Ibid. (88) 358.
90. Ibid. (91) 370.
91. Huchon, *George Crabbe and His Times,* 386-88.
92. Geoffrey Grigson, "New Letters from Jane Austen's Home," *Times Literary Supplement,* August 19, 1955, 493.
93. *Letters* (75) 292.
94. Ibid., 293-94.
95. Ibid. (92) 378.
96. *MW,* 397.
97. Ibid., 397-98.
98. *Letters* (93) 379.
99. *NA/P* (*Persuasion*), 100.
100. Ibid., 109.
101. Laurence Hutton, *Literary Landmarks of London* (New York, 1897), 34; also Harold Nicolson, *Byron, the Last Journey: April 1823-April 1824* (London, 1924), 274.

CHAPTER 8 — JANE AUSTEN AND SCANDAL

1. John Bernard Burke, *Landed Gentry* (London, 1939), 2302; also *LCR,* 206.
2. "Lord Saye and Sele," *Hampshire Chronicle,* July 18, 1788.
3. Sarah Chauncey Woolsey, ed., *The Diary and Letters of Frances Burney, Madame D'Arblay* (Boston, 1890), I, 130.
4. *AP,* 247.
5. Honan, 225-26, 429; also Austen family archives.
6. Sybil M. Rosenfeld, *Temple of Thespis: Some Private Theatres and Theatricals in England and Wales, 1700-1820* (London, 1978), 128.
7. *GH,* 100-105.
8. Ibid., 102.
9. Biographical information on the Rev. Thomas James Twisleton can be found in Rosenfeld's *Temple of Thespis,* 128-132; John Bernard Burke's

Peerage and Baronetage (London, 1913), 1714; David Verey, ed., *The Diary of a Cotswold Parson—Rev. F. E. Witts, 1783-1854* (Gloucester, 1979); G. F. R. Baker and J. Foster's *The Record of Old Westminsters* (London); the Rev. Henry Isham Longden's *Northampton and Rutland Clergy* (1942), 59-60; *Times* (London), October 10-11 and 24, 1788; and F. L. Bevan's *A History of the Diocese of Colombo* (London, 1946), 43-46. Twisleton's obituary appeared in the *Gentleman's Magazine*, March 1825, 275. His divorce papers from the former Charlotte Anne Frances Wattell are on file in the record office of the House of Lords in London.

10. Ibid.
11. *Letters* (84) 334.
12. *PA*, 102.
13. The fullest account of Mrs. Elizabeth Craven, including all quotations used in my account, can be found in *RCA*, 7-9, 72-73.
14. Ibid.; also "Coats of Arms in Berkshire Churches—Arms in Kintbury Church," in *Berkshire Archaeological Journal* (1934), 57-59; and *Wiltshire Visitation Pedigrees* (Staples), 189.
15. The fullest account of the trial of Mrs. Leigh-Perrot is to be found in Sir Frank Douglas MacKinnon, *Grand Larceny, Being the Trial of Jane Leigh-Perrot, Aunt of Jane Austen* (Oxford, 1937); also see Albert Borowitz, "The Trial of Jane's Aunt," in *A Gallery of Sinister Perspectives* (Kent, OH, 1982) 89-121; "Account of the Trial of Mrs. Leigh-Perrot," in *The Lady's Magazine*, April 1800; "Mrs. Leigh-Perrot Stands Accused," in *GH*, 82-95; and "Mrs. Leigh-Perrot (wife of James Leigh Perrot, cousin of Rev. Thomas Leigh)," in *Notes and Queries* (November 1947), 474-75.
16. Jack Ayers, ed., *Paupers and Pig Killers—The Diary of William Holland, a Somerset Parson* (Gloucester, 1984), 29.
17. Original manuscript in the collection of the University of Florida.
18. Sarah Markham, "A Gardener's Question for Mrs. Leigh-Perrot," *AR* (1981), 11-12; also Sarah Markham, *A Testimony of Her Times: Based on Penelope Hind's Diaries and Correspondence 1787-1838* (Salisbury, 1990).
19. Ibid.
20. Ibid.
21. Gilson, 89.
22. *Letters* (30) 106.
23. Ibid. (32) 113.
24. Information quoted from a letter from I. J. Lewis, Borough Librarian, Reading Borough Council (May 26, 1976) containing notes from A. M. Broadley and Lewis Melville, eds., *The Beautiful Lady Craven* (London, 1914).

25. Lesley Blanch, ed., *The Game of Hearts: Hariette Wilson's Memoirs* (New York, 1955), 22, 73, 78-79.
26. *MW*, 437; also *DNB*, 43.
27. *Letters* (34) 120.
28. Roger Fulford, *The Royal Dukes: The Father and Uncles of Queen Victoria* (Duckworth, 1933), 253-260.
29. *Letters* (27) 95.
30. Ibid. (36) 127-28.
31. The fullest account of Edward Jervis Ricketts's 1797-99 divorce from Mary-Cassandra Twisleton is on file in the records office of the House of Lords in London.
32. Tom Winnifrith, "Jane Austen's Adulteress," *Notes and Queries*, 1990, 19.
33. *Letters* (52) 197.
34. Ibid. (Chapman's note to this letter).
35. Ibid.
36. "Nisi Prius," *Hampshire Chronicle*, August 1808, 4. The record office of the House of Lords in London also has extensive files on the Powlett-Sackville affair.
37. *MP*, 440.
38. *GH*, 141-42; Piggott, 23; *Gentleman's Magazine* (1812), 78-79; and *AP*, 85, 112.
39. *Letters* (70) 276-77.
40. Constance Wright, *Louise, Queen of Prussia* (London, 1970), 93-94, 107, 242-43; also D'Antraigues, "A Secret Agent, Under the Empire," *The Spectator* (Literary Supplement), October 14, 1893, 487-88; *Gentleman's Magazine*, July-December 1812, 79-80.
41. Ibid.
42. *Letters* (72) 280.
43. William Berry, *County Genealogies: Pedigress of the Families in the County of Hants* (London, 1833), 274.
44. John Bernard Burke, *A Genealogical and Heraldic History of the Commoners of Great Britain and Ireland*, II, 599-601; also *Letters* (Other Persons Index under Beckford and Middleton).
45. Brian Fothergill, *Beckford of Fonthill* (London, 1979), 281.
46. Ibid., 281.
47. Ibid., 169-70, 172.
48. *Letters* (78.1) 504.
49. Ibid. (see Index II Addenda); also Leslie A. Marchand, *Famous in My Time: Byron's Letters and Journals 1810-12* (Cambridge, 1973), II (1810-12), 286.
50. Ibid.
51. Malcolm Elwin, *Lord Byron's Wife* (New York, 1962), 163.
52. *Letters* (141) 485.

53. The fullest account in print of the Paget scandals are available in The Marquess of Anglesey, *One Leg: The Life and Letters of Henry William Paget, First Marquess of Anglesey* (New York, 1961). The original divorce papers are on file in the Record Office of the House of Lords in London and the Scottish Record Office in Edinburgh.
54. Ibid.
55. Ibid.
56. *Times* (London), November 17, 1815, 3, column 1.
57. *Letters* (14), Chapman's note to this letter; also *Letters* (123) 448-49, and *Letters* (1232), 448.
58. William R. O'Byrne, *A Naval Biographical Dictionary* (London, 1849), 26-27.

CHAPTER 9 — JANE AUSTEN'S JOURNEYINGS

1. *Life and Letters*, 25; also *GH*, 150-151.
2. *Life and Letters*, 25.
3. *MW*, 79.
4. J. J. Cooper, *Some Worthies of Reading* (Reading, 1923). 72.
5. Elizabeth Jenkins, "Some Banking Accounts of the Austen Family," *CR* (1954), 58-61; also Deidre Le Faye, "Three Austen Family Letters," *Notes and Queries*, September 1985, 333-34.
6. Sir David Waldron Smithers, *Jane Austen in Kent* (Westerham, Kent, 1981), 27-29.
7. Anna Austen Lefroy, "Description of Steventon Rectory in the Rev. George Austen's Time," *AR* (1975), 11-14.
8. *AP*, 132.
9. *MW*, 9.
10. Ibid., 44-47.
11. Ibid., 89.
12. Ibid., 128.
13. G. L. Apperson, *A Jane Austen Dictionary* (New York, 1968), 88-89.
14. *MW*, 43.
15. Ibid.
16. *Biographical Notice*, 7.
17. *MW*, 105.
18. Ibid., 142-43.
19. Ibid., 191.
20. *AP*, 28.
21. *Letters* (61) 236.
22. Ibid. (51) 186.
23. Ibid. (8) 7.

24. Ibid.
25. Apperson, *A Jane Austen Dictionary*, 80-81.
26. *Times* (London), Monday, August 29, 1796, 1, column 1.
27. *Letters* (4-7) 8-18.
28. Ibid. (5) 11.
29. *AP*, 124.
30. *Letters* (6) 14.
31. Ibid. (7) 18.
32. Ibid., 17.
33. Ibid., 18.
34. *MW*, illustration facing page 242.
35. Gilson, 442-43.
36. *NA/P* (*Northanger Abbey*), 109.
37. *GH*, 124.
38. Marshall, 167.
39. *Letters* (17) 49.
40. Sarah Howell, *The Seaside* (London, 1974), 37.
41. *Letters* (17) 49.
42. Ibid., 60.
43. Ibid.
44. Ibid. (22) 70.
45. *Bath Herald and Register*, Saturday, June 29, 1799, 3.
46. *Letters* (21) 67.
47. Gilson, 441.
48. *AP*, 197-98; 205-6.
49. *GH*, 35-36; 73-74.
50. *Letters* (37) 131.
51. Howell, *The Seaside*, 31.
52. "Sidmouth and Jane Austen," *CR* (1958), 136-38.
53. Emma Austen-Leigh, *Jane Austen and Bath* (London, 1939), viii.
54. *FP*, 66.
55. King's Library, *Jane Austen 1775-1817. Catalog of an Exhibition Held in the King's Library Reference Division 9 December 1975 to 29 February 1976*, note on Item 87.
56. Richard Arthur Austen-Leigh, *Jane Austen and Southampton* (London, 1949), 11, 37-38; also *Letters* (56) 215.
57. King's Library, *Jane Austen 1775-1817*, note on Item 87.
58. Sir Egerton Brydges, *The Autobiography, Times, Opinions and Contemporaries of Sir Egerton Brydges* (London, 1834), II, 41.
59. King's Library, *Jane Austen 1775-1817*, note on Item 87.
60. *Letters* (39) 139.
61. Ibid., 140.

62. Ibid.
63. Ibid.
64. *SS*, 33.
65. *Letters* (39) 142.
66. *AP*, 31.
67. *Letters* (45) 163.
68. *Letters* (45) 163; (47) 167, 169; also F. P. Lock, "Jane Austen and the Seaside," *Country Life Annual*, 1977, 115.
69. R. J. White, *Life in Regency England* (London, 1963), 130-31.
70. *Letters* (35) 123.
71. *OFH*, 278.
72. *A Short Description of the Parish and Village of Adlestrop in Gloucestershire with a Rough Plan of the Village* (Adlestrop, 1975[?]); Mavis Batey, "In Quest of Jane Austen's 'Mr. Repton,'" *Garden History*, vol. 5, no. 1, Spring 1977, 19-20; and Mavis Batey, "Jane Austen at Stoneleigh Abbey," *Country Life*, December 30, 1976, 1974-75.
73. S. C. Kaines Smith, *Stoneleigh Abbey* (Derby, 1930[?]).
74. Edward Malins, "Humphry Repton at Stoneleigh Abbey, Warwickshire," *Garden History*, 1977, 21-29.
75. *AP*, 237-47.
76. Ibid., 247.
77. Ibid.
78. Ibid., 141.
79. Elizabeth Jenkins, "Birth of a Legend," *CR* (1965), 289-94.
80. Donald Greene, "The Orignal of Pemberley," *Eighteenth Century Fiction*, October 1988.
81. *Letters* (51) 191.
82. *Annual Register* (London, 1808), 53; also information furnished by the Royal Archives at Windsor.
83. *Letters* (52) 194.
84. Ibid. (53) 203.
85. Ibid. (52) 195.
86. National Trust, *The Book of Box Hill* (London, 1969), 24.
87. P. G. Skinner, *St. Nicholas Church, Great Bookham* (1971), 19; also "Miss Austen's Country," *The Spectator* (1875), 1225-26.
88. *Letters* (85) 337.
89. A. C. Turberville, *Johnson's England* (Oxford, 1933), 118.
90. *Letters* (79) 306-307.
91. Gilson, 53.
92. J. B. Priestley, *The Prince of Pleasure and His Regency, 1811-20* (London, 1969 [1971]), 85.
93. B. C. Southam, ed., *Jane Austen: The Critical Heritage, I, 1811-70* (London, 1968), 116.

94. National Trust, *The Book of Box Hill*, 24.
95. *Letters* (62) 242; also *Letters* (Authors Books and Plays Index).
96. Leslie A. Marchand, ed., *Lord Byron's Selected Letters and Journals* (Cambridge, 1972), 85.
97. *Memoir of Miss Austen*, ix.
98. *Aunt*, 14.
99. Ibid.
100. *MW*, 363.
101. William Cowper, *The Retirement* (1782), quoted in Howell, *The Seaside*, 18-19.

Chapter 10 — Jane Austen and Religion

1. *MW*, 453-54.
2. Andrew Finley Walls, "Miss Austen's Theological Reading," *Anglican Theological Review*, 1965, 50.
3. *Letters* (103) 410.
4. *Biographical Notice*, 8.
5. Ibid.
6. B. C. Southam, ed., *Jane Austen: The Critical Heritage, I, 1811-70* (London, 1968), 95.
7. *Memoir*, 153.
8. *The Loiterer*, No. II, Saturday, February 7, 1789, I, 12.
9. Frank Brady, *James Boswell, The Later Years: 1769-1795* (New York, 1984), 478-79.
10. Sir Egerton Brydges, *The Autobiography, Times, Opinions and Contemporaries of Sir Egerton Brydges* (London, 1834), I, 136-37; also II, 39-40.
11. Brabourne, I, 15-16.
12. Steventon Baptismal Register.
13. *Sailor Brothers*, 114.
14. J. Wickham Legg, *English Church Life from the Restoration to the Tractarian Movement* (London, 1914), 361-62.
15. *MW*, 445-446.
16. Ibid., 147.
17. Ibid., 232.
18. Gilson, 445.
19. Information furnished by Canon Frederick Bussby, Canon Residentiary of Winchester Cathedral, July 26, 1980; also *Princeton University Library Chronicle*, 162-63; and W. K. Lowther Clarke's *Eighteenth Century Piety* (London, 1944), 9.
20. *Letters* (8) 19.
21. Ibid. (32) 115.

22. *MW,* 232.
23. *Letters* (37) 133.
24. *MW,* 440.
25. *Letters* (40) 144.
26. Ibid. (41) 146.
27. Ibid., 147.
28. Ibid. (47) 169.
29. Frank W. Bradbrook, *Jane Austen and Her Predecessors* (Cambridge, 1966), 34-39, 42-45.
30. *Letters* (57) 219-20.
31. Ibid., 220.
32. Ibid. (58) 222.
33. Ibid. (59) 225.
34. Ibid., 227.
35. Ibid.
36. Ibid., 227-28.
37. Ibid. (66) 260.
38. Ibid. (64) 252.
39. Ibid. (133) 467.
40. *DNB,* XIII, 865.
41. *Letters* (65) 256.
42. Ibid.
43. Ibid. (103) 410.
44. Ibid. (106) 420.
45. *Oxford Dictionary* (Oxford, 1933/1978), III, 328-29.
46. *Letters* (78) 305.
47. Ibid. (64) 251.
48. Ibid. (65) 258.
49. *MW,* 439.
50. Southam, ed., *Jane Austen: The Critical Heritage,* 117.
51. Ibid., 122-123.
52. *Letters* (81) 314.
53. Ibid. (85) 339.
54. Ibid. (Authors, Books, and Plays Index); also *NA/P* (*Persuasion*), 318.
55. *Letters* (101) 406.
56. Ibid. (108) 422.
57. Ibid. (99.1) 508.
58. Ibid., 507.
59. Ibid. (145) 493, 495.
60. Ibid. (147) 498.
61. *Biographical Notice,* 4.
62. *Letters* (Appendix), 514, 516.

Bibliography

"Account of the Trial of Mrs. Leigh-Perrot." *The Lady's Magazine*, April 1800.

Ackerman. *Repository of Arts*. London, 1813.

"AEsop." *Sporting Reminiscences in Hampshire, 1745-1862*. London, 1864.

Altic, R. D. *The Shows of London*. London, 1978.

Anglesey, The Marquess of. *One Leg: The Life and Letters of Henry William Paget, First Marquess of Anglesey*. New York, 1961.

Annual Register. London, 1808.

Apperson, G. L. *A Jane Austen Dictionary*. New York, 1968.

Austen, Caroline Mary Craven. *My Aunt Jane Austen*. Winchester (Jane Austen Society), 1952.

———. *Reminiscences*. Edited with an introduction by Deirdre Le Faye. Winchester (Jane Austen Society), 1986.

Austen, Henry Thomas. "Biographical Notice of the Author." Prefixed to the first edition of *Northanger Abbey and Persuasion* (1817). Reprinted in *The Novels of Jane Austen*, ed. R. W. Chapman. Oxford, 1923 (1972), vol. 5, 3-9.

———. "Memoir of Miss Austen." Prefixed to the edition of *Sense and Sensibility* published by Richard Bentley in 1833, v-xiv.

Austen, James. *The Loiterer*. Oxford, 1789-90.

———. Manuscript album of James Austen's miscellaneous works. Owned by the Jane Austen Memorial Trust, Chawton. Numbers have been assigned to the individual poems as they appear in sequence in the volume.

Austen, Jane. *Jane Austen's Letters to Her Sister Cassandra and Others*. Edited by R. W. Chapman. Oxford, 1932. Reprinted (with corrections) 1959, 1964, 1969.

Austen, Jane. *The Novels of Jane Austen*, six volumes. Edited by R. W. Chapman, revised by Mary Lascelles. Oxford, 1971-1974. *Emma*, 1971; *Minor Works*, 1972 (with revisions by B. C. Southam; original printing 1954); *Northanger Abbey and Persuasion*, 1972; *Mansfield Park*, 1973; *Pride and Prejudice*, 1973; *Sense and Sensibility*, 1974. All references to Jane Austen's novels are from these volumes.

Austen, Jane. *Volume the Third*. Edited by R. W. Chapman. Oxford, 1951.

Austen-Leigh, Emma. *Jane Austen and Bath*. London, 1939.

———. *Jane Austen and Steventon*. London, 1937.

Austen-Leigh, James Edward. *A Memoir of Jane Austen*, second edition. Ed. R. W. Chapman. Oxford, 1926, rep. 1967.

———. *Recollections of the Early Days of the Vine Hunt.* London, 1865.

Austen-Leigh, Mary-Augusta. *James Edward Austen-Leigh: A Memoir.* Privately printed, 1911.

———. *Personal Aspects of Jane Austen.* London, 1920.

Austen-Leigh, Richard Arthur. *Austen Papers*, 1704-1856. London, 1942.

———. *Jane Austen and Lyme Regis.* London, 1941.

———. *Jane Austen and Southampton.* London, 1949.

Austen-Leigh, William, and Richard Arthur Austen-Leigh. *Jane Austen, Her Life and Letters: A Family Record.* London, 1913 (1965).

———. *Jane Austen: A Family Record.* Revised and enlarged by Deirdre Le Faye. London, 1989.

Austen-Leigh, William, and Montague George Knight. *Chawton Manor and Its Owners.* London, 1911.

Ayers, Jack, ed. *Paupers and Pig Killers—The Diary of William Holland, a Somerset Parson.* Gloucester, 1984.

Baker, C. H. Collins. "Lady Chandos' Register." *Genealogists' Magazine* 10 (1947-50), 255-64, 299-309, 339-52.

Baker, G. F. R., and Foster, J. *The Record of Old Westminsters.* London.

Batey, Mavis. "In Quest of Jane Austen's `Mr. Repton.'" *Garden History*, vol. 5, no. 1 (Spring 1977).

———. "Jane Austen at Stoneleigh Abbey." *Country Life*, December 30, 1976.

Bath Herald and Register, various dates.

Berkshire Archaeological Journal, 1934.

Berry, William. *County Genealogies: Pedigrees of the Families in the County of Hants.* London, 1833.

Bettany, Lewis, ed. *Diaries of William Johnston Temple*, 1780-1796. Oxford, 1929.

Bevan. F. L. *A History of the Diocese of Colombo.* London, 1946.

Bigg-Wither, Rev. R. F. *Materials for a History of the Wither Family.* Winchester, 1907.

Blakiston, J. M. G. "Flaxman's Monument to Joseph Warton: Its Genesis and Evolution." *Winchester Cathedral Record*, no. 42, 1973.

Blanch, Leslie, ed. *The Game of Hearts: Harriette Wilson's Memoirs.* New York, 1955.

Borowitz, Albert. "The Trial of Jane's Aunt." In *A Gallery of Sinister Perspectives.* Kent, OH, 1982.

Brabourne, Edward, First Lord. *Letters of Jane Austen.* 2 vols. London, 1884.

Bradbrook, Frank W. *Jane Austen and Her Predecessors.* Cambridge, 1966.

Brady, Frank. *James Boswell, The Later Years: 1769-1795.* New York, 1984.

Broadley, A. M., and Melville, Lewis, eds. *The Beautiful Lady Craven.* London, 1914.
Bryant, Arthur. *The Age of Elegance, 1812-1822.* London, 1975.
———. *The Years of Endurance, 1793-1802.* London, 1942.
———. *The Years of Victory, 1802-1812.* London, 1945.
Brydges, Sir Egerton. *The Autobiography, Times, Opinions and Contemporaries of Sir Egerton Brydges.* London, 1834.
Burke, John Bernard. *Extinct and Dormant Baronetcies of England.* London, 1838.
———. *A Genealogical and Heraldic History of the Commoners of Great Britain and Ireland.* London, 1823-1838.
———. *Landed Gentry.* London, 1937, 1939, 1952.
———. *Peerage and Baronetage.* London, 1865, 1900, 1913, 1917, 1970.
Bussby, Cannon F. *Jane Austen in Winchester.* Winchester, 1969.
Carpenter, T. Edward, *The Story of Jane Austen's Home.* Jane Austen Memorial Trust, 1954.
Cecil, David. *The Stricken Deer or the Life of Cowper.* Indianapolis, 1930.
Chapman, R. W. *Jane Austen: Facts and Problems.* Oxford, 1948 (1970).
———. "Jane Austen's 'Warren.'" *Times Literary Supplement,* May 14, 1931.
Chawton, Hampshire, Church of St. Nicholas. Parish registers.
Clarke, W. K. Lowther. *Eighteenth Century Piety.* London, 1944.
Cole, Herbert. *Beau Brummell.* New York, 1977.
Coleridge, Samuel Taylor. *Biographica Literaria.* 1907.
Collins, Arthur. *The Peerage of England* (Brydges edition, London, 1812), II, s.v. "Powlett of Winchester."
Cooper, J. J. *Some Worthies of Reading.* Reading, 1923.
Cope, Sir Zachary. "Dr. Charles Haden (1786-1824), a Friend of Jane Austen." *British Medical Journal,* April 16, 1966.
———. "Dr. Thomas Percival and Jane Austen." *British Medical Journal,* 1969.
———. "Jane Austen's Last Illness." *British Medical Journal,* July 18, 1964, 140, 182-83.
———. "Who Was Sophia Sentiment? Was She Jane Austen?" *The Book Collector,* 1966.
Cowper, William. "The Task," vi, 150.
Crawford, Thomas. "Boswell's Temple and the Jane Austen World." *Scottish Literary Journal,* vol. 10, no. 2, December 1983.
D'Antraigues, "A Secret Agent, Under the Empire." *The Spectator* (Literary Supplement), October 14, 1893.
Dark, Sidney. *Twelve Royal Ladies.* New York, 1929.
Dictionary of National Biography. Edited by Sir Leslie Stephen and Sir Sidney Lee. London, 1885-1900; 1921-22.
Dumfermline, (Lord) James. *Lieutenant General Ralph Abercromby K.B., 1793-1801: A Memoir by His Son.* Edinburgh, 1864.
Earney, H. W. "The Man Who Caused the American Revolution." *Hampshire Magazine,* October 1982.

Elwin, Malcolm. *Lord Byron's Wife*. New York, 1962.
Emden, C. S. "Oriel Friends of Jane Austen." *Oriel Record*, 1950.
Fielding, Henry. *The History of Tom Jones, A Foundling*.
Footerman, Sharon. "The First Fanny Price." *Notes and Queries*, June 1978, 217-19.
Foster, Joseph. *Alumni Oxonienses 1715-1886*. London, 1887.
Fothergill, Brian. *Beckford of Fonthill*. London, 1979.
Freeman, Jean. *Jane Austen in Bath*. Winchester (Jane Austen Society), 1969.
Fulford, Roger. "Address Given by Mr. Roger Fulford at the Annual General Meeting 1957." In *Jane Austen Society Annual Report*, 1957.
———. *The Royal Dukes: The Father and Uncles of Queen Victoria*. Duckworth, 1933.
Gentleman's Magazine, London, various dates.
Gilson, David John. *A Bibliography of Jane Austen*. The Soho Bibliographies. Oxford, 1982.
Greene, Donald. "The Original of Pemberley." *Eighteenth Century Fiction*, October 1988.
Grigsby, Joan. "The House in Castle Square." *Annual Reports of the Jane Austen Society*, 1978.
Grigson, Geoffrey. "New Letters from Jane Austen's Home." *Times Literary Supplement*, August 19, 1955.
Halsband, Robert. "The Female Pen." *History Today*, October 1974.
Hampshire Chronicle, various dates.
Herold, J. C. *Mistress to an Age*. London, 1959.
Hill, Constance. *Jane Austen: Her Homes and Her Friends*. London, new edition, 1904 (1923).
Honan, Park. *Jane Austen: Her Life*. New York, 1987.
———. "Jane Austen and Marriage." *Contemporary Review*, November 1984.
Howe, Evelyn. "Amateur Theatre in Georgian England." *History Today*, October 1970.
Howe, M. W. DeWolfe. "A Jane Austen Letter." *The Yale Review*, vol. 15, October 1925-July 1926.
Howell, Sarah. *The Seaside*. London, 1974.
Hubback, J. H. "Pen Portraits in Jane Austen's Novels," *The Cornhill Magazine*, July 1928.
Hubback, J. H., and Edith C. Hubback. *Jane Austen's Sailor Brothers*. London, 1906.
Huchon, Rene. *George Crabbe and His Times*. London, 1907.
Hutton, Laurence. *Literary Landmarks of London*. New York, 1897.
Irons, Keith. *Steventon and the Austens*. Steventon, 1975.
"Jane Austen," *Times Literary Supplement*, September 17, 1954.
"Jane Austen," *St. Paul's Magazine*, March 1870.
Jane Austen Society. *Annual Report*, 1966-1991.

Jane Austen Society. *Collected Reports,* 1949-1965, with an introduction by Elizabeth Jenkins, 1967.

Jenkins, Elizabeth. "Birth of a Legend." In Jane Austen Society, *Collected Reports,* 1965.

———. "Extracts from the Monrning Chronicle." In Jane Austen Society, *Collected Reports,* 1964.

———. *Jane Austen: A Biography.* London, 1938.

———. "Some Banking Accounts of the Austen Family." In Jane Austen Society, *Collected Reports,* 1954.

Jordan, Ellen. "Mansfield Park," *Times Literary Supplement,* June 23, 1972.

Kaines Smith, S. C. *Stoneleigh Abbey.* Derby, 1930(?).

Kaplan, Deborah. "Henry Austen and John Rawston Papillon." In Jane Austen Society, *Annual Report,* 1987.

King's Library. *Jane Austen 1775-1817. Catalog of an Exhibition Held in the King's Library Reference Division 9 December 1975 to 29 February 1976.*

Knatchbull, Lady. "Aunt Jane." *The Cornhill Magazine,* 1947.

Kunitz, Stanley, and Howard Haycraft. *British Authors of the Nineteenth Century.* New York, 1936.

Lane, Maggie. *Jane Austen's Family, Through Five Generations.* London, 1984.

Lang, Paul Henry. *George Frederic Handel.* New York, 1977.

Laudermilk, Sharon H., and Teresa L. Hamlin. *The Regency Companion.* New York, 1989.

Le Faye, D. G. "Anna Lefroy's Original Memories of Jane Austen." *Review of English Studies,* August 1988.

———. "Recollections of Chawton," *Times Literary Supplement,* May 3, 1985.

———. "Three Austen Family Letters," *Notes and Queries,* September 1985.

———. "Tom Lefroy and Jane Austen." In Jane Austen Society, *Annual Report,* 1985.

Lefroy, Anna Austen. "Description of Steventon Rectory in the Rev. George Austen's Time." In Jane Austen Society, *Annual Report,* 1975.

Lefroy, Helen. "Strangers." In Jane Austen Society, *Annual Report,* 1982.

Lefroy, J. A. P. "Jane Austen's Irish Friend: Rt. Hon. Thomas Langlois Lefroy, 1776-1869." *Proceedings of the Huguenot Society in London.* London, 1979.

———. "A Walloon Family, Loffroy of Cambray." *Proceedings of the Huguenot Society in London.* London, 1966.

Lefroy, Thomas Langlois. "The Late Chief Justice Lefroy." *Dublin University Magazine,* vol. 79, January 1872.

Legg, J. Wickham. *English Church Life from the Restoration to the Tractarian Movement.* London, 1914.

Leigh, Agnes. "An Old Family History." *National Review,* no. 49, 1907.

Leslie, Shane. *George the Fourth.* Boston, 1926.

L'Estrange, Rev. A. G. *A Life of Mary Russell Mitford.* New York, 1870.

Litz, A. Walton. "The Loiterer: A Reflection of Jane Austen's Early Environment." *Review of English Studies,* August 1961.

Lloyd, Alan. *The King Who Lost America.* New York, 1971.

Lock, F. P. "Jane Austen and the Seaside." *Country Life Annual,* 1977.

The Loiterer, various dates.

Longden, Rev. Henry Isham. *Northampton and Rutland Clergy.* 1942.

"Lord Saye and Sele," *Hampshire Chronicle,* July 18, 1788.

MacKinnon, Sir Frank Douglas. *Grand Larceny, Being the Trial of Jane Leigh-Perrot, Aunt of Jane Austen.* Oxford, 1937.

Malins, Edward. "Humphry Repton at Stoneleigh Abbey, Warwickshire." *Garden History,* 1977.

Marchand, Leslie A. *Famous in My Time: Byron's Letters and Journals 1810-12.* Cambridge, 1973.

———, ed. *Lord Byron's Selected Letters and Journals.* Cambridge, 1972.

Markham, Sarah. "A Gardener's Question for Mrs. Leigh-Perrot." In Jane Austen Society, *Annual Report,* 1981.

———. *A Testimony of Her Times: Based on Penelope Hind's Diaries and Correspondence 1787-1838.* Salisbury, 1990.

Marshall, John. *Royal Naval Biography.* London, 1823-35. *Supplement.* London, 1827-30.

Marshall, Mary Gaither, ed. *Jane Austen's Sanditon: A Continuation with "Reminiscenses of Aunt Jane" by Anna Austen Lefroy.* Chicago, 1983.

Matthew, B. *The Music of Winchester Cathedral.* London, 1974.

Melville, Lewis. *The First Gentleman of Europe.* London, 1906.

Midgley, W. "The Revd. Henry and Mrs. Eleanor Austen." In Jane Austen Society, *Annual Report,* 1978.

"Miss Austen's Country." *The Spectator* (1875).

Modert, Jo, ed. *Jane Austen's Manuscript Letters in Fascimile. Reproductions of Every Known Extant Letter, Fragment and Autograph Copy, with an Annotated List of All Known Letters.* Carbondale and Edwardsville, IL, 1990.

Moorman, Mary. *William Wordsworth: A Biography. The Early Years 1770-1803.* Oxford, 1957.

———. *William Wordsworth: A Biography. The Later Years 1803-1850.* Oxford, 1965.

"Mrs. Leigh-Perrot (wife of James Leigh Perrot, cousin of Rev. Thomas Leigh)." *Notes and Queries.* November 1947.

National Trust. *The Book of Box Hill.* London, 1969.

National Trust. *The Vyne.* London, 1973.

Nicolson, Harold. *Byron, the Last Journey: April 1823-April 1824.* London, 1924.

Nicolson, Nigel. *The World of Jane Austen.* London, 1991.

"Nisi Prius." *Hampshire Chronicle.* August 1808.

O'Byrne, William R. *A Naval Biographical Dictionary.* London, 1849; revised enlarged edition 1859-61.
Oxford Dictionary. Oxford, 1933/1978.
Oxford Dictionary of Quotations. Oxford, 1979.
Phillips-Birt, D. "Jane Austen and Old Portsmouth." *Country Life Annual,* 1966.
Piggott, Patrick. *The Innocent Diversion: Music in the Life and Writings of Jane Austen.* London, 1979.
———. "Jane Austen's Southampton Piano." In Jane Austen Society, *Annual Report,* 1980.
Pilgrim, Constance. *Dear Jane: A Biographical Study of Jane Austen.* London, 1971.
Pinion, Francis Bertram. *A Jane Austen Companion: A Critical Survey and Reference Book.* London, 1973.
Plumb, J. H. *The First Four Georges.* New York, 1937.
The Poetical Register and Repository of Fugitive Poetry, vol. 2, 1802. London, 1803.
Pope, Alexander. "An Essay on Man."
Poyntz, William. *Diary of Kempshot Hunt, 1791-03.* Royal Library, Windsor.
Priestley, J. B. *The Prince of Pleasure and His Regency, 1811-20.* London, 1969 (1971).
Princeton University Library Chronicle. Winter 1964.
Prosser, G. F. *Select Illustrations of Hampshire.* London, 1883.
Pryme, Jane Townley, and Bayne, Alicia. *Memorials of the Thackeray Family.* London, 1883.
Pyne, W. H. *The History of the Royal Residences.* London, 1819.
Ragg, Laura M. "Jane Austen and the War of Her Time." *Contemporary Review,* 1940.
Reitzel, William. "Mansfield Park and Lovers' Vows." *Review of English Studies,* 1933.
Reynolds, Sir Joshua. *Catalog of Pictures by the Late Sir Joshua Reynolds Exhibited by the Permission of the Proprietors in Honour of That Distinguished Artist and for the Improvement of British Art.* London, 1813.
Richards, George, and Shadwell, Charles. *The Provosts and Fellow of Oriel College.*
Richardson, Joanna. *The Disastrous Marriage.* London, 1960.
———. *George the Magnificent: A Portrait of King George IV.* New York, 1966.
Rosenfeld, Sybil M. *Temple of Thespis: Some Private Theatres and Theatricals in England and Wales, 1700-1820.* London, 1978.
Sadlier, Michael. *The Northanger Novels: A Footnote to Jane Austen.* English Association Pamphlet No. 68. Oxford, 1927.
———. *Things Past.* London, 1944.
Sawtell, George. "Four Manly Boys." In Jane Austen Society, *Annual Report,* 1982.
Scholes, Percy A. *The Oxford Companion to Music.* Oxford, 1970.
Shelley, Percy B. *Sonnet: England in 1819.*
A Short Description of the Parish and Village of Adlestrop in Gloucestershire with a Rough Plan of the Village. Adlestrop, 1975(?).

"Sidmouth and Jane Austen." In Jane Austen Society, *Collected Reports,* 1958.
Skinner, P. G. *St. Nicholas Church, Great Bookham.* 1971.
Smithers, Sir David Waldron. *Jane Austen in Kent.* Westerham, Kent, 1981.
Southam, B. C., ed. *Jane Austen: The Critical Heritage. I: 1811-70.* London, 1968.
———, ed. *Jane Austen's "Sir Charles Grandison."* Oxford, 1980.
Steventon, Hampshire, Church of St. Nicholas. Parish registers.
Stirling, A. M. W., ed. *The Diaries of Dummer.* London, 1934.
Stubbings, Frank. "Samuel Blackall and Jane Austen." *Emmanuel College Magazine,* quartercentenary issue. Oxford, 1984.
Thoyts, Rev. F. C. *A History of Esse or Ashe, Hampshire.* London, 1888.
Tillotson, Kathleen. "Jane Austen." *Times Literary Supplement,* September 17, 1954.
Timbs, John. *Clubs and Club Life in London.* London, 1967.
Times (London), various dates.
Tucker, George Holbert. *A Goodly Heritage: A History of Jane Austen's Family.* Manchester, 1983.
Turberville, A. S. *Johnson's England.* Oxford, 1933.
Turner, Barbara Carpenter. *Winchester.* Southampton, 1930.
Venn, J. A. *Alumni Cantabrigienses.* Cambridge, 1922.
Verey, David, ed. *The Diary of a Cotswold Parson—Rev. F. E. Wiits, 1783-1854.* Gloucester, 1979.
Walls, Andrew Finley. "Miss Austen's Theological Reading." *Anglican Theological Review,* 1965.
Warner, Charles Dudley, ed. *Library of the World's Best Literature Ancient and Modern.* New York.
Watkin, David. *The Royal Interiors of Regency England.* London, 1984.
Watson, Vera. *Mary Russell Mitford.* London, 1949.
Watson, Winifred. *Jane Austen in London.* 1960.
———. "Two Chelsea Doctors." *The Lady,* vol. 27, October 1960.
Webster's Biographical Dictionary. Springfield, MA, 1971.
White, R. J. *Life in Regency England.* London, 1963.
White, T. H. *The Age of Scandal.* Harmondsworth, 1962.
Williamson, V. A., G. W. S. Lyttelton, and S. L. Simeon, eds. *Memorials of Brooks's, 1764-1900.* London, 1907.
Willis, Arthur. "Last Days of a Great House." *Hampshire Chronicle,* May 30, 1970, 5, columns 1 and 2.
Wiltshire Visitation Pedigrees.
Winifrith, Tom. "Jane Austen's Adulteress." *Notes and Queries,* 1990.
Woodsworth, Mary Katherine. *The Literary Career of Sir Samuel Egerton Brydges.* Oxford, 1935.
Woolsey, Sarah Chauncey, ed. *The Diary and Letters of Frances Burney, Madame d'Arblay.* Boston, 1890.
Wright, Constance. *Louise, Queen of Prussia.* London, 1970.
Young, Percy Marshall. *Handel.* London, 1947 (1965).

Index

A

B

C

D

G

H

L

N

O

W